D0113883

ECONOMICS HANDBOOK SERIES

SEYMOUR E. HARRIS, EDITOR

CAPITALISM

ECONOMICS HANDBOOK SERIES

SEYMOUR E. HARRIS, EDITOR

Hansen · MONETARY THEORY AND FISCAL POLICY
Hoover · THE LOCATION OF ECONOMIC ACTIVITY
Schelling · NATIONAL INCOME BEHAVIOR
Sweezy · SOCIALISM
Wright · CAPITALISM

Capitalism

David McCord Wright

Professor of Economics
and Lecturer in Law
University of Virginia

FIRST EDITION

NEW YORK TORONTO LONDON
McGRAW-HILL BOOK COMPANY, INC.
1951

CAPITALISM

Dedication

In Memory of
JOSEPH A. SCHUMPETER
Teacher, Critic, and Friend

WHILE I WAS writing this book I occasionally wondered to whom I would dedicate it. That doubt has unhappily been settled by the lamented death of my great teacher, Joseph A. Schumpeter.

I have dedicated this book to him. No recognition that I could give would sufficiently acknowledge my indebtedness to his insight—nothing adequately describe his great personal kindness to me. But lest there be misunderstanding, I must add a few words of explanation.

One of Schumpeter's most winning characteristics was his attitude toward dissent. To obtain his respect you were not necessarily obliged to agree with him; you had only to understand him. Thus we did not always think alike by any means. He often amused himself by lecturing me on my incurable American optimism. Frequently, I believe, he merely felt that I was less "crazy" than most of my contemporaries.

Speaking more specifically, I felt, and still feel, that modern conditions have created needs for modern man which are legitimate and which his economics have not always met. And it seemed to me that those needs could be satisfied, within reason, without too greatly impairing the framework of capitalism and of democracy.

Schumpeter's position is difficult to pin down. Nevertheless, as I understood him, he did not dispute the *technical* possibility of the sort of system I had in mind. His position was rather a sort of ideological determinism. If you made change A, this would probably lead people to demand change B, and so on. In stabilizing the system, even relatively, we risked an incurable transformation of it. The masses, or, more accurately, the intellectuals who proselytize them, could not be trusted to rest at a happy mean. Democracy and capitalism would alike perish from their own success.

Now whether Schumpeter's assessment of human nature, and the trend of modern ideology, will prove more accurate than the less pessimistic views I have sometimes dared entertain is something which only history can decide. Also, as I have said, it is by no means clear just how ironclad an antithesis Schumpeter really had in mind. I shall therefore merely sum up my own position. What the actual outcome of a given historical situation may prove to be should not, I submit, affect our convictions of what ought to be. Believing that we do not *have* to plunge into despotism on the one hand nor yet unmitigated insecurity on the other, I should feel myself unworthy of my country and my people to indulge in premature despair or to fail to do all I could to point the way toward a possible and desirable solution.

David McCord Wright

Preface

ANYONE who undertakes to "outline" capitalism is likely to find himself immediately classed as a dogmatic adherent of unmitigated *laissez faire*. In order to avoid misunderstandings of this kind, I should like to begin by quoting the following passages from the conclusion of this book: "One of the great wastes of any war, be it an international or an intellectual one, is that the energies which might normally be used for improvement are drained off into defense. Personally the writer finds the most distasteful aspect of modern discussion to be the extent to which one has to spend one's time stating the problem rather than trying to answer it. . . . It would be so much better to be able to explore the many ways available to us for reducing conflict—instead of having to keep insisting that a minimum of conflict will always remain. I would so much prefer to occupy myself in discussing techniques of stabilization—rather than in insisting that stabilization, in a growing world, can never be perfect. But the thing which keeps us from doing what we *can* do is the assumption of some people that we may easily achieve the impossible. Once, to be sure, we understand the problem and know our values we can go ahead toward improvement. In this connection, I should like to call attention to the many areas of social action indicated in the present volume: Work to conserve natural resources, to improve aesthetic and cultural standards, to make society sufficiently stable, to increase opportunity for all, and to prevent the concentration of too much power in single hands—all this furnishes an ample outlet for anyone's energy. But as long as we are obsessed with the idea that by some apparently quick, easy, single change all our other aims will be automatically realized, then we are diverted from constructive action. Exploration of the limits of action is often a necessary prelude to successful action. It must be confused with a policy of complacent inactivity."

The material in this book has been assembled according to a carefully integrated plan, and it will help, I think, to explain that plan at the beginning. The reader will naturally want to know why certain topics have been brought together in this special order, and I will, accordingly, begin with a brief general survey of the whole project.

First of all it should be remembered that the book was not written as anything more than an outline. The subject is so vast and so complicated that there is scarcely any possible middle ground between a terse presentation of major issues and a treatise in fourteen volumes. It is necessary, therefore, to stick pretty closely to an explanation of basic problems alone.

A book so designed cannot of course attempt detailed answers to all the thousands of specific questions which might be raised. Perhaps when an author starts on his fourth book some latitude is permissible. I should like those who want a more detailed explanation of my point of view to refer to my earlier books, especially *Democracy and Progress*. But even if we do confine ourselves to a summary and explanation of the major problems, the result, I submit, will be found to be far more constructive than might at first appear.

"Those who wish to defend capitalism," it has been said, "had better study socialism." With at least equal justice one can say that "those who wish to inaugurate socialism, or even centralized comprehensive planning, had better study capitalism." "Planning" today derives a great part of its emotional force not from the idea that it is a better way of going *at* problems, but from a notion that once we inaugurate general planning there simply will *be* no problems.

Such an approach, especially from the point of view of the socialist or the general planner, is most unfortunate. Anyone really studying the specific tasks of practical planning (and the author has had considerable experience in that line) will soon discover that planning per se is not a solution of problems but a technique for approaching them. Sometimes this "planning" technique may be better than the "market" one, sometimes worse. But if the administrators of the plan—socialist or otherwise—are not prepared for their difficulties and come into power supposing themselves possessed of a magic word which will automatically banish all obstacles, they will immediately find themselves involved in disastrous and avoidable errors. Much modern discussion reads as if changing automobiles would move the bumps out of the road. Let us try here, first, to discover what the "bumps" are, and, next, how many of them are put there by capitalism, as such, and how many are due to more fundamental forces.

Following out this general plan, we begin in the first chapter by discussing the communist doctrine of the "withering away of the state." The reason for starting in this way is that it is obviously foolish to discuss what *type* of "state" or politico-economic system is desirable until we have first decided whether it is necessary to have *any* social system at all.

But the discussion in the first chapter is not directly related to capitalism and is not intended to be. The chapter is designed to indicate the framework within which *any* social system—socialist or capitalist—must operate. Nevertheless, in discussion of the communist doctrine a number of basic materials and ideas are collected regarding the psychological sources of insecurity and pressure groups, the nature of man, and so on, which will be fundamental to the rest of the book.

Chapter 2 is also not written with direct reference to capitalism. Our first chapter refers in considerable part to a stationary society. Chapter 2 takes up explicit consideration of the problem of social growth. We ask what are the attributes which any society must have in order to permit rising living standards and economic development.

When we come to Chapter 3 the main elements of the politico-economic problem, common to all societies, should be clear, and it is possible to begin the specific comparison of the techniques (social systems) by which the problem may be approached. Chapter 3 is therefore devoted to sketching in the way in which capitalism goes at the various problems outlined in the two previous chapters.

Chapter 4 is vital and the core of the book, but it cannot be fully understood without the background of the previous chapters. In Chapter 4 I state certain reasons which lead me to believe that a regime of relatively competitive capitalism is the most democratic and, over the long run, the most productive system. In this connection I should like to point out that, although my work has had its share of unsympathetic criticism, no hostile reviewer has ever yet mentioned, much less tried to rebut, my fundamental thesis of the narrowing of the self-selecting, noncompetitive group. As long as that issue is not directly faced—and as yet it has not been—I do not feel criticisms so far made are very conclusive.

This basic thesis of the narrowing of self-selecting groups may be misunderstood in two ways. First of all, the narrowing takes *time*. The experience of five, ten, or even twenty years is not sufficient. There should be two, and better still three, professional generations. Next, even the self-selecting group may be capable of a predominantly parasitic development. That is to say, such a group may take over and apply the major ideas of a more competitive and creative society and thus *appear* to be developing. But were it not for the *outside* competition, the self-selecting institutional organization would not long remain capable of spontaneously generating social development.

The plan of the second half of the book is easier to follow and does not need detailed explanation. Three of the major problems of capitalism are developed: The business cycle (in relation to the Marxian labor theory of value), "monopoly," and stabilization.

The stabilization chapter, especially, should convince the reader of the author's willingness to make all reasonable concessions to the social demands of our time.

But these demands are not always consistent with one another and in our last chapter we try to sum up some of the factors which will affect the future of capitalism. Will there be a "euthanasia" of capitalism, an explosion, or a new era of development?

The author wishes to thank the following publishers for permission to quote from the material noted: Atlantic Monthly Press, "Composers Must Eat"; Columbia University Press, *The Problem of Employment Stabilization*; Harper & Brothers, *Freedom and the Administrative State*; Harcourt, Brace and Company, Inc., *The Economics of the Peace, Essays in Persuasion, Technics and Civilization*; International Publishers Co., *Stalin on the New Constitution*; Lloyds Bank Review, "Liberty, Equality, and Full Employment"; Oxford University Press, *From Max Weber, The Theory of Capitalist Development*; Vanguard Press, Inc., *State and Revolution*; Yale University Press, *Ideological Differences and World Order.*

I also wish to thank the following who have given much time and effort to criticism: Dean Edward S. Mason of the Harvard School of Public Administration and Dr. Arthur F. Cole of the Harvard School of Business Administration, both of whom read the entire manuscript. In addition, Dr. Clare Griffin of the University of Michigan, Dr. A. Powell-Davies of All Souls' Unitarian Church, Washington, D.C., Dr. Marcus Mallet of the Department of Philosophy, University of Virginia, and Dr. Thomas Hammond, professor of Russian history at the University of Virginia, all read parts of the book. None of these gentlemen is, of course, responsible for any views here expressed. The Institute for Research in the Social Sciences of the University of Virginia also rendered important financial assistance.

Let me stress once more that the present book is not intended to be in any sense exhaustive. My aim has been, first, to present some of the chief problems of the modern world and second, to stimulate the reader to further thought and effort on his own. If that much is accomplished the book will have been worth doing.

David McCord Wright

University of Virginia

January, 1951

Contents

Editor's Introduction

FOR YEARS many teachers of economics and other professional economists have felt the need of a series of books on economic subjects which is not filled by the usual textbook or by the highly technical treatise.

This present series, published under the general title of The Economics Handbook Series, was planned with these needs in mind. Designed first of all for students, the volumes are useful in the ever-growing field of adult education and also are of interest to the informed general reader.

The volumes are not long—they give the essentials of the subject matter within the limits of a few hundred pages; they present a distillate of accepted theory and practice, without the detailed approach of the technical treatise. Each volume is a unit, standing on its own.

The authors are scholars, each writing on an economic subject of which he is an authority. In this series the author's first task was not to make important contributions to knowledge—although many of them do—but so to present his subject matter that his work as a scholar will carry its maximum influence outside as well as inside the classroom. The time has come to redress the balance between the energies spent on the creation of new ideas and on their dissemination. Economic ideas are unproductive if they do not spread beyond the world of scholars. Popularizers without technical competence, unqualified textbook writers, and sometimes even charlatans control too large a part of the market for economic ideas.

In the classroom The Economics Handbook Series will serve, it is hoped, as brief surveys in one-semester courses, as supplementary reading in introductory courses, and in other courses in which the subject is related.

The Economics Handbook Series includes studies of capitalism, socialism, and Soviet economics. The study on socialism, by Dr. Paul Sweezy, probably the leading Marxist in the country, has been published. In the present volume, Professor David McCord Wright adds his study of capitalism. Professor Abram Bergson of Columbia University is writing the volume on Soviet economics.

In three previous books (*The Creation of Purchasing Power,* 1942; *The Economics of Disturbance,* 1947; and *Democracy and Progress,* 1948), Professor Wright had shown an unusual capacity to deal with technical problems of economics and yet to put economics in a framework of broader problems of our society. He shows his ability to do this in the current volume also. Since the author has written an introductory summary of his book, I shall merely adumbrate a few of the high lights. What is the ideology of capitalism, and how does capitalism fit into the problems of society and growth? What is the broad relevant social problem? What are the conditions for social growth? What are the diseases of capitalism? And how important are they? What is the relation of the constant quest for security with growth and freedom? These are the major questions in Wright's study of capitalism. The author would be the first to admit that capitalism is not free of disease and that more is required than a mere do-nothing program, but he is also relatively optimistic concerning the possibilities of capitalism. Monopoly, instability, and insecurity are the diseases which the author especially considers. Therapy is acceptable, he agrees, but surgery must not be so heroic as to deprive the system of organs essential for growth and freedom. The search for security may destroy the capacity to grow and may endanger freedoms. The reader might compare Wright's conclusions on these points with those of Dr. Paul Sweezy's aforementioned book on socialism.

Professor Wright has studied at the University of Pennsylvania, University of Virginia, and Harvard University, where he received his doctorate in 1940. He was trained in architecture, in law, and then in economics, is well versed in history and philosophy, and has had considerable experience in business and government. Able to write well and interestingly and with a strong concern for the anatomy and physiology of our economic system, Professor Wright was an obvious choice for our volume on capitalism in The Economics Handbook Series. A former attorney with the RFC and economic consultant with the National Resources Planning Board, he has taught at the U.S. Army School of Military Government, Columbia University, University of California, and Harvard University, and is now a professor of economics and lecturer in law at the University of Virginia.

SEYMOUR E. HARRIS

Part One

The Social Problem

CHAPTER 1

Government and the Social Problem

IF WE WERE really to try to cover the entire "social problem" in this book, our field would have to be much larger than that we will actually attempt. Not merely economics or government would concern us but also the problems of family, of religion, philosophy, taboos, customs, and so on. We shall mention all of these from time to time. But our major concern at this point is much more limited. What we are primarily interested in here is the relationship of economic life to the state, on the one hand, and to techniques and living standards, on the other. In this chapter we ask what are the principal problems which *any* politico-economic system will have to solve, while in later chapters we shall try to describe and appraise their capitalist solution.

We may begin by listing the major social problems which we contend must exist in any economic system. It is submitted that most American and English social scientists would agree that the following tasks are, for any important length of time,[1] universal: selection of rulers; arbitration of disputes; enforcement of decisions; production of goods needed to satisfy customary living standards; allocation of the goods once they are produced. To this list most thinkers (in the Western world anyhow) would probably add two more problems: How shall we *increase* our output of

[1] As will be shown later, small groups of individuals who have undergone special spiritual experiences may for short periods or, at most, a generation come to approximate a state of conflictless anarchy.

goods (raise living standards)? How shall we improve the *quality* of such goods and the lives of the people making them?

But before we can go further, we are met by a preliminary question of great importance which has to be disposed of. By no means everybody would agree that the list of tasks just outlined was truly universal. The Marxists in particular, or at any rate the Leninist Marxists, would deny that *every* culture had to provide for settling disputes or enforcing decisions.[2] Furthermore, some of them at least would even deny a universal need for maintaining distributional rules to allocate output. They would say that such tasks were the attributes of "the state" and that, if only private property were abolished and production "coordinated," men would gradually become so "good" that the need for coercive government would disappear. The implications of this error are so important and the role which it plays in stimulating enthusiasm for Marxism is so great that we are justified in devoting an entire chapter to it. Furthermore, many of the errors which we shall discuss here are not confined to Marxism but also underlie the opinions of many modern theologians and scientists. Quite aside from the rights and wrongs of Marxism the basic ideas of com-

[2] There are as many different kinds of Marxists as there are Keynesians. Marx himself once declared in disgust, "Je ne suis pas Marxiste." We shall not try to deal with all the subtle shadings of the literature but shall instead concentrate upon the Marx-Lenin-Stalin tradition which may be called "orthodox" Marxism. The two books most relied upon are the *Communist Manifesto* and Lenin's *State and Revolution.*

See the *Communist Manifesto,* end of Sec. II, "In the place of the old bourgeois society with its classes and class antagonisms, we shall have an association in which the free development of each is the free development of all."

Lenin, thinking of a certain Rousseau-like anarchy, said, "Democracy will disappear when the state disappears"—for democracy is a form of government. Lenin, *State and Revolution* (New York: Vanguard Press, Inc., 1929), p. 126. Again he said, Chap. IV, Sec. 2, "We do not at all disagree with the anarchists on the question of the abolition of the state as the *final* aim." (Italics supplied.)

munism have to be evaluated in getting a true idea of the relation of man to the state.

The Marxist Vision

In order to understand the Marxist vision, in its most sophisticated form, it is necessary to draw a very fine distinction between "government" in the sense of the *administration* of production, on the one hand, and "the state" in the sense of *coercive* action on individuals, on the other hand.[3] What the most intelligent Marxists mean is not that there will be no administrators in their ideal world but only that nobody will ever have to be forced to do anything. Spontaneously and voluntarily from native intelligence and sheer love for humanity everyone will see what ought to be done and do it—or see who the right man is to do the job and let him do it or voluntarily submit to his direction in a joint undertaking. The function of deciding disputes and *enforcing* the decision will "wither away." For though everyone is entirely free to do as he wishes, no one will "want" to be foolish or wrong. We will have no need for judges or policemen when all men are satisfied—for who then would want to steal or fight?

[3] See P. M. Sweezy, *Socialism* (New York: McGraw-Hill Book Company, Inc., 1949), pp. 131–133. Also Lenin, *op. cit.,* Chap. IV, Sec. 6, p. 187, "We set ourselves, as our final aim, the task of the destruction of the State, that is, of every organized and systematic violence, every form of violence against man in general. We do not expect the advent of an order of society in which the principle of submission of the minority to the majority will not be observed. But, striving for socialism, we are convinced that it will develop further into Communism, and side by side with this there will vanish all need for force, for the *subjection* of one man to another . . . since people will *grow accustomed* to observing the elementary conditions of social existence *without force and without subjection*. . . . Engels speaks of a *new* generation 'brought up under new and free social conditions, which will prove capable of throwing on the dust heap' . . . every sort of State . . . including even the democratic republican state." (Italics are Lenin's.)

All the Marxist says, that we have to do, therefore, in order to get "eventually" the equivalent of what a Christian would describe as the kingdom of God on earth is first to turn over all power to Marxist planners and then to abolish private property. For all conflicts, they maintain, trace back to private property. At first, in what the Communists call the "socialist" phase of Marxism, a strong government, army, and police force will definitely be required to deal with those who are still selfish. But soon everyone will become so good that this state (courts, police, and other means of coercion) will wither away. In place of the "old bourgeois society with its class antagonism we will have a world in which the free development of each is the free development of all." [4]

Clearly, if it were really possible to get such a priceless reward by such an apparently simple method, most of us would want to try that method. Therefore, just as a certain number of people keep buying wild-cat gold mines, so also a certain number will always be Marxists in hopes of realizing its glittering promise. But why would the mere adoption of Marxist economic "planning," accompanied by the abolition of private property, inevitably serve to usher in a reign of universal righteousness and love? Unfortunately it is just at this point that the Marxist writings become most elusive. Two main lines of approach may, however, be distinguished. The first line is static and ideal or psychological and has no relation to living standards or output. The second is dynamic and utilitarian and puts great emphasis on the economic productivity of planning. The first argues that men are made bad or selfish by the struggle for "private property:" substitute for personal profit the goal of "working for the state," and men will stop wanting to fight or to act selfishly.[5] The second has it that, if we introduce "planning," and abolish private property,

[4] *Communist Manifesto,* end of Sec. II. See also the quotation from Lenin *supra,* note 3.

[5] Lenin, *op. cit.,* p. 124.

the economy will become so productive that, even if people are still selfish, selfishness will become unimportant. For what difference will it make how much any man wants if there is more than enough of everything for everybody?

These two arguments, it should be noted, are independent and could be discussed independently. But they are sometimes combined in a very persuasive, but nevertheless mistaken, fashion. There is an important question of timing here. For we cannot assume that selfishness is going to be made irrelevant by plenty until *after* the "plenty" has been produced. As long as we stick to the "plenty" argument, we have got to assume that planning (and the abolition of private property) will somehow make possible an immense increase in production *even though* selfishness and egotism of many sorts survive—though not, to be sure, the chance to make a fortune. The author has known some Marxists, however, *first* to say that selfishness will be made *irrelevant* (though not removed) by planned plenty, and then, if you ask them why planning is going to produce plenty, the reply will be that it will do so because abolishing private property will make people unselfish. In other words people will become unselfish because they have plenty and have plenty because they have become unselfish. But just where, one may ask, does the process get started?

Planning "Plenty" and Pressure Groups

Let us begin with the widespread popular idea that "planning" or equal incomes, *merely as such,* will remove all problems of insecurity, pressure groups, and resistances to change. Evaluation of this notion is absolutely vital to all the rest of this book, for the one thing on which most of the people of the world seem to be agreed—nominally at least—is the idea that a rising living standard for the masses is desirable. And if men really do believe in the principle of growing output, then obviously a strong case is made out for whichever system can best handle the problem of growth.

In 1946 a group of sociologists questioned a population sample of Americans as to how much money they needed to make them "happier or more comfortable." Sixty-eight per cent of the sample were definitely dissatisfied, and these people wanted, on the average, an *eighty-six* per cent increase over their present incomes.[6] These figures are no doubt subject to many possible criticisms, but they do indicate something of the tremendous unsatisfied income wants which exist even in the United States—the richest country in the world.[7] Yet, as Hicks and Hart point out: "Enough can be 'redistributed' to mitigate the extremes of poverty . . . but substantial gains for the majority of the population must be sought in increased productivity." [8]

If we are really, then, to give "more" to more people, we need growth. But though the idea of the "economy of abundance" has sunk deep into the consciousness of the Western world, and though it often seems impossible to open any newspaper without reading glowing forecasts of the "abundance" which we, or at any rate our grandchildren, are going to enjoy, still there is one fact so obvious that it is almost always overlooked: Practically no one assumes that we can get this state of "abundance" merely by using the methods and working the machinery which we *already* have. Even the most rabid writers on the subject admit that there will have to be, at the least, a great *re*organization and *re*allocation of resources, while the more thoughtful members of the extreme left pin their main hope of abundance upon the joint effect

[6] Krech and Crutchfield, *Theory and Problems of Social Psychology* (New York: McGraw-Hill Book Company, Inc., 1948), p. 543.

[7] J. R. Hicks and A. G. Hart in *The Social Framework of the American Economy* (New York: Oxford University Press, 1945), p. 231, figure that the total excess of consumption over $5,000 a year amounts to only about 5 per cent of total consumption output.

[8] *Ibid.*

of a planned increase in the amount of machinery and equipment relative to labor, plus the introduction of new inventions, for example, atomic power.

But whether we are dealing only with the shifting around of equipment and men we already have or are talking about new growth and new invention, one thing is unavoidable. The process involves *change.* Men have got to be moved from one place to another, certain skills will become obsolete, while others will become more valuable, and so on. If planning is really going to give us "plenty," it has got to be able to manage readjustments of this sort in such a way that output will always keep far ahead of human desires. Let us therefore see whether the mere introduction of Marxist "planning" (or, for that matter, any other kind) will serve to eliminate conflicts and resistances to change.

Space is lacking for a minute dissection of Marxian exegesis. The Marxist structure may, of course, be softened down and "interpreted." Thus the author has known some apologists to imply that all that is meant by the withering away of the state is that "everyone accepts the necessity of planning." Such interpretations vibrate between tautology and nonsense. The myth which Marx taught and Lenin elaborated, the myth which has fired the minds of thousands of intellectuals, has been one of an eventual literal anarchy, obtained through a present strict control—the idea that *all,* or virtually all, economic (and social) conflict stems from the struggle of "bourgeois" (those who live on incomes from property) and "proletarians" (those who live on wages). We shall examine the psychological inadequacies of this opinion, and we shall show both its close connection with comparable defects in other elements of nineteenth-century thought, and the way in which such ideas, taken together, have led to quite dangerous misunderstandings of the social process—not only in some of the most radical and eccentric modern quarters, but also in some of the most respectable.

Dr. Lewis Lorwin, in summarizing the communist doctrine of

the class struggle, speaks of a social class as being to the Communist "an aggregate of persons who have the same *function* in the productive process and who therefore have the same source of income" (italics added).[9] While the actual words are Lorwin's, the definition quoted embodies an important and interesting ambiguity in the general Marxian outlook and also in much modern economics. This ambiguity is a confusion of the nature of the productive *function,* or income source, with the *manner* in which money is paid. In other words whether a man is a coal miner or an oil driller, whether he is a simple worker or a foreman or a vice-president, he is impliedly treated as having both the same *function* and the same income *source* simply because he receives wages rather than rents or dividends. To say, however, that all conflicts grow out of differences between "workers" as a group and "owners" as a group overlooks a multitude of possible sources of friction. The trouble is that only one small part of the complex motivation of humanity is considered. Even if we confine ourselves to "purely economic" ideas, the Marxist classification overlooks the possibility of "vertical" conflicts between *all* those in one industry and *all* those in another.

Vertical conflicts between rival industrial groups, each containing *both* "capitalists" and workers, have received considerable attention from economists, for example, Professor Lionel Robbins in his *Economic Basis of Class Conflict.*[10] In the liberal-left mythology, however, the problem is usually recognized as occurring only in capitalist context between owner and owner. The radical finds relatively little difficulty in seeing that under capitalism the *owners* of the oil industry (*i.e.,* of its capital) may be in conflict with the *owners* of the coal industry, for each group produces substitute products and the wealth of one inevitably implies some

[9] *Encyclopaedia of the Social Sciences,* Vol. III, p. 540.

[10] Lionel Robbins, *The Economic Basis of Class Conflict* (London: Macmillan & Co., Ltd., 1939).

diminution of, at the least, the potential wealth of the other. But it may be plausibly maintained that, if all capital were owned by the state, the obsolescence of individual units would be a matter of small consequence to "the workers" and resources would be allocated without serious conflict and in the best interest of all. There would be no "vested interest."

A good explanation of the pressure-group problem is furnished by Dr. E. D. Domar's essay on "Investment, Losses, and Monopolies." The passage is also interesting because of the implication that centralized planning could overcome or at least greatly ameliorate the dilemma. Domar writes:[11]

> We may imagine representatives of our big business, perhaps together with those from big labor, sitting around a table. All prospective investments are placed on a platter and passed around. The representative of General Motors might, for example, find all of them splendid, all with the exception of Kaiser-Frazer's new plan for expansion. He takes this one project off and passes the platter on. Pennsylvania Railroad has no objection to Kaiser-Frazer and to all other such projects, but it might decide to veto the St. Lawrence Waterway. Its views are seconded by United Mine Workers whose behaviour is undistinguishable from that of their business associates at the table. The platter moves on. . . . By the time the platter completes its trip around the table it is perfectly empty; all projects have been vetoed by one or the other participant. And there goes our prosperity.
>
> If the participants were small and weak, as they are supposed to be in an atomistic society, their vetoes would be just empty talk. On the other hand, *if the whole economy were ruled by one closely connected financial group,* the latter would not treat the level of income as independent of its own actions, and would find it profitable to invest and expand in many dif-

[11] From *Income, Employment, and Public Policy: Essays in Honor of Alvin Hansen* (New York: W. W. Norton & Company, 1948), p. 52.

ferent directions. . . . It would even pay the rest to compensate a particularly injured member for his losses in order to remove his opposition. [Italics added.]

The first thing which will strike an unbiased reader about this passage is the apparent assumption that private businesses really do get together in this way. Dr. Domar does not seem to realize that what he is really aiming at is a session of a government planning board or NIRA. But leaving that to one side, the basic inadequacy of the passage quoted is the idea that planning will virtually eliminate pressure-group conflicts. Marx puts the matter more strongly: "From the time," he writes, "when together with class domination and the struggle for individual existence, *resulting from the present anarchy in production,* those conflicts and excesses which arise from this struggle will all disappear . . . there will . . . be no need for the state" (italics added).[12] Evaluation of this statement will bring out the essence of our argument.

Let us suppose that the law requires that everyone be paid the same money income—no more and no less. Suppose that this happens in a relatively wealthy society and that the equal income thus received is enough to meet the "necessities" of life and allow for a margin of comfort. Would it not seem that everybody would then be "secure" and that there would no longer be pressure groups or social conflicts?

It is just at this point, however, that the Communists and many liberal socialists diverge. Many liberal socialists would say that equal income plus planning would certainly *reduce* conflict, but they would not necessarily say that conflict would ever disappear. But the Communists would say that equal money income, plus Marxist nationalization of industry, would eventually remove *all* conflicts and pressure groups. For the present we shall consider the extreme Marxist version.

[12] Lenin, *op. cit.,* p. 124.

The author believes that the trouble with many left-wing writers is that they have taken orthodox economics far too seriously! For the idea that planning, plus equal money income, will eliminate conflict is the direct bastard offspring of "economic man." In some of the cruder economic expositions an economic man is supposed to care for virtually nothing save money income (properly "adjusted" by a statistical price index of course) and to be willing to fight for practically nothing save money income. Now if such a view of human nature was correct, it would follow that, if everyone were guaranteed the same wage, the process of relocating men and resources, which is an inseparable part of the process of growth, would arouse no conflict of any kind. What difference, one would think, would it make to a man whether he lived in Los Angeles or in Pittsburgh if he got the same salary and prices were the same? What difference would it make if he were shifted from being a college professor to being a truck driver (or vice versa) if his salary were unaffected, prices remained the same, and hence his expenditure level was unchanged? Unfortunately, as soon as we bring the problem down to earth in this way, all sorts of problems are soon encountered and we can see at once the artificiality of considering income alone.

In the first place, even if we abolish money differences, great differences in perquisites may survive. What is the difference between going broke and losing your factory if you are a capitalist and moving out of a former tsarist palace into half a room if you are a commissar who has lost favor or whose skill has become obsolete? Suppose we go even further and abolish all perquisites? Still there would remain the secret sweets of power and the feeling of being a big shot.

The trouble is that money income (even after due allowance is made for price changes) is often only a small part of the sum total of human incentives and motivation. Resistances to change may often be grounded in forces far deeper than merely financial insecurity. Let us try to list some of the numerous nonmonetary, non-"economic" reasons which would lead people to oppose the transfers and the retraining which growing national income must imply.

In the first place, a man may like a given community, a given house, a given view, and not want to leave them. In the second place, he may be attached to a given group of friends, a given organization, or a given team of work mates. Third, he may have a special love of his work and a special pleasure in it. Finally, he may love power and prestige, and his particular source of power may be some line of activity which change threatens to make obsolete.

The love of friends and of places does not require much explanation. The love of one's work, however, does need a bit of elaboration. Under the nineteenth-century ideology men were looked upon as balancing a certain amount of work (disutility) against a certain amount of enjoyment or leisure or consumption (utility). Work therefore was conceived of as drudgery, and the aim of progress was to enable us to do as little of it as possible. The whole creative instinct of the human race was slurred over.

In a healthy society, however, work is not to be thus sharply set off against enjoyment. It is true that we can get tired from doing *too much* or too unpleasant work—just as we may get tired of eating too many bananas—and we may have to supplement the pure instinct of workmanship to get as *much* work out of a man as we wish. But this is *not* ground for making the sharp division between labor and consumption usual in economic and Marxian thinking. Work is still frequently *one* of a man's satisfactions. Just because a man gets tired of eating bananas if he has too many of them, we can't jump to the conclusion that it will make no difference to him whether he eats bananas or oranges. Just because he gets tired if he works *too long* at one job, we cannot jump to the conclusion that he would just as soon work at any other job.

As Krech and Crutchfield put it in their *Theory and Problems of Social Psychology,*[13]

> The worker whose painfully acquired skill has suddenly become useless and meaningless by some new invention or improvement in production methods finds himself facing very serious psychological problems. Not only must he learn new skills and routines of work, but his feeling of *personal worth and self-esteem,* based in many instances on his mastery of the now obsolescent skill, is threatened. [Italics added.]

When we add to frictions like these the love of power which many people have, the problem of finding a perfect solution becomes insuperable. It is all very well for Lenin to say that in the Marxist utopia "the authority of the government over persons will be replaced by the administration of things and the direction of the processes of production." [14] The trouble is one cannot direct and (more important) redirect the processes of production *without* directing people.

The trouble is that, in shifting resources or altering technical methods, we also alter work relationships, and in altering work relationships we also alter *power* relationships among the human beings who make up the work teams of the organizations involved. "Retraining" some men—especially young ones—could certainly *help* to minimize friction. The same would also be true of removing the fear of starvation or indeed of any reprisals on the consumption level of an individual. But though the sources of friction are *helped,* they are never wholly removed. What does a guaranteed consumption level mean to a politician compared with the loss of office or power, or to a physicist if balanced against the loss of his laboratory? A man who loves a special community may value contact with friends much more than a guaranteed ability

[13] Krech and Crutchfield, *op. cit.,* p. 540.

[14] Lenin, *op. cit.,* p. 125.

to buy beer. Similarly a man who loves a special job (or art) may value it more than a mere fixed income.

But it may be objected that we can "compensate" the individuals whose skills are made obsolete or who have to do unpleasant work. Again, however, infinite possibilities of disagreement are opened up. There are some people whose love for their work or power or friends or community may be such that *no* money could compensate them for their loss. Would Mr. Truman resign from the Presidency for a million dollars? I doubt it. Would Stalin move to Monte Carlo for the sake of a guaranteed income? It scarcely seems likely. But even on a more mundane plane, and even if there is *some* money sum which might induce many of us to leave our employment willingly, still the amount demanded by us, *as individuals,* to compensate our *subjective* valuations may appear utterly ridiculous to the rest of society and be far more than they are willing to pay. Hence, unless those inconvenienced by change are allowed to levy unlimited blackmail, many conflicts still remain possible.

Again there is a suggestion contained in some of the Marxist literature that everyone could be trained simultaneously to do anything and everything. As Dr. Bober puts it, "In a joint work in 1845 the two young revolutionaries [Marx and Engels] irresponsibly declare that under communism the worker will hunt in the morning, fish in the afternoon, rear cattle in the evening, and criticize after dinner." [15] But it does not take much thought to see that, even if everybody was intrinsically capable of being trained to do everything (which is surely a doubtful proposition—can the tone-deaf man be trained to sing?), the immense amount of time needed to train *everyone* to be *at once* a doctor, lawyer, physicist, actor, railroad engineer, truck driver, painter, sculptor,

[15] M. M. Bober, "Proceedings of the American Economic Association, Dec. 27, 1948," *American Economic Review,* May, 1949, p. 41; "Die Deutsche Ideologie" in Marx-Engels, *Historisch-kritische Gesamtanagabe* (Berlin: 1927–1932), Part I, Vol. 5, p. 22.

chemist, etc., in one lifetime would speedily use up the whole national income.

The Marxist is caught in a curious dilemma. If he argues that men, in modern industry, have all become interchangeable parts and therefore will not care what they are doing and hence will not form pressure groups, he is admitting that the instinct of workmanship and local attachments are going to be frustrated in his society. Furthermore, practically speaking, the interchangeable-part idea will not be true of the higher rank scientists and planners. On the other hand, if he admits the existence of the instinct of workmanship, he must admit the existence of potential class (group) conflict in the socialist state. Many an erstwhile happy man could be left stranded as a "back number," and no money salve is ever likely entirely to relieve his hurt. The scientist who wishes to introduce a new pattern, involving new resource allocations, will inevitably create potentialities of conflict whether there is planning or not. The "free development" of the man who wishes to continue in an obsolete industry or whose power depends on continuance of an obsolete industry can never be the free development of all—and this not from mere money drives but from far more deeply seated and complex psychological factors. Those UNESCO "scientists" who wished to avoid conflict by giving every man a chance for "personal growth and development" have failed to realize that one man's growth in *any* system may involve another's "insecurity." [16]

Is Plenty Ever Possible?

We are thus forced to the conclusion that the mere introduction of planning and the mere abolition of economic income differences do not of themselves abolish pressures which might lead individuals to restrictive or antisocial action. Men may be ego-

[16] Report of the UNESCO committee of "social scientists" on the causes of war. *Christian Science Monitor,* Aug. 28, 1948.

tistical about many things besides money, and these various *non-monetary* types of egotism may create quite as significant impulses toward conduct obstructing desirable social and economic change as the profit motive ever did. The problem of social change and growing living standards, therefore, cannot be solved, even under planning or equal incomes, unless we find some way of either persuading or else forcing the individual inconvenienced by change to yield to a process which disturbs *him* but which the rest of society considers desirable. In other words we arrive at the age-old ethical problem of getting the individual to bow to the public good.

It follows that in order to achieve "plenty" or in order to create a conflict-free world the Marxist society cannot simply rely on the "productivity" of planning but must also be possessed of some special *new* psychological formula which will solve the ethical problem that has puzzled humanists throughout the ages—a formula which will induce men to act *always* unselfishly even when pressures toward selfishness remain. We shall discuss in a moment the communist formula available for this ethical task, but before we go further, we may well ask whether plenty is *ever* possible?

By plenty, it should be understood, is meant not merely a great increase in productivity or a stable adjustment of economic life but a world in which *everyone* has quite literally *everything* he could want. To borrow an illustration from William James: "If there remained one cockroach" with an unsatified desire, the perfection of the universal harmony would be spoiled. The concept of Marxist plenty does not include cockroaches, to be sure, but it does include *everyone* human. Two basic objections, however, are usually made to the idea of absolute plenty. In the first place it is pointed out that historically the "satisfying" effects of a rise in production have nearly always, sooner or later, been wiped out by one or both of two things: a rise in people's wants or a rise in the birth rate. In the second place most people would agree that there are lots of other things which men desire and could fight about besides money or private property, and hence if we want to prevent serious fights and maintain order, we shall still need policemen or coercion of some sort if *all* we have done is abolish private property.

Modern Western societies have perhaps, for the moment anyhow, taken care of the problem of excessive birth rates. If anything, the problem may come to be how to get enough births. But the question of rising desires is more complicated. Even if we mean by "plenty," only plenty of things to take from the counters of stores, we still shall have to supplement increased production by a very thorough indoctrination of youth in order to keep people from wanting anything more than the standard of consumption their society can supply. It may well be asked whether conditioning of this sort can really be done without some coercion. But in addition to this problem there is another and more profound one: No society can ever have or produce enough of *certain* things to satisfy all the people who want them. For example, if several men love the same woman and she wishes to choose only one of them exclusively, the others must be disappointed. No amount of increases in the standard of living can *by itself* prevent conflicts from this source. "Is this the face that launched a thousand ships and burned the topless towers of Ilium? Sweet Helen, make me immortal with a kiss." Again if several men desire the privilege of serving the community in a certain special way and only one can hold the desired office, increased output of goods *by itself* cannot prevent conflicts from this source. "But as he was ambitious I slew him." We thus see not only that it is impossible to obtain rising living standards without *first* dealing with the problem of selfishness but also that living standards can never be raised so high as to give *everybody everything* they will want. Thus the idea of avoiding conflict *merely* by overwhelming people with gadgets cannot work. In any society the ethical problem must be dealt with directly.

Technological Levels and Social Action

Before, however, we reach the ethical problem which is the core of our discussion, there remains one point to be dealt with, which, like the last, is especially applicable to a stationary world. The reader may object that so far we have put all our emphasis on social *growth*. Why not stop social growth, it might be asked, and have a stationary society? Then there would be no insecurity and hence no pressure groups and hence no necessity for social conflict.

Unquestionably the complexity of the technical level and, still more important, changes in its complexity do affect the dimensions of the problem, and we shall have to come back to this point later on. Nevertheless, it remains true that, even if we put aside all ideas of further growth or further technical change, and even if we try merely to remain where we are as far as living standards and production methods are concerned, still there would be pressures toward social conflict and toward selfish and antisocial conduct which mere planning or equal incomes could not overcome.

The trouble lies in the fact that, even if the political "state" were nominally abolished, still there would remain the task of selecting, not political rulers (if you object to calling them by that name), but technical administrators. Even if governors of states were nominally abolished, superintendents of waterworks must remain. But this involves great possibilities of conflict and frustration. As long as men are different in their abilities and make-up, some will be better fitted to hold responsible *technical* jobs than others. There must be long and careful training and careful selection. The more complex the technology the more careful the selection. But to get men to undergo this training we must inculcate some ambition—if only to do a good job for the state. And then, since there must be a selection of candidates, we should have to frustrate some of the very ambitions we had ourselves created. Once more the free development of each could not be the free development of all. How is the stationary state going to be *kept* stationary? Is it reasonable to suppose that men who have had general access to *some* science and to the method of discovery will spontaneously refuse to speculate any further as to the working of the universe? The question almost answers itself. Technology could not be kept stationary without a technological inquisition such as Samuel Butler mentions in his *Erewhon,* accompanied by strong social taboos against innovation. And again the free development of each is not the free development of all. Indeed *free* development would be almost the last thing permissible in such a society.

Pressure Groups, Egotism, and the State

What new element does the Marxist have to contribute to the solution of the ethical problem—either in its personal aspects or in the matter of economic pressure groups? It is true that Marxism begins with the use of force and of the coercive power of government. But these, in the Marxist ideology, are supposed to be temporary expedients. Something more is required. Something in the mere atmosphere of Marxist socialism is supposed to be going to make people progressively "better" and less in need of "coercion" despite the fact that pressures toward selfishness will survive; and it is supposed that, as this factor operates, the need for government, courts, and police will gradually decline. Yet what factor will this be? We have seen that mere planning and the abolishing of private property and income differences will not abolish pressures toward selfishness and conflict. The answer, then, cannot be that Marxist planning will avoid situations producing drives toward selfishness. We cannot even say that it will avoid feelings of psychic insecurity on the part of the individual, especially those with the power and duty of making decisions. What the Marxist has got to say is that the slogan of "working for the state" will *ipso facto* produce so high an ethical tone that men will reach a stage in which they can be counted on *always* to subordinate their desires and their beliefs to a better individual and a better idea when one comes along—without ever having to be *made* to do so.

But *who* is to say what idea is "better" and what men are "best"? In this question we reach the essential core of the problem of government. Many people today have the notion that all wars are the outgrowth either of selfishness or of ignorance and misunderstanding. They often go further and say that all disputes between individuals result either from selfishness or from ignorance and misunderstanding. Unhappily it can be shown that neither of these ideas is true.

Suppose that we have a community which wants to increase its output and use new methods and new inventions. Suppose next that each person in the community has come to be possessed of a noble and disinterested zeal to do his or her very ultimate best to increase production and help the good of the state. Will such a community automatically be freed from the danger of conflict because of the ethical transformation of its citizens? Unfortunately not entirely. For still there may be disputes as to the best *method* of doing things.

The easiest way to get at the basic issue is to drop the loaded word "conflict" and substitute the word "disagreement." Can we have a disagreement-free world? Only if individuals are given an identical rearing and set of beliefs and, *in addition,* are also identical in psychic, intellectual, physical, and genetic make-up—which is impossible. Nor can there ever be a body of "scientific" knowledge on *all* subjects sufficient to settle *every* difference of opinion with such immediate, crushing, and irrefutable evidence as to leave no room for further dispute by the disgruntled. "You cannot," remarked Mr. Justice Holmes, "argue a man into liking a glass of beer." This is not to deny the immense value and usefulness of science but only to dispute either that it is all-embracing or that it is infallible in the form we find it handed to us by individual scientists or even individual experiments. The "unanimity" of scientists is an outsider's delusion. Even on their own narrow field physicists today simultaneously entertain two entirely different and entirely contradictory explanations as to the nature of light and are unable as yet to tell which is correct.

Complete absence of disagreement, then, is impossible. The question therefore arises: When do disagreements become overt conflicts? The Marxist would say, "When money interests are involved." Others might go a bit further and say, "When money *or* other self-seeking or vainglorious motives are involved." But neither statement would be complete, for both would assume that the essential origin of conflict was moral turpitude or ignorance. Conflicts, however, may *also* arise when the most magnanimous and unselfish of men are disagreed as to the *best way* of attaining noble ends upon which they are all agreed. And the nobler they are, the finer their nature, the deeper their love for humanity, and the more devoted their determination to serve the state the more they may fight!

For example, during certain periods of medieval history scholars tried to settle nearly all questions of fact by reference to the ancients—Aristotle, Galen, etc. Now as long as Aristotle and Galen were believed to be infallible, and in the (rare) cases in which they were so unambiguous as to admit of no differences in interpretation, this method did tend to give "peace," of a sort, among scholars. But we know now that Aristotle and Galen were often wrong. Without the courage of the *unselfish* dissenters, who were willing to fight traditional oracles, the progress of medicine and physics would have been indefinitely delayed.

A culture, therefore, which wishes to maintain adequate order will be obliged to set up some means for settling disputes no matter how moral the citizen. And accompanying this method of settlement there must be social sanctions—police, for example, or social ostracism or, say, banishment—whereby the minority can be coerced who are either too selfish or too *unselfish* but far-seeing (in their own esteem anyhow) to abide by the decision reached through the accepted method of settlement. This function as arbitrator, with its accompaniment by sanctions, constitutes the irreducible essence of the state. To be sure, such functions need not, in all cultures, take the centralized and immensely complex forms we see today. Yet in some embodiment or other the essential function always survives. What is a supreme court and an army in one culture may be only iron-clad custom backed up by "public opinion" and an occasional lynching or banishment in another. But it is the state just the same and will be found everywhere, albeit sometimes in attenuated form, until men become literally identical. Yet

> 'Tis with our judgments as our watches, none
> Goes just alike yet each believes his own.

Do not think to count always on appeal to a man's higher nature. He may reply "My higher nature tells me it is my duty to save the city, and even though everyone doubts me, and though the authorities and the votes have gone against me, they are wrong! I must keep fighting the citizens for *their* own good."

Final Summary and Conclusion

We may stop at this point and summarize our discussion. We have seen that the *mere* introduction of "planning" (Marxist or otherwise) or of equal incomes will not serve to eliminate insecurities, pressure groups, or conflicts in a growing world. Nor could we avoid the potentiality of conflict by "compensating" those inconvenienced by change (unless, of course, one were willing to pay unlimited blackmail). Any society, then, which wishes a higher living standard must find means of dealing with pressure groups directly. Again no matter how much the living standard may rise, there can never *always* be enough of *every* thing to satisfy *every* person. The ethical problems thus cannot be by-passed by increased output. Furthermore, even if we put aside rising living standards as a delusion and try only to stay where we are, still the problem of social conflict remains, for, first, the task of training *and* selecting technical administrators would survive (which we have seen inevitably involves possibilities of frustration and conflict) and, second, it would be necessary to take coercive measures from time to time to stop those who are seeking to discover or use new methods and new scientific truth. Finally there survives a concluding insoluble problem in the fact that even with the highest motives men will disagree from time to time as to methods. Conflict may be rooted in *un*selfishness.

The preceding argument proves that save for short intervals, in small communities of especially "moral" individuals, there must always be some residual "state" power in every culture. It does not, however, prove that the need for such power may not vary enormously from culture to culture. Nor need it be taken as proving that the complexity of society and the need for the *coercive* state must always increase in the same proportion. We do not need to end in entire pessimism—contemplating a world that is *only* dog eat dog.

Once we concede, indeed, that absolute freedom from social conflict and from coercive action is impossible, then we may find it possible to work out numerous schemes for *mitigating* conflict. And it may turn out that *relative* absence of conflict, like relative happiness, can be best obtained by not searching for it too frantically and too directly. In the author's opinion the man who is least likely to obtain happiness is the man who gets up in the morning and asks himself tensely, "What shall I do to be happy today?" And the state least likely to escape the need for coercion is the state which seeks to avoid conflict by trying to ensure uniformity of opinion.

Agreement to disagree may be a better way of avoiding conflict than intense pressure toward agreement. Social order does not require absence of disputes. It need require only general agreement as to the means of settling them. If men are pretty well agreed as to the "fairness" of their general scheme of political and social life, *most* of those adversely affected will yield without violence and the need for coercion is proportionately reduced—though never wholly eliminated.

In the same way if the economic administration of society is split up among numerous units accompanied by a philosophy of give and take in a system permitting constant adjustment, there may be less of serious conflict or less of frustration than if all economic life is swallowed up in some vast leviathan. Thus by recognizing the inevitability of some disagreement and conflict and permitting it to occur in numerous *secondary* ways within a framework of generally accepted rules of the game, we come *nearer* avoiding serious coercion and cruelty (*i.e.,* get less of it) than if we try to avoid conflict entirely by forcing all men into the same mold or subjecting all of them to the same minute authority.

Two fallacies, however, are today being used to turn us away from the approach just sketched. The first confuses relative absence of bureaucracy and absence of *overt* conflict with the absence of basic coercion. This idea often leads to "back-to-the-land" schemes or to *de facto* advocacy of regimes of state. It would be easy to sketch a society which *looks* stateless. Such a society could be organized on a very primitive, very simple technological level and governed by a few simple, well-understood, and absolutely not-to-be-questioned assumptions, customs, and values. Under such circumstances selection of rulers might conceivably be made by rather haphazard methods largely unrelated to personal merit or ambition, for example, seniority, inheritance, etc. And since everybody would know his foreordained place in the scheme, few would need waste time worrying about it. As long as there was no change, *overt* conflict would be at a minimum. Children would have to be trained to conform, a few dissenters occasionally eliminated, but for the rest, surface calm would be maintained by the frustration of all impulse toward novelty. Yet though administration would be at a minimum, coercion (and frustration) *could* be at a maximum—and certainly could not disappear.

The second fallacy of modern social life is the idea that we can avoid all conflict and make men spontaneously and uniformly good if we protect them from all save the "right" opinion—it being assumed that there is a single right opinion on every subject which can be definitely, unequivocally, and spontaneously recognized by all free men. This is the basic mistake of Marxism.

The communist ideology, indeed, appears to be the worst possible combination for the avoidance either of the administrative *or* of the coercive state. If the Marxists were content with a stationary, primitive economy, they could, we have seen, reduce administration to a minimum and come close to eliminating *overt* conflict—though not coercion or frustration. But communism emphatically desires a high industrialism and is nearly as naïve as any Main Streeter in its faith in salvation by gadgets. Also if the Marxists were content only to reach a certain level of technology and then stop, they might hope to preserve a steady routine, though scarcely to dispense with administration. But the Marxian promise, at least in its modern communist version, is one not only of industrialism but of *developing* industrialism—an outlook idealizing scientific discovery—yet insisting it conform to the "party line"—the current interpretation of an ambiguous social oracle. To glorify change and yet restrict it; to stimulate the restless inquiry of the West and then expect it to conform spontaneously to the vague rules of a complex and evasive gospel concerning whose meaning there may, in utmost good faith, be scores of different interpretations; to feel an utter, fierce conviction that the salvation of mankind depends upon the survival only of the correct (your) interpretation, surely there could not be a social outlook less likely ever to dispense with coercion or eliminate conflict.

CHAPTER 2

Requirements of Social Growth

SO FAR we have done no more than point out some of the basic and universal rudiments of the problem of government and economics. Our discussion may have seemed a little remote. But before deciding what *type* of politico-economic system we might want, it was clearly necessary to decide whether we were obliged to have any system at all. We found, however, that as long as men are not perfectly good, perfectly wise, and, still more important, perfectly identical, the potentiality of conflict-creating disagreement remains. Socialism does not eliminate forces pressing men toward selfish action. Furthermore even were men unselfish, there still would remain the possibility of conflicts undertaken nobly, unselfishly, and in good faith concerning the best way of doing things. There is no infallible oracle which could cover and settle *all* possible sources of disagreement. It follows that in all types of society there must be methods, however informal, by which urgent questions can be determined and disputes settled. And there will also be a need for the invocation, at times, of social sanctions to force the dissenter or the criminal into line. This task of arbitration and enforcement constitutes the irreducible essence of "the state."

But though we have only begun to investigate the complexity of the politico-economic problem, our analysis already shows clearly how much the idea of growth increases the ramifications of the task. We have listed the universal elements of the problem as selection of rulers, arbitration of disputes, enforcement of decisions, production of goods, allocation of goods. But we pointed out that in the Western world two more problems were widely stressed: increasing the output of goods, improving the quality of these goods and the lives of the people making them. In the present chapter we shall leave the political problem largely to one side and concentrate for the time being on the economic and social requirements for growth and change under any type of system.

Considering the importance of the subject the requirements of social growth have received extraordinarily little explicit or systematic treatment, and most of what has been written has made small attempt at institutional generality. Business apologists have usually assumed that the mere institution of private property, in and of itself, was somehow magically responsible for all social development. On the other hand, left-wing writers have treated the growth impulse as being the automatic outgrowth of science and have concentrated on negative factors in capitalism tending to hold growth back.

Our thinking has been additionally hampered by the tendency of "pure" economic theorists, until recently, to concentrate upon problems of "equilibrium" rather than expansion. Economic and social life has been frequently envisaged as a quiet pond into which a rock is dropped from time to time rather than a continuing *process* of change and development. This emphasis on equilibrium has encouraged the tendency of "welfare" economists to put far more stress upon the way the national income is divided than upon the way it is increased.

Our task in this chapter will, therefore, be a twofold one: first to give a systematic presentation of the essentials of economic growth and second to express our theory of growth so broadly that it will be applicable to nearly all types of developing human society. We want to avoid ideological provincialism. Until we outline the basic general principles, there is no point in dissecting particular systems.

The requirements of social growth are submitted to be eight in number. They are as follows: natural resources, labor, knowledge and education, saving, enterprise, ideology, a degree of stabilization, criticism. Let us run over them in turn.

Labor, Resources, and Knowledge

Not many people, no matter what their political opinions, will dispute the statement that at the present time, at the least, increased output requires some labor, some natural resources, and a great deal of knowledge. There is a danger, however, that, in concentrating upon economic and technological problems or the discovery of *new* knowledge, education as such will be overlooked. Yet each generation is a "new invasion of barbarians." Human knowledge and human cultures do not perpetuate themselves. Books do not simply walk out of a library and force people to read them. The ideas they contain must be taught. Any civilization, then, will decline which fails to transmit to its younger members the key ideas of its culture. And this remains true no matter what economic system we adopt or what momentary success our society may have in increasing the output of turbines or stepping up production of atomic power.

Saving

But in speaking of knowledge and education we are still dealing with things which, in principle at least, are universally conceded. Really fundamental misunderstandings and disputes do not begin until we come to the next item in our list: saving. Here we encounter a curious paradox. As long as socialists are out of power, they are apt to deride and to minimize the need for saving, for socialist theories of capitalist crises are almost always underconsumption ones. But as soon as they come into power, the need for great expansion to implement their welfare promises usually forces a revision of their slogans and they appeal frantically to the masses for increased saving. In order, therefore, to postpone ideological frictions as long as possible let us begin with a very primitive, simple, and noncontroversial example.

Mankind has been described as a "tool-using" animal. Suppose we took a group of the strongest, most intelligent, most vigorous, and most highly educated young women and men in our society. Suppose we stripped them naked and dropped them into a primeval forest or on a desert island. What good would all their knowledge or their vigor do them—they would barely survive, or they would die—*unless* they used their knowledge and their strength to begin to recreate approaches toward some of the weapons, the tools, the shelters, and the equipment they once knew. And the eventual comfort they attained would be directly related to the stock of equipment they could create.

But next let us split the group into two. One group, we may suppose, goes in for playing games and admiring sunsets. It is willing to make out on such bits of food as it can get by picking berries or by casual, hand-to-mouth hunting without weapons of any sort. A second group, however, is more vigorous, more energetic, and more anxious for eventual food and comfort. The members of this second group are willing to spend less time playing and to eat fewer berries for a while in order that they may use the time and energy thus made available to make, let us say, crude ploughs for cultivation or bows and arrows or other primitive weapons to help in their hunting. Such people would be the first savers and the first investors. They have saved because they have gone without some of the enjoyment and some of the immediate food which they *might* have had if they had not spent their time trying to make tools and weapons. They are investors because they use the energy thus set free in order to make lasting items of equipment or "means of production" which will ultimately give them a higher living standard. In this crude and simple example we have the ultimate essence of the basic problem of successful saving in any society. No country, be it capitalist, socialist, or communist, can hope for economic growth unless it is willing to forego part of its potential consumption and enjoyment in order to accumulate more skills, more machinery, and more equipment. Furthermore, once a society, however crude, has accumulated a stock of equipment upon which its standard of living depends, it not only cannot grow without some saving but also it cannot even stand still unless it is willing to spend enough of its energy to replace its stock of equipment as it wears out.

Unsuccessful Saving

Socialist critics insist correctly, however, that we cannot apply to complex modern civilizations primitive examples such as have just been given without making great allowances for the different institutions under which the process is carried on. It will be noticed that we spoke in the previous paragraph of *successful* saving. Now saving is frequently *un*successful, and on this point hinges a great portion of the disputes of the modern economy. Among the institutions which at once help to make saving easier, and at the same time can help most to frustrate its purpose, is the use of money. Speaking very crudely, each bit of money may be thought of as a ticket or vote controlling a certain tiny portion of the stock of labor and resources which a society has available. When we spend our money on clothes, on food, or on other immediate gratifications, we are "voting" to keep resources busy producing the things which satisfy personal wants. In the same way if we save money and use it to build a house for ourselves or to buy a share of stock in a company which wishes to expand, we are voting to keep people busy in the production of more equipment for society, in other words, more saving and more investing. But if we get money and neither spend it nor invest it but simply leave it under the mattress or in the bank and the bank does not make offsetting loans, then, in the first instance anyhow, we are voting to keep certain men and resources *idle*. The process of saving without either spending or investing is called "hoarding" and unless our hoarding happens to be offset by someone else's spending or investing (for example, the bank's) we are, by hoarding, helping to force our society into a state of unemployment or else of dislocation.

It is easy to see, then, why saving is always such a source of dispute. Every society which wants to grow will have to save, and socialism can no more avoid this than can any other type of community. But on the other hand, simply because some saving will always be needed for growth does not mean that every bit of money actually saved will be used for growth as some capitalists like to imply. Such an inference would be quite misleading. In the world which we know, the impulse to save under certain circumstances not only may fail to benefit the individual doing the saving but also may actually serve to cause unemployment and dislocation for other people. But if capitalist apologists are apt to be one-sided, so also the socialists are equally biased in their way, for socialists or left-wing writers are apt merely to dwell on the fact that money hoards at some particular time are not being used for productive investment. They seldom allow themselves to ask why. But in failing to ask why they leave out half the question. "Oversaving" can equally well be described as "underinvestment." Every honest economist must grant that sometimes private savings can run to waste in an economic system. But is this always the fault of capitalism? Might not a somewhat similar process occur under socialism? Questions like these lead us on to the next item on our list.

Enterprise

One of the most popular and most mistaken assumptions of modern thought is the idea that scientific discoveries are somehow self-implementing. It seems often supposed that, once an idea has taken shape in the brain of a scientist or been discovered in his laboratory, it will automatically become embodied in practical use without requiring anything more than routine effort on the part of a few individuals. Such an idea is entirely mistaken, no matter what sort of social system we are dealing with, for just as books acting alone have no power to get themselves read without the intervention of some human agency, so also scientific ideas and scientific discoveries require special effort before they are given practical use. Furthermore, the scientist or man of ideas may not be the type of person likely to do a good job of putting across a new way of going about things. There are many obstacles to be overcome, and the contemplative lover of pure wisdom, having made his discovery, may be content to stop at that point. In the first place one must deal with simple stupidity or ignorance, but these are only a small part of the basic task. Far more important is the ingrained dislike which a large proportion of the human race seems to have for new ideas or ideas which disturb the routine of its existence. Men's minds have a tendency to become set in given molds, and the man who attempts to disturb these preconceptions will encounter little mercy from those whom he is trying to stimulate. In the case of science one might think that all that is needed is an opportunity for conclusive experiment. But frequently on one pretext or another even the chance to *show* that one is right is at first denied. The history of science, for example, the life of Pasteur, is full of cases of this sort. In such cases it may be said with little fear of successful contradiction that the opponent has already become subconsciously convinced of the validity of the new notion but is unwilling to allow an experiment which would deprive him of face and hurt his ego.

Obstacles to change, however, are not merely of the subtle, psychological type just sketched. They may also be directly economic, and because selfishness under capitalism is usually associated with money and private property, many people jump to the conclusion that the abolition of private property would abolish frictions of this sort. We have, however, in the preceding chapter seen that this is a mistake, and there is no need to repeat the argument here. But when one considers that pressure-group problems of some sort are universal and adds to this the unwillingness of people to abandon their mental preconceptions, we can see that under any society it must require a certain amount of special force, energy, and insight to put across a new social or technological combination. In some cases, for instance the Pullman car, the inventor is also the man who "puts across" the new idea. But in a number of cases, as already indicated, the man who is interested in pure research is psychologically unfitted for the struggle needed before his ideas are put into use. He either will let his discoveries languish or will willingly turn them over to someone else before they are ever introduced. Accordingly, a special name is needed for that type of man, in any society, who not only thinks up new ideas *or* adopts the ideas of others but who, *in addition,* is willing to run the risk and undergo the frequent social onus and difficulties involved in putting across a new social or technological pattern. Such men we will call "enterprisers" or "entrepreneurs." [1] It must be understood that, though in using the word entrepreneur we are employing a term with capitalist connotations, we do not confine its meaning in this book only to capitalism. *Anyone* in *any* type of society who evolves a new technical, artistic, or social program *and* puts it into practice is an entrepreneur. Viewed by this definition, Stalin and Lenin are enterprisers and indeed Josef Stalin, no less than Henry Ford, becomes one of the most remarkable entrepreneurs of social history. Furthermore, just as all entrepreneurs do not have to be businessmen, so also all businessmen are not necessarily entrepreneurs. We are following here the terminology of Professor Schumpeter in his *Theory of Economic Development.* In that book Schumpeter draws a sharp distinction between "managers" on the one hand and "enterprisers" or "entrepreneurs" on the other hand. A manager to him is the type of official or leader who in any society merely

[1] Cf. J. A. Schumpeter, *The Theory of Economic Development,* Opie, trans. (Cambridge, Mass.: Harvard University Press, 1934), pp. 74 *ff.*

carries out routine decisions or operates within the frame of a routine technology and value.[2] He may have a great deal of power, for the distinction is not one concerning legal right or official position. The only thing a "manager" cannot do and still be called a "manager," under our terminology, is to explore *new* paths or to revise the general framework of preconception within which he is operating. When he does that, he becomes in our terminology an entrepreneur, and unless a social system, whatever its name, manages to contain within itself a certain number of these entrepreneurs, it cannot hope for change.

Yet we must remember that without change there cannot be an indefinite amount of social growth. Not only do we need to save a certain amount in order to create new capital goods, new machinery, and new equipment, but in addition we must be constantly varying and improving the type of machinery and equipment which we are trying to install. If you doubt this, think what sort of standard of living the United States would be enjoying today if we were forced to go back to the techniques which were used, say, in 1870 and had limited ourselves during all the past half century to a mere endless multiplication of the methods standard at that time. Progress comes through change, and change is not automatic. Unless there are individuals who are willing to see the possibilities around them and to put them across, the ideas of the scientist and the philosopher will remain forever sterile. After all, the Greek philosophers were quite familiar with the steam engine—as an amusing toy.

The recent successes of some great cooperation and government bureaus have led some writers, including Schumpeter himself, to suggest that the entrepreneurial function is becoming more "automatic" and that "personality and will power" no longer count for as much as they formerly did.[3] This, I submit, is again a one-sided

[2] *Ibid.*, p. 77.

[3] Schumpeter, *Capitalism, Socialism, and Democracy* (New York: Harper & Brothers, 2d ed., 1946), p. 132.

delusion. Whenever we find a great organization initiating some strikingly novel change in technique or policy, the change can always be related back to some individual—often in a subordinate position—who is "spark-plugging" the group.

Ideology

But we have not yet completed our list of the requirements of social growth. For just as saving in the long run is likely to become sterile or even harmful unless there are entrepreneurs who can put it to work, so also entrepreneurs by themselves will be helpless if they are put in a society which does not allow them to exercise their peculiar gifts. Not only do we need resources, labor, knowledge, saving, and enterprise—also we need a social ideology which will permit all these factors to operate together. A favorable cultural atmosphere is one of the most important and one of the most usually overlooked requirements for economic growth.

Fish, someone has said, are not likely to be the first to discover the existence of water. The individual who moves within a given cultural pattern is apt to take it so much for granted that he is quite incapable of either appreciating its nature or estimating its importance. Yet there cannot be a more vital subject. Nations, cultures, and societies are held together by basic sets of symbols, preconceptions as to what constitutes justice and the good life, what constitutes good form, what type of conduct can be relied upon in the "moral" individual, and so on.[4] Every tribe, whether it is the dwellers on the island of Madagascar or on the island of Manhattan, has such a set of symbols or complex of sets of symbols. Detailed description of such sets is the task of the anthropologist and sociologist. All we shall try to do in this book is to sketch very briefly some of the characteristics which a social symbolism must have if it is to permit of social growth.

[4] Cf. Clyde Kluckhohn, *Mirror for Man* (New York: McGraw-Hill Book Company, Inc., 1949).

The basic problem of symbolism and change is one which constantly recurs. In essence it is the task of balancing sets of qualities never wholly harmonious yet all indispensable for successful civilization. Harmony-in-growth involves the successful combination of routine versus adventure, order versus change, security versus insecurity, equality versus achievement, sovereignty versus freedom, and so on. There must always be rulers of some sort, and they must have a frame of reference within which they can operate and a set of sanctions to support their position. But these sanctions and frames of reference can never be allowed to become too "set" if we want continued growth. Furthermore, even considering the matter from a purely neutral point of view, too absolute a degree of power by itself is not likely to be a good thing over the long pull. A dictatorial individual or caste is especially likely to become set in its preconceptions and to admit of little change. Thus sovereignty and democracy have to be reconciled under some working agreement. As Professor Whitehead puts it, a race makes progress which combines reverence for its symbols with courage in their revision.[5] Enterprisers cannot function in a society which has an absolutely fixed and unchanging order and code of symbolism. But on the other hand, it is equally true, though not so usually realized, that they also cannot function in a society of pure anarchy. There must be a very special balance of social qualities.

Economists have usually seen this problem in terms of two contrasting qualities which we may call the "principle of harmony" and the "principle of conflict." Many of the earlier "orthodox" economic theorists, for example, David Ricardo, stress the harmony of individual and social welfare. For example, Ricardo remarked in 1810 in his famous pamphlet on the *High Price of Bullion,* "Happily, in this case, as well as in most others in com-

[5] Alfred North Whitehead, *Symbolism* (New York: the Macmillan Company, 1927). The whole final chapter (III) of Whitehead's book is recommended to anyone who wishes to understand civilization.

merce where there is free competition, *the interests of the individual and that of the community are never at variance*" (italics added). But thirty years later economics has become more sophisticated, and François Bastiat, though second to none in dogmatic belief in *laissez faire,* brings out the opposite problem in language almost foreshadowing that of Thorstein Veblen.[6]

> The separation of occupations, which results from the habits of exchange causes each man, instead of struggling against all surrounding obstacles to combat only *one* . . . it hence results that this man looks upon the obstacle which he has made it his profession to combat, for the benefit of others, as the immediate cause of his riches. The greater . . . this obstacle, the more he is remunerated. . . . The reasoning of all producers is, in what concerns themselves, the same. As the doctor draws his profits from *disease,* so does the ship owner from the obstacle called *distance* . . . the cloth manufacturer from *cold* . . . the schoolmaster lives upon *ignorance,* . . . Here is presented to us an ingenious machine, which cuts down the oak, squares it, . . . and forms them into casks. The obstacle is thus diminished and with it the fortunes of the [cask makers]. We must prevent this [the obstructionists cry]. Let us proscribe the machine!

The truth of the matter is, of course, that, as we saw in the previous chapter, elements of *both* conflict and harmony are always present and always necessary. Henry Ford, by inventing a cheap automobile, undoubtedly made a great fortune for himself. But he also greatly raised the general standards of production. That is the principle of harmony. Yet on the other hand, by the making of cheap cars, many of the manufacturers of more expensive models were ruined. Here is the principle of conflict. We shall try to develop this balance of qualities as this study unfolds. It is enough to say here that socialist cultures are likely

[6] François Bastiat, *Sophisms of the Protective Policy,* McCord, trans. (New York: G. P. Putnam, 1848), pp. 32 *ff.*

to overstress the need for order whereas capitalistic cultures are apt to put too much emphasis upon the value of change.

Stabilization

What is true of ideology is also true of economic policy, and accordingly, we have listed as our seventh standard of economic growth a certain "degree of stabilization." It will be argued later that perfect security and perfect stability are incompatible with continued growth. Yet on the other hand we have seen that saving may run to waste and cause unemployment. Why such maladjustments occur will require a special chapter for explanation. It should, however, be clear even at this point that a failure to confine economic upheaval to tolerable limits may result in an appalling waste of social energy and needless wrecking of millions of lives. It is quite conceivable, under some circumstances, that the whole gains of an expansion could be lost in an unnecessary resulting unemployment. Thus rapid growth necessarily requires some policy of stabilization.

Criticism

We come now to the last and one of the most important requirements for successful social growth. Yet it is also the requirement which the economist is least qualified to treat. We must mention it, however, to keep our treatment in proportion. This requirement is "criticism." By criticism I mean insistence upon *qualitative* standards of social development. Convenient as it may be to define progress, or growth, as the mere rise in the value of output per head, any honest economist must admit the incompleteness of such a criterion. Mere change as such can just as well be change toward evil as change toward good. Mere increase in output can be increased garbage as well as increased sources of better living.

Criticism, then, is vital. Yet it is important to realize that a mere shift in social organization, for example a shift to "planning," does not necessarily imply the adoption of a different or even of a higher standard of criticism. Hitler could plan quite as much as Clement Attlee. As the author has pointed out in connection with Mr. R. H. Tawney's *Acquisitive Society,* a professional society does not in itself involve any special value principle.[7] After all, the professional society could be a society of professional murderers. It is easy enough to abolish the capitalist system, but whether or not that will automatically usher in the reign of the true and the beautiful is quite something else again.

Summary and Conclusion

It is time to stop and summarize our argument for this chapter. We set out to outline the fundamental requirements of social growth for any economic system. These we grouped under eight heads: labor, natural resources, knowledge and education, saving, enterprise, ideology, a degree of stabilization, and criticism. It must be stressed again that this list is not merely limited to capitalism but applies to any form of culture. The topics were related in the following manner: Natural resources, labor, and knowledge are generally admitted to be needed for social growth. But we pointed out that there were further requirements, for example, saving. By saving was meant only a failure to use all of one's productive potential to satisfy immediate personal wants. Man, we pointed out, is a tool-using animal, and unless he is prepared to devote part of his energy to keeping up his stock of equipment, his society cannot even stand still. Even more important, if he wishes to have social growth, he must put aside a certain amount of his production for the making of additional instruments to increase output. But while some degree of saving is a necessary

[7] David McCord Wright, *Democracy and Progress* (New York: The Macmillan Company, 1948), p. 49.

condition for social growth, it is not by itself a sufficient one. Just because *some* saving must be done in order to produce *some* investment, we cannot jump to the conclusion that every dollar actually saved will actually lead to increased production of machinery and equipment. Saving, we saw, frequently runs to waste.

The usual left-wing reaction to this fact is to suggest that we cut down on the saving. But another inference is quite as logical. Instead of cutting down on saving, we may try instead to remove the barriers which are preventing investment. Now the most important factor needed to employ saving is the one which we have called enterprise. Enterprisers were defined as those men who, besides seeing or discovering new technical or social patterns, also have the energy and determination to put these ideas into action. Saving which merely resulted in the piling up of a heap of the same goods would soon become useless. Without constant discovery and the *use* of these discoveries, the national income cannot grow. Thus the role of the enterpriser, whether he is called a commissar, a bureaucrat, or a businessman, is one of the most important factors in social development.

But enterprisers cannot function in a culture which is hostile to change, and this fact led us to a sixth requirement of social growth, namely, the cultural problem of finding ideologies which would permit sufficient freedom of action to new ideas while maintaining adequate order. Successful ideology involves a balance between the principle of harmony and the principle of conflict. Finally it was pointed out that rapid growth was likely to entail instability and that, if we were not prepared to confine this instability within reasonable bounds, much of the social gain of rapid growth would be lost through unemployment and other wastes. Rapid growth in any type of social system is likely to imply a stabilization problem, and some degree of stabilization is an essential of rapid growth. Perfect stability, however, cannot be combined with rapid growth.

As our last requirement for successful social growth, we listed the factor of criticism. By this we meant only to call attention to the fact that mere increase in material output is no guarantee of genuine social progress. Qualitative standards of criticism are necessary if we are to prevent our production from being merely the production of junk. We may summarize then once more the eight requirements of successful growth: labor, natural resources, knowledge and education, saving, enterprise, ideology, a degree of stabilization, criticism. Our next task will be to see how capitalism goes about dealing with these problems.

CHAPTER 3

Capitalism and the Social Problem

JUST AFTER the Second World War, so the story goes, an American officer asked a Russian officer to have dinner with him at a restaurant. The dinner was good, and the Russian said, "You must have had to order this weeks ahead to get so good a meal." "No indeed," said the American, "I just walked in." The Russian was astounded. "How did they know," he said, "that anyone was coming in to order this particular meal?"

Most of us are so accustomed to the daily miracle of production functioning apparently without a guide that we are impressed only when the system goes wrong. But from the point of view of historical perspective the Russian's attitude was the right one. The "normal" state of mankind, if we merely take a majority vote of cultures over the known range of history, is either planned despotism or oligarchy or else unchanging primitive society governed by iron-clad custom. It is only in the past hundred and fifty years of recorded history that we know of anything different continuously existing on a large scale, and if we could really take a long view, we should not be surprised that things sometimes go wrong. We should be astonished only that they ever went well.

The major reasons why the economic system sometimes explodes and what can be done about it will be discussed in a later chapter. In the same way the problems of "monopoly," "frictions" of adjustment, and so on will be taken up in Part II. But for the present, maladjustments are left largely to one side. Our job now is to explain how the system *does* work to the extent that it does. In the same way we postpone major emphasis upon the political problem to the next chapter. Our task will be first to sketch the economic organization of a capitalist society—how goods get produced and distributed—and next to ask what are the features of capitalism which make for continued growth, that is, how does it approach the problems of saving, enterprise, and incentives generally discussed in the previous chapter. Finally we shall suggest, very briefly, some of the characteristic cultural attitudes toward life, the family, etc., which have accompanied and may have helped to maintain a capitalist culture.

Production and the Pricing System

Looking at capitalist production and distribution from the point of view of "democracy," we see a wide divergence immediately appear. The organization of each working unit seems to be more or less authoritarian, for until recently, the power of the manager to direct the processes of production has been (subject to certain rules of law) theoretically absolute. On the other hand the organization of distribution, though not equalitarian, has been otherwise quite democratic. The capitalist "market," even if not exactly the ideal and utopian blessing which some have described, is nevertheless a very sensitive mechanism for relating the pattern of production to the spending of the consumer.

We shall show in the next chapter that the contrast just outlined between capitalist production and distribution is not nearly so sharp as we have made it. Even leaving aside trade-unionism, law, and conscience, the theoretical absolutism of the capitalist manager has always been subject to many checks. But for present purposes the structure of production inside each given organization need not be elaborated. We shall concentrate instead upon the working of the capitalist pricing system—the method by which it is decided what goods shall be produced and who shall get them—since this is the most unique feature of the capitalist process.

For many years there was in this country, and still is, an

organization called the "League for Industrial Democracy" whose slogan is "production for use and not for profit." To many people the linking together of increased democracy with abolition of the profit motive will seem no more than common sense. Yet there are others who disagree and who would say that the profit motive in a capitalist market was an extremely democratic thing. Let us try to see why this is so.

The clue to the problem lies in the analogy between votes and money which we touched upon in the previous chapter. In effect, the capitalist market can be looked upon as a perpetual election to decide what shall be produced. Money forms the votes, advertising the campaign literature; and the election returns, determining which business shall stay in operation and which shall go out, are set by profit and loss.

Sooner or later this economic election serves to eliminate the more unwanted products and to guide producers into uses which people can be persuaded to pay for. It functions in the following way. If there are too many people making bicycles, the price of bicycles will tend to fall and eventually some of the bicycle makers will shut down. People will thereupon try to get jobs in other lines and other businesses. Conversely, if the production of a particular good has not been expanded as much as consumers wish, profits will probably be high and there will be a tendency for those who are making less money in other lines to move into the field which beckons with unusual rewards. Monopolistic groups of workers or businessmen may, it is true, arrest this process of adaptation. People may make mistakes, changes may not offset each other smoothly or may lag, and there may be a consequent depression. Nevertheless the analogy with political democracy is exceedingly strong even to its imperfections, and before we go further, it will help to compare some of the complaints often made regarding the economic market with some weaknesses of political systems.

One of the most widespread criticisms of the modern economic market is that capitalistic advertising is not always truthful. Who, however, could maintain that political speeches are always truthful? Again, products, it is said, are often "sold" to the public rather than spontaneously demanded by it. Is this not often true of political programs? Next people will say that certain capitalist businessmen have special influence over the market. But do not certain political leaders have special influence over the political market? Finally some people object that they are forced to choose among the alternatives presented to them and cannot simply have anything that they wish. They are, in other words, forced, to a considerable extent, to choose among the goods actually in the stores; and unique or unusual tastes may have to go unsatisfied. But also in political life are not most of us obliged to choose among the candidates presented to us in a given campaign rather than "running our own man"?

There is another way in which the consumer is sometimes said to be "coerced" into buying what he does not want. This is the charge, quite prominent in modern marketing literature, that capitalist producers tend to burden the consumer by making him buy unnecessary services and gadgets when many of us, if we had a chance, would prefer something cheaper. In time of price control and "concealed" inflation compulsory "extras" are, of course, one method of evasion. But leaving inflation aside, the analogy here is very close to the problem of minority pressure groups in political life. When two major candidates are about evenly balanced, it often follows that they will try to woo some small minority group which, under the special circumstances, holds the deciding vote. Both sides acting alone would have nothing to do with this minority point of view, but because it happens to hold the balance between them, they will both try to make terms with it. Thus it may happen that a relatively small splinter group will have much more real influence over an actual decision than the vast majority of both sides. A somewhat similar problem is found in the economic market when competition is keen and the alternatives about equally balanced. An enterprising businessman may add a particular service to attract just the small minority of undecided individuals who can be induced to switch their purchases. His competitor, equally anxious to reach the undecided buyer, will follow suit, and thus, as with rival politicians trying to outbid each other with promises, rival businessmen will try to outbid each other in services. The tastes of a minority are thus to some extent imposed upon the majority. But it is difficult to see how this phenomenon can be abolished either in politics or in economics without abolishing the democratic process itself. And though multiplication of services may frequently be hailed as an indication of monopoly, it is actually usually an indication of competition—though not, of course, academic "pure" competition.

Perhaps, however, the feature of the economic market which most troubles many modern thinkers is its association with "competition" and hence with "greed," with "conflict," with "struggles," and with "selfishness." Nietzsche's "blonde beast," Darwin's and Spencer's survival of the "fittest," and a number of other ferocious similes easily come into mind. The Victorians tremendously overemphasized this aspect of social life in their *theory*, and it is impossible to deny the existence of elements of aggression and predation in *fact*. But the trouble with many modern criticisms of the market or of the "pricing" system is that they spring from too one-sided an understanding of the meaning of "competition." Let us, for the moment, look at another side of the coin, admittedly incomplete also but which has at least *as much* partial validity, in describing the market, as does the "reign of tooth and claw."

Competition in the last analysis means trying to excel. One can try, it is true, to excel at greed or torture, but one can also try to excel at unselfishness or service. The ambiguities that lurk in the word are well illustrated in Samuel Butler's remark that we "should all strive hotly to be as lukewarm as possible." Competition is competition whether the end is noble or base. The author has often heard it argued that men should not "compete" because the fellow who does not do so well may have his "feelings hurt." But the trouble with this idea is that, if we really mean it, then everybody should try to do no better than average in every task and, if he really wants to be "moral" and avoid hurting anyone's feelings, he should try to do even worse than average. The socialist commissar who does a better job of being a socialist commissar than other socialist commissars may hurt their feelings. The doctor who does a better job of doctoring than other doctors may cause other doctors to feel frustrated. "Aggression," thus defined, comes to be practically synonymous with achievement, and the aim of striving "hotly to be as lukewarm as possible" comes to mean that everyone will try to do an equally poor job.

There is no need to elaborate this difficulty. In the world we live in some rivalry can be shown to be essential. If we don't accept this idea, then we ought to abolish political elections and give the Presidency of the United States not to the best man or even to a reasonably able man but simply to the man who wants the job most—whether he is a moron or not. The question of whether or not rivalry is permissible in a given case depends, therefore, not on the existence of competition or rivalry *as such,* but on the *end* of the particular rivalry, the types of means used *toward* the end, and the social *results* of the whole process. Now if we take this point of view and choose only among various types of rivalry, then surely one can think of worse forms of rivalry and competition than rivalry and competition as to who shall *serve* the public best. And there can be worse reasons for allowing a man to earn a large income than that he has managed to produce cheaply (*e.g.,* Henry Ford) something that the public shows it wants. Particularly is this the case if we dislike coercion. Always remembering the need for general standards of decency and health, competition as to who shall best give the public what it is persuaded it wants may seem better than competition as to who shall best force the public to take what it doesn't want. The economic market, despite its explicit incorporation of the idea of competition, has thus a strong service and cooperative element as well as an element of predation, and it is in thinking of this aspect of the case that Alfred North Whitehead—a man with no overweening love for *laissez faire*—entitled his chapter on commercial societies "From Force to Persuasion." [1]

Whatever our value judgment as to ultimate desirability may come to be, one fact is beyond dispute. The alternative to abolition of the pricing system must be the adoption of some system of rationing. And socialist critics have invariably been forced back into one of two positions. Either they maintain, as does Dr. Lange, that socialism can set up a competitive market similar to capitalism, in which the tastes of the consumer can be reflected, or else they will argue that freedom of choice among goods is very much overvalued and that it would be better for the consumer to be allowed to buy only what was "good" for him.[2] Some approach to a pricing system would appear to be inevitable in any economy —socialist or capitalist—which subscribes to the liberal value of trying to give the consumer what he wants to buy when he wants it.

In later chapters we shall mention the ideas of the mathematical welfare school of economists who hope by a series of elaborate adjustments of incomes and prices to get a more satisfactory total result. All we are trying to do here, however, is to explain in brief outline how the system works. And before completing our task we should return to the question with which we began: Why did the restaurant know the American was going to come in and order that particular meal? The answer is, of course, that the restaurant could not possibly have known any such thing. Nevertheless, the

[1] Alfred North Whitehead, *Adventures of Ideas* (New York: The Macmillan Company, 1933), Chap. V.

[2] Oskar Lange, "On the Economic Theory of Socialism," *Review of Economic Studies,* 1936–1937, p. 123. Lange suggests that the relevant commissars "play" at competition.

system does run after a fashion, and the question is how. The answer, of course, lies in past experience and the working of the law of averages. The operator of an establishment gets to know, through experience over the years, approximately what types of goods will be asked for and when. Men, like electrons, cannot have their *individual* paths predicted by scientists or social scientists. But taken as a group, their behavior becomes somewhat more predictable, and as long as changes are not too sudden or too violent, the pricing system is capable of adjusting itself to them. We have here, however, one important point for the analysis of the business cycle. If change comes too fast, the profit-and-loss mechanism cannot be expected to adjust itself within a tolerable length of time and severe maladjustments may ensue. We shall discuss the implied problem of stabilization later on.

Incentives and Growth

The mention of disturbance easily leads to the problem of growth. It is not enough merely to explain the way in which a given output is distributed among the people of the country. We want equally well to know how the total of ouput is increased. Such an inquiry, as we saw in the previous chapter, immediately leads to the problems of savings and of incentives. We need to ask what are the methods which capitalism has used to recruit savings, enterprise, and energy, while in our next chapter we shall ask if there is any special feature of the capitalist institutional organization which can be used to account for the extraordinarily rapid development of the capitalist epoch.

The problem of incentives in a democratic society is a very difficult one, for if democracy means literal equality, then any form of distinction is undemocratic. Even if we follow Jefferson and interpret "equality" to mean equality of *opportunity,* still we are faced by the fact that, if men are unequal in their original endowment, equality of opportunity must result in eventual *inequality* for the more able individual. Worse yet, if there is any inequality among parents, something of this inequality will be transmitted to the children, so that the known child of a successful father, in any system, is likely to receive at the very least a slight degree of preferential treatment.[2a] Even if the father himself tries to prevent this, there will nevertheless be assiduous flatterers anxious to take special advantage of the connections which the son may afford. On the other hand, however, there has never yet been a society which did not find it necessary to reward special effort in special ways. We are thus, therefore, faced with a problem which has no perfect solution but which admits of a wide variety of treatment. Let us see how the problem is approached under capitalism.

It is difficult to summarize capitalist incentives neatly at the present time because the course of social legislation has greatly altered or (if you will) impaired them. We are now in a period of transition, and to some extent we are still the beneficiaries of conduct whose rational basis has been largely removed by law. We shall, however, begin by outlining what might be called the "classic" capitalist incentives, stopping from time to time to show how they are being modified.

Basic in the capitalist folkways has been what may be called the "family epic." A man was supposed to work hard to provide for his family. He was also supposed to save and to acquire property in order to give his family and children a "better start." The capitalist life scheme involved at least three generations—parents, children, and grandchildren. Calvinist emphasis upon relatively plain living made the prime incentive accumulation *and* transmis-

[2a] Dr. Arthur M. Schlesinger, Jr., remarks that "at twenty-eight young Vassily Stalin was a major general, an eminence possibly not due entirely to merit." *The Vital Center* (Boston: Houghton Mifflin Company, 1949), p. 75.

sion rather than mere "enjoyment," *i.e.,* spending of the individual's present income.

As a result the typical capitalist upper classes have been among the most abstemious in history, and there has been supposed (for example, by Lord Keynes) to be a very close correlation between the distribution of wealth and the amount of saving.[3] Reference to abstemiousness, however, will immediately evoke violent reaction among many moderns. Numerous instances of prodigality and waste are frequently enumerated. But as always in such matters, we must speak in terms not of absolutes but of *comparisons.* That capitalist magnates and middle-class people also often have wasted and still waste money to some extent could scarcely be denied. But compare Palm Beach with ancient Rome or with King Solomon or the great Mogul or even the fêtes of Versailles.

Even today the capitalist has but one wife at a time and eats only one meal at a time, while large-scale concubinage is discouraged. It remained for Solomon to have a thousand wives and for the Romans to eat six meals at a sitting—delicately disposing of the remainder in the *vomitarium.* As soon as we put the matter in relative terms and terms of history, the facts speak for themselves. Moreover, in the evaluation of "waste" there are many intangibles. The Taj Mahal is frequently regarded as one of the most beautiful buildings in the world. One is not sure, however, but that Thorstein Veblen would not have considered it a monumental example of conspicuous waste. Certain it is that some historians have maintained that the Emperior Shah Jehan, in

[3] Cf. J. M. Keynes, "The Capitalist classes were allowed to call the best part of the cake theirs and were theoretically free to consume it, on the tacit underlying condition that they consumed very little of it in practice. The duty of 'saving' became nine-tenths of virtue and the growth of the cake the object of true religion." *The Economic Consequence of the Peace* (New York: Harcourt, Brace and Company, Inc., 1920), p. 20. Few brief surveys can surpass Keynes' brief sketch of capitalism in this chapter.

order to build it, so depleted the resources of his country as to bring on a famine.[4]

Returning, however, to the problem of incentives for saving, corporate saving at the present time has taken a place in this country as a major source of saving paralleling the individual motives now so heavily hampered (as will be discussed later) by tax laws. Some have even gone so far as to argue that the presence of corporate savings and investment makes the whole structure of private incentives obsolete. There are two main points here, however, which must be borne in mind.

In the first place the fact that corporations will give us *some* saving does not prove that they will necessarily give us *enough* saving. Even today corporate saving amounts to only about one-third of the total. We must therefore consider, to some extent at the very least, the problem of saving incentives for individuals. The confusion usually made here is one which economists will recognize at once as the confusion of absolute with marginal supply. A price which will give us *some* of a good may not be the price which will give us *as much* of it as we want.

The second point regarding private incentive takes us from the question of incentives for saving to the question of incentives for enterprise. A modern corporation, it is often argued, is no longer greatly influenced by profit considerations. Many people maintain that, once the corporation has attained commanding position, it wishes merely to maintain its life over a long period and aims, if it considers profit at all, merely at some sort of long-run "fair" average. Just, therefore, as corporate savings are said to make the need for savings incentives obsolete, so also the type of "profitless" corporate expansion just sketched is said to make the need for personal-enterprise incentives obsolete. But before we

[4] F. Yeats-Brown, *A Pageant of India* (Philadelphia: McCrae Smith Company, 1942), p. 121. Whether or not the building of the Taj actually "caused" the famine is certainly open to doubt. But the simultaneous presence of so much magnificence and so much famine seems unquestionable.

can accept this doctrine, we have a long way to go. In the first place the incentives which suffice for the slow, steady growth of a number of large-scale firms may yet not be the incentives which will call for the degree of rapid, independent, and changeable growth which has, in the past at least, been one of the principal factors in capitalist development. The small firm depends very largely on profits as a source of capital, and if these profits are taxed away before they can be invested, the expansion of the smaller firm is proportionately hampered. Effects of this sort will be discussed in greater detail in our chapters on monopoly and the business cycle.

One important oversight, however, frequently made in connection with problems of this sort deserves more discussion. This oversight is the tendency to personify the corporation and to consider it as having an independent existence other than the existence of the executives who operate it. Such a mode of thought is, of course, sometimes legitimate, but surely, after Mr. Thurman Arnold's remarks on the folkways of capitalism, we need not carry it to an extreme. We are too apt to forget that enterprises are initiated and corporations managed by people. No corporation ever did anything. The people in a corporation do whatever it does. If they have no incentive to act as good corporate officers, the incentive of the corporation is also reduced. As far as many professions go, there can be little question that the income tax has had a serious effect on incentives—why not the profession of being an executive? If individual inducements to enterprise are reduced, corporate inducements also must suffer some loss.

Fashionable doctrine in recent years would have it that businessmen work chiefly for fun and prestige. They are said to bring home a profit as a hunter brings home his trophy, and the chance of a very small one appears to be thought enough to get a man out in the vilest weather. The author does not deny the importance of the creative and prestige features to capitalist motivation. We cannot, indeed, understand the system unless we make allowance for impulses of this sort. But here are other motives also. As Dr. Kenneth Boulding reminds us, the entrepreneur has not merely a choice between profit and loss. He has a choice between action and nonaction as well.[5] In some cases a man may work harder with a high profit and income tax in order to amass a fortune in spite of the exactions of the government. But in other cases he may not. The greater the extent to which the pleasures of leisure and cultivated hobbies are preferred, the more likely will the tax be to discourage business activity. But Boulding's argument, at its lowest terms, would seem to indicate that there would be at the least a *margin* of possible entrepreneurial action concerning which income- and inheritance-tax laws, by making it more difficult to transmit an estate, cast a balance in favor of leisure.

Recurring to the hunting example, it might well be asked if the professional hunter would bring in quite so many birds if he knew that nine of every ten would be taken away. And we may conclude that the steadiest capitalist motives have been as follows: The corporation still in the active, expanding stage is more interested in retaining earnings, paying off debts, and expanding operations than in paying out dividends. The usual capitalist individual has been more interested in the accumulation of a fortune than in the enjoyment of income. Furthermore, he has been interested in the accumulation of a fortune largely in order to transmit it to his children.

Passing from incentives to personal activity to problems of social growth, we must ask what provision the capitalist system makes for stabilization and for criticism. We find that these two points constitute perhaps the weakest aspects of the whole scheme. Capitalist thought makes little explicit recognition of the problem of a general collapse. The usual ideas of profit motive can be used to explain shifts from one line to another, but they do not help us greatly if we want to understand a *general* col-

[5] Cf. Kenneth E. Boulding, "The Incidence of a Profits Tax," *American Economic Review*, September, 1944, p. 567.

lapse of most industries at the same time. In so far as orthodox capitalist thought has given explicit recognition to the problem of *general* depression, it has been supposed that a slump could be cured by price reduction or wage reduction. The *mathematical* logic of this orthodox position has never been successfully overthrown. Nevertheless, both Keynes and his followers have established, beyond the possibility of doubt, that we cannot be sure that the spontaneous mechanism of lower prices and lower wages will bring a depression to an end within a *reasonable* (*i.e.*, tolerable) length of time or within the margin of instability which the electorate will permit. We must discuss this problem of stabilization in detail in later chapters.

In the same way that the capitalist outlook makes little allowance for stabilization, it also makes little explicit provision for criticism. The blame here, however, lies not so much upon the shoulders of capitalism as upon the outlook of the eighteenth-century philosophers and illuminati from whom came the basic ideals on which our system is based.[6] From the eighteenth century comes that overwhelming reliance upon quantitative scientific standards which is one of the greatest difficulties confronting those who wish to insist upon quality at the present time, as well as the tremendous overemphasis upon the reasonable and rational nature of mankind which has underlain so much economic thought. But

[6] Even Lewis Mumford gives some partial recognition to this factor. Cf. the following: "The important thing to bear in mind is that the failure to evaluate the machine and to integrate it into society as a whole was not due *simply* to defects in distributing income, to errors in management, to the greed and narrowmindedness of the industrial leaders, it was also due to a weakness of the *entire philosophy* upon which the new techniques and inventions were founded" (italics supplied). Lewis Mumford, *Technics and Civilization* (New York: Harcourt, Brace and Company, Inc., 1934), p. 283. Though Mumford seems to have been primarily thinking of economics in this passage, I would suggest that a more searching analysis would relate the one-sidedness of the economics to the scientific attitude which the economics was trying to emulate.

changing economic systems, as we have already pointed out, will not by *itself* serve to introduce any newer or more effective value principles into social life than those which our society already has. And conversely, a shift in ethical and social ideas *within* the present economic system might be of far more value in securing our aim.

There remains a final point which we must consider in discussing the mechanism of capitalist societies, and that is: How does capitalism choose its leaders? Since the typical capitalist social structure has been democratic, we need not discuss the selection of political leaders. What we deal with at this point is the question of the selection of economic leadership. Here, too, we strike a very vulnerable point in the system. For the capitalist ideology makes no explicit provision for the selection of leaders. Professor Schumpeter always maintained that there was no such thing as an entrepreneurial "class." The leaders are supposed to be very largely *self*-selected. This does not mean that the system is necessarily a bad one but only that it is peculiarly vulnerable to attack from those who wish to rationalize the position of each individual within the social scheme. Broadly speaking, it may be said that according to the ideology of *laissez faire* a successful businessman gets to be a successful businessman by *being* a good businessman. The idea is one of constant turnover—of a system sufficiently decentralized to permit many unwealthy young men to "make good," of the emergence from the *ranks* of the more able leaders of production and distribution. The less able, even though initially wealthy, are thought of as being constantly left to one side through competition, and the more able, as advanced by the same method. To be sure, as businesses have become larger and more bureaucratic in their organization, this spontaneous method of leadership selection has been seriously modified. Nevertheless, capitalist selection of leaders remains relatively spontaneous and from the point of view of the academician, with his elaborate hierarchy and set of "objective" tests, very irrational.

We may use here a bit of terminology borrowed from Max Weber, the great German sociologist. Weber contrasted "bureaucratic" leadership with something which he called "charismatic" leadership. Charismatic comes from the Greek word "charisma" meaning "gift of grace" and refers to the spontaneous or self-selected leader who seizes the opportunity which happens to be presented to him. Now although Weber's considerable anti-capitalist bias prevented him from applying the charismatic concept to capitalism to any great extent and though it induced him to reserve the word almost entirely for politics, it can, I believe, nevertheless be said that on the whole capitalism, in its classic phase anyhow, was an example of charismatic rather than bureaucratic leadership and exhibited all the consequent attributes of relative spontaneity and discontinuousness as contrasted to orderly routine.[7] We shall come back to the effect of this point on social growth in our next chapter.

Some Notes on the Cultural Attitudes of Capitalism

We have now completed our brief sketch of the essentials of the capitalist *mechanism* and its incentives. We have mentioned the pricing system, the family epic, the profit motive, the weakness regarding stability and criticism, and the nonrational or at least nonroutine, but relatively effective selection of economic leadership. Now we must ask: What are the qualities of mind and character which have been most esteemed in the capitalist outlook? In other words, what is the capitalist scheme of life and values? This is a point concerning which the technical economist, as such, has not much that he can say. Yet capitalism is no more the mere existence of some private property, or some profit, than democracy (as we shall see in the next chapter) is the mere

[7] See *From Max Weber: Essays in Sociology,* H. M. Gerth and C. Wright Mills, trans. and eds. (New York: Oxford University Press, 1946), pp. 67, 91.

holding of an occasional election. The various economic mechanisms and the various incentives sketched so far are only part of a general scheme of reciprocal attitudes and beliefs. And though we do not yet know enough to describe these ideas in full or to be able to say confidently just which is relatively the most essential, still some mention must be made of the problem—both to stimulate the reader to further thought and to keep our treatment in reasonably balanced perspective.

In the present volume we are dealing primarily with a capitalist civilization that is already a going concern, just as in the author's earlier *Democracy and Progress* attention was fixed upon a democracy that was already a going concern. Such an approach by-passes the really terrific problems of the transition from primitive societies to capitalism, but to deal with them at all adequately would require several complete books in itself. It decidedly remains to be seen whether primitive cultures and cultures of deeply alien mental and religious background can develop overnight or even over centuries the delicate balance of attitudes which culminated after a thousand years of piecemeal growth into north European, Anglo-American democracy and capitalism.[8] We have

[8] In this connection, however, it is worth remembering that the shattering effect of industrialism on a primitive people need not always be the result of "low" wages or "exploitation" but rather of the primitive tribe's complete ignorance both of the necessary attitudes and of the necessary health requirements of a more complex life. For example, people with incomes capable of supporting them in health and comfort may die from malnutrition due to ignorance. But the problem goes far beyond so simple an example.

It has been suggested that the Japanese absorbed Western notions so quickly because they had *already* largely shifted from a customary to a price economy before Perry's expedition. See M. Takizawa, *The Penetration of the Money Economy in Japan* (New York: Columbia University Press, 1927).

The industrialization of Soviet Russia, however, has scarcely been altogether idyllic. Professor Alvin Hansen has suggested that England in the

given the name "entrepreneur" to the man who "puts over" social or technological change in any society. But, under capitalism (that is, while it exists) entrepreneurship has mostly taken a "capitalist" slant; that is, the men initiating change have mostly been interested in scientific and industrial change. The question which the social sciences are not yet able to answer satisfactorily is: Why did their minds turn in that direction?

Confining ourselves, however, to a well-established, going-concern capitalism, it is easy to give a list of the more obvious features which such cultures have generally shown.[9] Capitalist cultures, as already indicated, have been cultures emphasizing the "rational" and the "scientific." They have had a wide tolerance and respect for the attitudes and desires of the average man. Capitalist intellectual life, instead of despising material comfort, cleanliness, health, and "good" (though not "extravagant") living, has, on the contrary, generally applauded advances in these lines. The general current of nineteenth-century capitalist life, furthermore, was not so much nonreligious as possessed of a religion which often applauded and at least approved worldly economic activity and profit making.

We must not, however, follow the Victorian theorist in concentrating all attention on the "heroic" factor of capitalist life and the factor of struggle. Despite the excesses of the early industrial revolution, capitalist cultures have been characterized not merely by competitive elements but also—notably in Anglo-American life—by strong elements of mutual forbearance—in other words,

---

early nineteenth century and Russia today are both examples of countries which, under widely differing techniques and surroundings, were pushing industrialism too fast. Nor is the ultimate independent productivity of the Soviet experiment yet established.

[9] Cf. Thomas C. Cochran, "Role and Sanction in American Entrepreneurial History" in *Change and the Entrepreneur,* prepared by the Research Center in Entrepreneurial History, Harvard University (Cambridge, Mass.: Harvard University Press, 1949), p. 153. This whole symposium will be of intense interest to those studying the problems.

not merely self-respect but respect for the other fellow also. And there has been a strong, continuing, and very valuable flair for voluntary, informal association in group effort—both in "emergencies" and upon occasions specified and understood in the folkways.

Accompanying this general pattern one finds a framework of law similarly elastic and often ambivalent but insisting both upon respect for the individual and his "property" *and* also upon the sovereign rights of the community in "health, safety, and morals" —concepts continually expanding. It is very difficult to isolate anything in the nature of cause and effect here. People in a capitalist society saved and invested, some will say, because their property was relatively protected by the law. But on the other hand one could equally well argue that the citizens of a capitalist state insisted upon the protection of property by law because *they* were the kind of people who saved and invested or who hoped someday to be able to save and invest.

Hen-or-egg arguments of this type are not merely intellectual curiosities. For example, one finds in South America both some private property and some elections, but strong surviving medieval, feudal, and classical elements in Latin-American culture have prevented the development of any very important indigenous capitalist entrepreneurship and of any very stable "democratic" government.[10] The wealthy upper classes of Latin-American states probably do not conform very closely to our description of the typical "abstemious" middle-class capitalist. But if their "propensity to save and invest" is low—as is often alleged—may this not be related to the general insecurity of property in an unstable political environment? Yet conversely, may not excessive "conspicuous consumption" help to make the political structure unstable?

In mentioning points of this nature we wish merely to stimulate

[10] Cf. Philip D. Bradley, "Entrepreneurship in Latin America" in *Change and the Entrepreneur*, p. 37.

the reader's thought and investigation on these lines. But before returning to more "purely" economic problems the author would like to point out some of the attributes of the capitalist idea of the "good life." It should be stressed once more that all businessmen are not entrepreneurs any more than all entrepreneurs, under our terminology, are businessmen.[11] We wish here, therefore, not to imply a sweeping generalization covering every dweller in a capitalist state or even every businessman but only to point out what might be called some "typical" attitudes.

In the first place it might be said that in a typical capitalism the qualities most admired have been energy, self-reliance, and independence. The responsibility of a man for his own acts, for providing for his family, and so on, were stressed to a high degree. Capitalism presents the same ambiguous attitude toward the cosmos shared by the Calvinist and the scientist. A great faith in overriding natural law is combined, for all practical purposes, with an equal emphasis upon the personal independence and freedom of the individual. One of the forces working against the capitalist ideology today is the modern tendency to see each individual man as a helpless mechanical automaton. In the capitalist scheme of life the individual is looked upon not merely as shaped by life but also to some extent as shaping *it* for himself.

One final characteristic of capitalist ideology seems to the author to be of extreme importance. The typical active entrepreneur and the creative artist—types usually considered to be widely divergent—share one basic attitude: Both conceive of the good life in terms of *activity* rather than idle enjoyment, serene routine, or contemplation. The usual description of capitalist motives is thus not adequate. One of the most important clues to the entrepreneur's behavior is that he *enjoys* his work. It is true

[11] It must not be supposed that the manager-entrepreneur distinction is a clear-cut black-and-white one in real life. Cf. Arthur H. Cole, "Entrepreneurship and Entrepreneurial History" in *Change and the Entrepreneur*, p. 85.

that in the preceding section the author was at pains to rebut certain extreme inferences drawn from the idea, but the notion of enjoyment-in-activity is a basic one for capitalism.[12] Browning, whatever his personal politics may have been, represents a basic capitalist point of view *par excellence*. His poems are filled with quotations praising the life of action. For example:

> And the sin I impute to each frustrate ghost
> Is—the unlit lamp and the ungirt loin.

or

> One who never turned his back but marched breast forward
> Never doubted clouds would break. . . .

Goethe, too, stressed the value of activity and effort as in the conclusion of *Faust*.

But in this connection there is one peculiarity of the capitalist ethos that deserves special notice. Most noncapitalist entrepreneurs are apt to be social innovators working for the achievement of some *final* social pattern. They thus inconsistently, but effectively, combine the *present* enjoyment and excitement of initiating *change* with the intellectual satisfaction which many people seem to derive from carrying in their minds an ideal picture of a single eternally fixed social type. "Entrepreneurs" of this persuasion never appear to stop and think how unhappy their psychic successors will be once the unchanging system has been established. Who would be more unhappy in a mature and massively orthodox socialism than some future Mr. Laski!

It is one of the outstanding features of capitalism that it is an ideology providing for *continual* growth and change. Its culture has been specially geared to the problem of maintaining reasonable order in a world of constant adventure. For it is not simply routine activity—the work of the artisan—that has been prized but activity in initiating *change*. The capitalist entrepreneur in

[12] Cf. T. V. Smith, "The New Deal as a Cultural Phenomenon" in *Ideological Differences and World Order*, F. S. C. Northrop, ed. (New Haven: Yale University Press, 1949).

making his change is not, unlike many of his radical equivalents, necessarily seeking to make further changes largely impossible.

But precisely here we find one of the most important aspects of the modern crisis. Behind all special problems and criticisms it may well turn out that a great part of modern dissatisfaction with capitalism springs from a profound change in social ideals. Oriental standards of security and routine appear to be gaining in the Western mind. This hidden conflict of modern value is well shown by a comparison of two passages—one from Lewis Mumford's *Technics and Civilization,* the other from Alfred North Whitehead's *Adventures of Ideas.* Writes Mr. Mumford: "Technically speaking, changes in form and style are symptoms of immaturity; they mark a period of transition. The error of capitalism as a creed lies in the attempt to make this period of transition a permanent one." [13] Against this we may set Alfred North Whitehead: "There can be no real halt of civilization in the indefinite repetition of a perfected ideal. Staleness sets in . . . a race preserves its vigor as long as it harbors a real contrast between what has been and what may be . . . without adventure civilization is in full decay." [14]

That some synthesis is in order goes without saying.[15] But how curious a development when the idea of eternal changelessness is hailed as venturesome and radical, the idea of adventure and youth as reactionary and conservative!

[13] Mumford, *op. cit.,* p. 396. Mumford concludes as follows: "As soon as a contrivance reaches technical perfection there is no excuse for replacement on the ground of increased efficiency." Though what "technical perfection" means aside from "efficiency" I find hard to imagine. Let me hasten to say, however, that Mumford shares Veblen's ambivalent attitude toward change and that other passages can be cited praising it. Nevertheless, the fundamental structure of his ideals (as with Veblen) tends toward the stationary and the authoritarian.

[14] Whitehead, *op. cit.,* pp. 368, 360.

[15] Such a synthesis is, of course, explicity provided by Whitehead, for example, in *ibid.*

The Protective Myths of Capitalism

Every system functions under the shelter of certain common beliefs and attitudes. It is no valid criticism of these attitudes and beliefs that they are not always literally or universally true. Even Plato in outlining his ideal republic was obliged to set up a myth of iron, brass, and golden men in order to reconcile his citizens to the fact of inequality which he proposed to enforce so rigidly. A test of two systems of ideals is not whether either one of them is absolutely correct but which is the most nearly correct and also which on balance conforms most closely to the values of the chooser. It is evident that so strenuous a system as that we have just outlined must have had to have a particular set of ideas permitting it to function.

The beliefs which have helped most to contribute to the achievements of American capitalist democracy are submitted to be as follows: first, the belief that capitalism is more productive than other systems; second, the belief that it gives more opportunity. This is closely allied with the Horatio Alger "rags to riches" story and the idea of "three generations from shirt sleeves to shirt sleeves." Next is the relative democracy of American manners and the *comparative* classlessness of American social life. Closely bound up with this is the idea that capitalism gives a man what he wants rather than what somebody else thinks he ought to have.

At the present time every one of these ideas is deeply under attack. It is said, first of all, that planning would be more productive and more secure than capitalism. We shall discuss this point in our next chapter. Next the idea of rags to riches, the idea of consumer sovereignty, and the idea of relative democratic classlessness are all under attack.[16] It cannot be denied that there are

[16] Cf. William Miller, "The Recruitment of the American Business Elite," *Quarterly Journal of Economics,* May, 1950. To evaluate Miller's argument completely would require a careful dissection of his statistical technique. But even at face value it does not, I submit, prove anything more than that our system is not perfect. One must judge *relatively.*

many defects in the American scene, most especially in relation to certain minority racial groups. Barring that question, however, it is submitted that the major portion of left-wing criticism misses the fundamental point. The question is not whether there is *some* inequality of opportunity in this country or whether there are *some* discernible class structures, structures of habits, and so on. The question is rather: Are conditions in this country better than in other countries? In this regard I believe that the United States can show up very well on any fair comparison. Constant turnover in the make-up of our dominant upper income group has been very noticeable all during the past century and a half. If it is charged, as some have done, that it is now more difficult for a man to be a "success" than it was before, it may well be asked if this is due to any defect of capitalism or if it may not be related to certain unintended but very serious defects of the left-wing redistributive program. We shall discuss this point later on. In the same way the man who wishes to stress uniformities of taste imposed by the surroundings in which he lives can easily show that a great number of people in such and such an income group buy such and such goods. But again one must ask: How much freedom do people in *other* cultures have to express themselves, and how much real opportunity is there in *other* nations to pass from group to group? Even the primitive societies of the South Seas, so often spoken of as if they had represented the democratic ideal, were in fact intensely class- and custom-ridden societies under an iron rule.[17]

But beyond and behind all these criticisms, there are really two

[17] The myth of idyllic anarchy dies hard. Thus Lewis Mumford writes, "Men will be back once more in the Edenlike state in which they have existed in regions of *natural* increment" (italics supplied). Mumford, *op. cit.*, p. 279. The features of the South Sea culture which our sophisticates like to forget are (1) control of the minutest concerns of life by iron custom and caste, (2) population control by infanticide. I refer, of course, to the culture as it existed before deteriorating. But cf. footnote 8.

basic points. In the first place, as we have already stated, there has come to be a school which increasingly doubts the validity of the idea of *striving* or of "success" of any kind. These people are not willing to face the connection between achievement, effort, and inequality in *any* form of endeavor, however lofty in itself. Michelangelo's nose, for example, was not broken by some capitalist usurer trying to collect a debt but by a fellow pupil, Torregiani, an artist, who was jealous of the extravagant praise which Michelangelo's works were receiving.

The second point is a basic defect of all society. Capitalism has certainly on average been one of the most productive systems ever known. One can say this without committing oneself to any belief as to whether planned systems might not conceivably have been better. But though a society can make everybody twice as rich as he was before, there is no way of making everybody twice as rich as everybody else. In other words, what many people want is not absolute but *relative* prosperity, not to be better off than they are now but to be better off than somebody *else* down the street. Yet since *everyone* cannot possibly be a *relative* "success" at the same time, the author has heard it said that there can be no stability in our (or any other) society until the majority of men once more believe in the possibility of a good life apart from *relative* material prosperity.[18] In other words, our culture does not make adequate provision for the psychic needs of the less successful. Whether it is possible, however, to provide for such needs without outlawing achievement (of any kind) also is indeed one of the most profound questions of all social life.

[18] I am indebted to Dr. O. H. Taylor of Harvard for this suggestion.

CHAPTER 4

Democracy, Capitalism, and Growth

IN THE preceding chapter we sketched in general terms the essential features of the capitalist economic organization. We also made certain suggestions regarding its characteristic ideology. Now we wish to relate this organization and its ideology more specifically to the problems of democratic government and economic growth. How far can society go in altering economic organization without affecting political values such as "tolerance" or "justice"? How far can we go in stabilizing change without bringing change to a halt? The problem is obviously a vital one. Practically nobody believes today in unmitigated *laissez faire,* and, on the other hand, fewer and fewer Americans, even American intellectuals, remain orthodox Stalinite Marxists. But are we justified in lumping together all the vast variety of potential social patterns that lie between a municipal waterworks and the Russian Gosplan? A more serviceable analysis is needed, and in this chapter we shall try to work out some of the standards which may perhaps be relevant.

The Meaning of Political and Social Democracy

If we want to decide whether a given system is or is not democratic, we must first make up our minds what democracy is. Yet three principal concepts of political democracy are now disputing the future of the world. The first and crudest is the idea of majority rule—no matter what—the unqualified right of the 51 per cent.[1] The second and the most finespun is the Marxist concept of "dictatorship of the proletariat." Marxist concepts of democracy, during the "socialist phase" at any rate, completely invert usual Anglo-American ideas and define "democracy" as *de facto* rule *of* the majority *by* a self-selecting minority acting in what it conceives to be the "best" interests of society as a whole.[2] Finally there is the American constitutional concept of democracy, largely derived from Thomas Jefferson, which defines democratic government ultimately as a rule of "justice" and "tolerance" but which, by an act of faith, feels that such justice and tolerance are most likely on average to be obtained through electoral government restrained by the people's conscience and a bill of rights.

We adopt in this book the Jeffersonian compromise. A concept of democracy in terms of mere majority rule is always open to the objection that, if democracy is only majority rule, then any

[1] Majority rule, "no matter what," easily turns into dictatorship. Max Weber in his celebrated conversation with Ludendorff seems to have evolved a concept of democracy which (to an Anglo-American) would appear to have the worst features of both systems.

WEBER: Do you believe that I think this swinish condition which we have at present is democracy?

LUDENDORFF: If you talk that way, maybe we can reach an agreement.

WEBER: But the preceding swinish condition was not a monarchy either.

LUDENDORFF: Then what do you mean by democracy?

WEBER: In a democracy the people choose a leader in whom they trust. Then the chosen leader says, "Now shut up and obey me." People and party are then no longer free to interfere in his business.

LUDENDORFF: I could like such democracy.

WEBER: Later the people can sit in judgment. If the leader has made mistakes—to the gallows with him!

But, how do you get rid of such a dictator without catastrophe or revolution? See *From Max Weber: Essays in Sociology,* H. H. Gerth and C. Wright Mills, trans. and eds. (New York: Oxford University Press, 1946), p. 42.

[2] But we have shown in Chap. 1 that the "socialist" phase will be permanent or, rather, that the withering away of the state is impossible.

mob, however savage, is democratic—as long as it is a majority. Rule of the majority *by* a self-selected minority, on the other hand, unless one makes the assumption that a particular group is somehow to be endowed with eternal virtue and infallibility, is the open door to tyranny. The Jeffersonian concept, however, does not attribute infallibility to rulers, people, or courts but hopes by their mutual "checks and balances" to keep the opportunity for "injustice" to a minimum.

Words like "justice" and "tolerance," however, do not in themselves carry very precise meaning unless implemented by some implicit code of values. It may be said, in effect, that the human personality has many different attributes and potentialities and that the expression of some of these attributes is highly prized and considered "just" in one culture and "unjust" in others. Our Western concepts of justice derive, however, in the main from the Judaic-Socratic-Christian humanist tradition which has so profoundly shaped our culture. They have centered around such ideas as giving every man a "chance" to "make the most" of himself, of love and respect for the other fellow, of a minimum of "pushing around" and a high value upon persuasion rather than coercion.

Unfortunately, however, the economic implementation of these ideas is open to a wide variety of interpretation. One of the most technical and, historically, one of the most important economic standards of "democracy" is the labor theory of value which will be discussed later. But in order to show the complexity of the general notion of economic democracy we shall list here five other economic standards, two of which are usually stressed by conservatives, two by radicals, and one by both but *all* of which are in some measure recognized by nearly all factions.

The five aspects which we shall discuss may be listed as follows: (1) democracy of control, (2) democracy of status, (3) democracy of welfare, (4) democracy of choice, (5) democracy of aspiration and opportunity. By democracy of control is meant the right to participate in elections. "Decision making" it is called, though not always very accurately, and left-wing writers often charge that, since the worker is free as a citizen "because" he has a vote in the management of his government, he is *not* free as a worker because he does not have a vote in the management of his job. Democracy of status, our second standard, refers to the idea of "equality," and here, too, the left often takes it to mean literal equality of income: the "one man, one vote, one dollar" idea of democracy.

The third standard, however—democracy of welfare—is appealed to by both sides. What it means, in effect, is that Western democratic cultures have usually put a high value upon the idea of a rising standard of living, and in this connection the capitalist will point to the record of capitalism as accompanying a rapid rise in productivity while the radical speaks of the "greater" gains to be realized through planning.

Two more standards remain, both of which receive great stress from the left even though they are also favorites of more capitalist writers. The first of these is democracy of choice—the ability to choose among the professions available to one and to spend such income as one has upon the things one feels one wishes. This, of course, is one of the principal arguments for the pricing system.

Our fifth and final standard is democracy of "opportunity" and "aspiration." It means a chance for each man to make the "most of himself." Such a standard may sound simple, but in fact it is one of the most difficult to handle of all the aspects of democracy, for, as pointed out in the previous chapter, it frequently runs into direct conflict with what is often called equality of status. If two men are inherently "unequal" and they are given an "equal" chance, will they not wind up unequal in their status whatever the particular field they have chosen? Most thoughtful socialists have accepted this dilemma and argue merely that socialism will give the widest possible opportunity. The Marxists at present also favor great differences in income and opportunity, though, as always, they still speak of an "eventual" utopia in which everyone will be equal and there will be no need to select.

Economic Sources of Democracy

Throughout the present chapter we shall find it necessary to refer to one or another of the five democratic standards we have just listed. It is not, however, necessary at this point to discuss more precisely just what particular attributes we are going to give to the idea of "justice" or "tolerance." We want, for the moment, to discuss the problem on its operative rather than its substantive level. The question we wish to ask is this: Granted that the democratic ethic requires that men's personality and activities be protected in certain ways, how does democracy go about giving this protection?

The answer which seems obvious enough to most people is that, in a democracy, men are protected from injustice by their ability to vote in elections. In other words, "democracy" of "control" is all that is needed. But is a vote really sufficient? Suppose, for example, that we adopt a system of "cooperative management" whereby each worker is given a vote in the operation of the plant. Will this vote by itself automatically serve to protect every individual against injustice and intolerance? Must there not be other qualities and mechanisms also present? Let us try to give a more specific list.

The first requirement for economic and social democracy, and probably the most important, is the one concerning which the economist has the least that is authoritative to say. This requirement concerns the character and ideology of a people. If they are lazy, unhealthy, or weak; irresponsible or shortsighted; stupid, ignorant, or superstitious; timorous or insecure psychologically, then democratic government will not function. The best such a people can hope for is that luck will send them an occasional "good" dictator. But good dictatorships seldom stay good. Here, as in the preceding chapter, immense problems of transition are implied for "backward" people, which here, too, we are obliged largely to omit.

But on the other side of the coin it is clear that, if a people are energetic, healthy, and intelligent; if they feel responsible for the working of their government and are willing to exert themselves from time to time to see that it conforms to their ideas of justice; if, furthermore, they combine these qualities with certain notions of mutual tolerance and self-respect, then they will have a much better chance at creating an effective and progressive democracy.

There are thus at least two variables here—on the one hand the level of character and ideology, and on the other hand the economic and political organization. It follows that the problem is never wholly mechanical but rather a matter of *mutual* inter-determination. Nevertheless it is clear that, while nations differ widely in characteristics, they never achieve an angelic average. *Given,* therefore, a people's general character and traditions, some environments might conceivably make democratic government unworkable for them while under others they might find it quite easy. Thus, while a "democratic" people may survive more regulation than a less "democratic" one, we must in all cases take care lest we load the scales too heavily. And avoidance of such over-loading involves a much more careful analysis of the real function-ings of political democracy and its relationship to economics than has been fashionable for some time.

We begin with the assumption that majorities (and minorities) can sometimes be unfair and unwise, and we ask ourselves what economic factors should be present to give a favorable chance to a man who feels himself unjustly treated by the authorities in his electoral unit (political or industrial) or who wishes to obtain the reversal of a majority decision which he feels unwise. In order to bring out sharply the essentials of the problem we shall assume, furthermore, that initially, at least, all the usual political guarantees are present.[3] Men cannot be arbitrarily thrown into jail for criticizing the government. There is freedom of speech. The courts are open for reasonably impartial adjudication of the usual private grievances between citizens. Elections are regularly held. Under such circumstances what difference does it make how we organize economic life? Are not civil liberties adequately protected?

If the community is small and intimate, if the people are reasonably fair-minded and intelligent, if, in addition, the injustice complained of is a rather clear violation of local mores, or if the new policy being agitated is not a wide departure from accepted ideas and involves no very serious economic reorganizations, then it is probable that relatively little energy will be needed to make effective protest and that mere political guarantees may suffice. But once we leave limited and favorable cases of this sort, the author submits that a purely political analysis is insufficient. He contends, instead, that in the majority of cases two further factors should be present both of which have important economic implications. These factors are, first, economic *independence* for the rank and file and, second, independent *competition* among the leaders.

Let us consider the matter first from the point of view of a would-be leader who wishes to "put across" a given program. It will not suffice if he is merely allowed to talk his head off against a blank wall of centralized administrative complacency and among a cowed population. The voters not only must have a vote but must also be willing to use it. But if a man's *economic* livelihood comes to depend upon his voting for a given political faction, then an important element of coercion is given to the "ins." A mere secret ballot will not suffice. A man's sympathies and to some extent his vote easily become known. Simple refusal to tell

[3] If one is in a position to control the elections by economic dominance, then the political guarantees may all be removed, for even the Constitution may be amended and the size of the Supreme Court legally altered.

how one voted, for example, may be a suspicious circumstance. And even an outright lie may not serve.

Another problem involved is that leadership in a difficult cause is usually a full-time job and that a leader must eat. He, too, has to have some economic independence. Now if the would-be leader has private finances of his own, for example, if he is a rich man like Franklin D. Roosevelt, this problem is taken care of. But such a solution would restrict leadership in protest to a very few. Clearly if a man opposing the authorities has no means and no salary, he must live off contributions from the rank and file. And again *they* must have enough independence (and enough means) to keep him going.

Thus looking at the matter from the point of view of the leaders we see that economic independence is an important factor in effective democratic action. Without it the voters may be pressured into "toeing" the line in spite of their convictions, and they may be hindered to a considerable extent from supporting the opposition "organization." In cases of outrageous abuse, of course, the electorate may act in spite of potential economic coercion, but the greater the economic dangers of protest, the greater the amount of courage needed to act and the greater the degree of injustice and frustration likely to be tolerated.

So much for the economic independence of the voters. Let us next consider the need for independent competition among leaders. In order to evaluate this force properly we must understand the limitations of "primitive" democracy. In the first place not everyone appears to have the psychological drives and the other aptitudes needed to make a good leader. The *direct* participation of all the people in government and administration is a physical impossibility. Once past the small town meeting and usually even then, the rank and file are generally obliged to choose among ideas and leaders presented to them rather than acting directly. Sometimes a given general policy springs so directly from popular values that a spontaneous general pressure grows up in its favor. But even in such a case detailed implementation of the policy cannot be carried on by the entire electorate.

Thus if a man is not physically, economically, or psychically able to become a leader himself, he must find someone to lead his protests for him. And if all the leaders belong to the same group and follow substantially the same policies, the average citizen will often be left helpless. There must thus be both independent *competing* leaders and a rank and file possessed of some economic independence.

We may sum up our argument by saying that effective democratic action, whether in a union or a political election, depends upon the *right of counterorganization* and that this right of counterorganization depends upon economic independence plus competing leadership. Mr. Joseph Rosenfarb, a well-known trade-union theorist, writes: [4]

> For ideas to spread and to become accepted they must be transmitted from the conceiving individual to others and then perhaps from the minority to the majority. For that purpose initiative in organization is necessary, which is another quality of leadership . . . employers have frequently found it unnecessary to eliminate all union members but only the leaders.

Rosenfarb's ideas are, however, capable of a far wider application than he gives them, and it is time to apply our political analysis to some more specifically economic examples. Let us come back once more to the case of "cooperative" management. Let

[4] See Joseph Rosenfarb, *Freedom and the Administrative State* (New York: Harper & Brothers, 1938), pp. 101–102. See also *ibid.*, p. 101: "Only in small organizations is it possible to get the whole membership, or even any substantial portion of it, into one meeting place. In consequence, the mass of the people . . . are on the periphery of power." Rosenfarb's book is an extraordinary one in its combination of keen political insight with complete economic fogginess. We shall refer to it several times, since Mr. Rosenfarb, an ardent trade-unionist and "planner," cannot be accused of bias against government. This makes his political concessions all the more important.

us suppose that all the workers in a plant belong to the union and that they elect their officers who run the plant. Does this not seem an ideal example of democracy? Unfortunately a good deal more analysis is needed.

Suppose, once more, that a man disagrees with the policies of the union officials running the plant or feels that they are being unjust to him. But suppose next that, if he begins to organize a protest, the union officials against whom he is complaining can have him dropped from the union and from his job. How effective a protection of the rank and file will the mere holding of an occasional election be then? Neither of the elements we are speaking of is likely to be present. As long as we consider only the single organization in isolation and rule out the possibility of getting other jobs in other organizations, the voters in the union election will not have economic independence. Also the leadership is likely to be very close-knit.

Some people feel that, if the workers are given "job security" as against both the employer and the *union,* and if they cannot be dismissed without a hearing before some "impartial" tribunal, the problem of democratic action will be met. But unfortunately it is doubtful if such a plan would be fully adequate. How much can *one* man do against a single, very centralized, and powerful organization? If he drops his other concerns to push a given cause, will he not soon furnish those in control with technical grounds for dismissing him? Job security means security in the *job.* It does not mean security to go out experimenting and agitating against the leadership (union or employer) controlling your job. "He is neglecting his work," they can say. "He is a troublemaker." And effective leadership is apt to become a full-time occupation.

Again, security in routine gives no guarantee of a chance for advancement. A man may discover that all chances for promotion have been cut off by the group he is attacking. If he is ambitious, this is bound to affect him. Even if security of promotion by seniority is guaranteed, that also will be subject to some minimum work requirements—requirements which the active leader may well be accused of violating.

Finally, the mere existence of *job* security (even as against both the union and the employer) does not guarantee the presence of adequate alternative leadership. To be sure the leaders inside an organization *could* be in a state of quarrelsome rivalry so that a member of the rank and file could find someone to press his cause. But in the first place, if jobs and promotion alike may depend on "toeing the line" politically, such a state of independent rivalry is not likely. And in the second place, an organization thus split up into warring factions is not likely to be very effective in achieving its *corporate* purpose. There is a potential conflict, therefore, between the centralized coordination often required for the efficient performance of general purpose and the degree of rivalry among leaders needed to give minority ideas and groups a chance.

For all these reasons an analysis which concentrates all its emphasis upon job security *within* organizations is seriously deficient. Job-security schemes, even if we are willing to swallow the stagnation of techniques which they are likely to entail, do not give the necessary element of economic *independence* which is so important a factor in the power of counterorganization. Mere security in routine for the rank and file of some massively centralized system will not adequately safeguard the emergence of the effective new leadership upon which real democracy depends. We have got to take a broader view.

Fortunately, however, it is not necessary as yet to confine one's thinking to intraorganizational problems. When there are many independently competing organizations, the man who finds himself oppressed or frustrated by a given leadership or group may often be able to shift, without too great economic loss, to some *outside* organization. The presence of *alternative* job opportunities may thus come, at times, to be a quicker and easier remedy for injustice than elaborate agitation or pleading within a given unit. Furthermore the presence of independent competitors will make possible a less disruptive *competition among leaders* than the mere factionalism of office politics.

Accordingly we conclude that one of the most important sources of economic independence and hence of effective political democracy is, not mere job security inside an economic unit, but *external* competition accompanied by a reasonable possibility of economic *transfer*. We suggest that independent "pluralism" of this sort—the external competition of leaders in different units—is of tremendous value, not only because of its effects as a help toward economic independence but also because it furnishes perhaps as workable a compromise as is possible between the always somewhat rival ideas of "freedom" on the one hand and efficiency on the other.

At the present time there is a deal of talk of "participation" as a value, and by this is often meant "cooperative" management, or the right of the workers to vote upon management policy. Now it follows from our analysis that, if a worker does not have a chance to shift jobs, and if he could lose the job he has by agitating too strenuously against his leadership, whether union or employer, the mere fact of an occasional election would not be very significant. For real counterorganization would be exceedingly difficult.

Let us, however, consider for the moment not merely counterorganization but also the question of efficiency. Worker management has seldom made for large-scale efficiency. As *The London Economist* put the matter, cooperative management has not made for large-scale efficiency for the same reason that few if any armies have ever been able to function effectively for very long if their officers were elected by the troops and subject to their recall.[5]

[5] See "Old Boss Writ Large," *The London Economist,* Vol. 154, p. 1001 (June, 1948): "The main argument against the direct control of industries by those who work in them—whether the doctrine is christened syndi-

The competitive system, however, with its independent pluralism, recognizes the need for authority within an organization yet tempers it by the fact that no one is obliged to remain within any

---

calism or guild socialism—is that it does not work, any more than the various experiments that have been made throughout history to run an army by delegates from the ranks have ever worked."

See also, and from a very sympathetic observer, the following remarks by Lord Lindsay of Birker (made a peer by the Labour government): "One of the most persistent ideals of early trade unionism was that of the 'self-governing workshop,' in which the distinction between the management and the managed had entirely disappeared. Unfortunately experiments made of setting up such workshops have always, or nearly always, been inefficient. It is interesting to note that the Russians started with the same idea—that the worker, the ordinary simple worker at the bottom, should run the business—and they have had, in the interests of efficiency, progressively to give up any such notion."

Also: "What I am concerned to point out is that the making a business in itself democratic is not the same problem as making the management of an industry responsible to the community as a whole. Either of these problems could be solved without solving the other."

Again "Discussion *for* us is not the same as discussion *by* us."

Lord Lindsay of Birker, "The Philosophy of the British Labor Government," in *Ideological Differences and World Order,* F. S. C. Northrop, ed. (New Haven: Yale University Press, 1949), pp. 261–262, 265. Since Lord Lindsay is a very sympathetic critic, his concessions are of special value.

I should also like to point out that the feeling of participation is in large part a function of size and of time. Cf. Krech and Crutchfield, *Theory and Problems of Social Psychology* (New York: McGraw-Hill Book Company, Inc., 1948), p. 549: "Some unions, whose battles are in the far past, no longer offer their members an exultant sense of progress . . . other unions operate as a tight bureaucracy."

Also *The London Economist,* Vol. 154, p. 1055 (June 26, 1949), commenting on the dock strikes, "This union has the worst record of unofficial strikes because its enormous *size,* wealth and power place its leaders in a position so exalted that only an exceptional man can keep in close touch with the rank and file. Consequently the Union has, in the minds of its members, become an entity as remote as the government *or the employer.*" (Italics supplied.)

given unit. Nor need we suppose that *everybody* has to shift to impress those in authority. As soon as any sizable margin of men begin to leave, intelligent leadership will heed the signal. If leadership is not intelligent, it may begin to lose ground altogether. The mere knowledge that such a shift is possible may be of immense importance, for it may give just the courage needed to stiffen opposition.

In the remainder of this paper we shall treat some of the problems raised by our analysis. How, for example, can we ensure that it will always be reasonably possible for people to transfer from one line to another? At the moment, however, we wish only to make our basic point. Security schemes *inside* an organization will not suffice to ensure the economic independence and immunity of competitive leaders which is one of the basic requirements of democratic government. Without external competition (competition *between* organizations) strong pressures toward technological stagnation and political authoritarianism are alike engendered.

But now we come to the root question: Granted the political analysis just given, will not the extreme centralization of power and leadership implied by certain kinds of economic planning eliminate most of the free competition of leaders on which democracy largely depends? Let us again quote a trade-union answer. Rosenfarb writes:[6]

> It need not be feared that the administrative class (in a comprehensively planned state) will become the omnipotent dictatorial class. As in every other broad class or form of power there would be internal pyramids of power within it in the form of agencies in constant competition with each other. Has the fact that the Army and Navy are both subdivisions of the government precluded them from being longstanding bitter rivals? The problem is not how to create rivalry but how to mitigate it and to effect cooperation for common purposes.

[6] Rosenfarb, *op. cit.*, p. 124 .

As far as the author knows, this is the only serious attempt that has as yet been made to answer the general line of political analysis we have been describing. It therefore deserves the most careful consideration. For what the passage quoted seems to be saying is that competition and rivalry among leaders is the guarantee of freedom, yet that we need not competition but cooperation in order to get efficiency. In this paradox one has the fundamental problem and fundamental danger of our civilization.

Planning, Democracy, and Growth

The most basic choice that the planners of any society have to make is whether they do or do not want more growth. Almost anybody can run a stationary culture. But when growth begins, the whole picture changes. The explosive element in modern life, one could almost say, is not so much the atomic bomb as the widespread desire and belief that we can combine the serene routine of a mystic with the rising living standards of industrialism.

Quite a good philosophical argument can be made that a rising standard of living is a snare and a delusion. The Buddhists may quite possibly be correct in stating that wisdom is found in the putting aside of desire rather than the attempt to satisfy it. But there is a problem here, if not of political honesty, certainly of political effectiveness. The left wing—in practical politics at least—does not promise to do a different job, economically speaking, from capitalism but to do the capitalist job *better*—not, for example, to "slow down" housing in the interest of stability but to give *more* houses (and more everything) and still give more security. Yet if the expectations of the people are disappointed, will not the disappointed masses turn toward more extreme governments—right or left? The tendency will be for a government which fails to live up to promises either to lose popular support and be forced out or else to maintain itself by slowly ceasing to be liberal and making increasing resort to propaganda, censorship, and repression. In other words, if our planning government is voted in on a promise of giving a rising living standard, it will (*as long* as it remains democratic) have to deliver the goods in a reasonable time or else go out. This means that any successful liberal planning government must be able to solve the problem of economic growth.

Just here, however, comes the most important single difficulty. Planning is advocated today not merely to give "plenty" or to satisfy consumers but also to give "security." Political and economic writers have talked of *social* security and most of them realize that that is all the security they can give. But to the general public "security" means personal security, and this is usually taken to mean that nobody will ever have to change jobs unless he wants to move to one he thinks is "better," that nobody actively at work will ever have any changes in wages except increases, and that nobody will ever be fired except for the most egregious misconduct. Unfortunately, however, it can very easily be shown that, if we really try to implement this strict popular meaning of security, we cannot possibly have more growth.

When an economist tells a political scientist that the *complete* advance guarantee of absolute security or even of absolute "full" employment must almost certainly mean indefinite rationing, priorities, and price control, the political scientist is apt to assume (or so the author has usually found it) that the economist is implying bad faith or stupidity on the part of those doing the planning. Fortunately, however, it requires no very esoteric economic theory to explain the practical point at issue.

The fact is that, whether we are dealing with a socialist, a generally planned, or a capitalist society, if we want higher living standards and if we want to make some effort toward satisfying the consumer, we shall immediately have a forecasting problem. As long as output is not growing, past experience is a fairly reliable guide. But as soon as we start to expand, it will be necessary for those in control, whether they call themselves commissars, bureau chiefs, union officials, or businessmen, to go beyond mere repetition and draw up estimates of the future pattern of wants during the next planning period. Yet if they guess incorrectly, there can be great dislocation. For example, if the board thinks consumers will want washing machines and allots numerous materials to that industry only to find housewives buying vacuum cleaners instead, there will probably be considerable disturbances, shortages, and (without control) price adjustments.

There is, however, a further point usually overlooked in modern literature which is overwhelmingly important. This is not merely the *variability* but also the *unpredictability* of consumer wants in an expanding and unrationed society.[7] Those who think about the problem at all usually assume that, during an expansion, demand for all goods will go up in approximately the same proportion. For example, they tend to suppose that the board could order, say, a general 20 per cent increase of output by all industries and leave it at that.

Unfortunately such a symmetrical and predictable expansion is largely impossible in an unrationed world. In some industries, for instance, salt, a 20 per cent increase in output would probably pile up a great surplus inventory; in other cases, so small an increase would be quite inadequate. There exists overwhelming statistical evidence that, even if no new inventions are made, and even if advertising were abolished, the pattern of consumers' wants would shift disproportionately and often unpredictably.[8]

[7] Compare Albert Lauterbach, *Economic Security and Individual Freedom, Can We Have Both?* (Ithaca, N.Y.: Cornell University Press, 1948), p. 65.

[8] Cf., for example, Arthur F. Burns, *Production Trends in the United States since 1870* (New York: National Bureau of Economic Research, Inc., 1934); Solomon Fabricant, *The Output of Manufacturing Industry, 1890–1937* (New York: National Bureau of Economic Research, Inc., 1940); David McC. Wright, *The Economics of Disturbance* (New York: The Macmillan Company, 1947), Chap. III. Also *Survey of Current Business*, January, 1950.

Sometimes the total would add up to "more" than full employment, and then we would have pressure toward inflation; other times to less, and then we should, if we did nothing about it, have unemployment. But no type of industrial organization is likely to do a perfect job of anticipating wants. What would be needed for a perfect job would be an X-ray eye to read off the consumer's wants for next year—even before he had formed them.

Yet it follows directly from the incontrovertible fact that simple expansion will affect different industries in differing degrees that simple growth of the national income—in and of itself—will upset the routine operation of various industries. Some businesses may even be ruined by prosperity. If national income doubles, manufacturers of kerosene lamps will scarcely double their sales. The chances are that most of their customers would switch over to electricity. Mere growth, then, will inconvenience many vested interests. Not only does this mean the capitalist vested interest of the businessman in his dividends but also, as we have seen earlier, the socialist vested interest of the bureaucrat in his job and the laborer in his skills. Change can render many a formerly happy man a "back number," and no mere money salve is going to relieve his hurt.

From the urge to security, however, comes the problem of pressure groups. It is often argued by mathematical and statistical economists that, even though we cannot guarantee each individual man security in *his* particular wealth, skill, or prestige structure, still we can at least make sure *in advance* that the total of industrial changes will always add up to full employment. The economic logic of such schemes is usually absolutely impeccable. Only when we consider the politics of it do doubts begin to shape.

The trouble is that, if we want always to have an absolute and advance guarantee of, say, 97 per cent full employment, we must set up a group of men who will serve as traffic cops for new investment. This does not mean that full employment may not very often exist spontaneously. It is only that perfect *advance* knowledge and calculation cannot be had without centralized control of change. Nobody's property or plant, in the beginning anyhow, needs to be government-seized or -operated, but all further growth has to come under rigid government control. No major expansion of any industry can take place without a clearance from the central investment planning board. No government agency can expand its projects without clearing through them. They will be in a position to decide on the expansion of almost every town, every region, every business.

Yet while centralized advance planning of this sort is admittedly the only way *always* to be sure of perfect stability, it does not answer the problems of either democracy or growth. There are two main defects. In the first place to give a single small group of men such enormous power over the economic prospects of every city, town, manufacturer, union, and government bureau would make possible a degree of economic reprisal against dissenting groups and regions difficult to reconcile with the political analysis with which we began. In the second place the control bureau would probably be subject to so many influences from pressure groups of all sorts, seeking to preserve their own special positions, that the total of economic growth might well be choked off in a general stalemate.

Cotton farmers would want to expand the output of oleomargarine; dairy farmers to prevent it. The West might want to build up new plants; the East might want to prevent it. Coal miners would object to hydroelectric plants; railroad workers and sailors to oil pipe lines; Massachusetts to the expansion of southern mills; the South to retaining industry in the North. We should repeat on a national scale the log-rolled stagnation which has accompanied every tariff act ever debated in Congress. We conclude that the advance guarantee of absolute individual security cannot be combined either with effective democracy or with rising living standards.

Innovation and Aspiration

In tracing the unstabilizing effects of growth, negatively speaking, we have, however, left aside one of the most important elements of social growth. Not only do rising living standards cause change, but also they are brought about through change. Without new inventions, we have seen, our standard of living would soon cease rising. But in touching upon the problem of invention we reach what might well be called a solar plexus of civilization. It is the point at which the structure of planning, the structure of political life, the structure of power, and the structure of growth all overlap in one supremely important complex of energies to produce that creative activity on which any vigorous culture depends. The essential fact is that inventions both good and bad are seldom spontaneous either in discovery or in application. Even their intellectual comprehension is not sufficient to produce practical use. Both for discovery and for use, the environment favoring inventions must usually have certain special characteristics.

Growth comes through change. But change comes through *independent* minds. That type of planning which concentrates upon producing only a smooth routine is not likely to give much encouragement either to intellectual or to economic independence. For independence and invention, by producing growth and change, also produce disturbance. Here we touch upon our fifth standard of economic democracy—democracy of aspiration—a chance to rise on independent terms.

At the present time many forces are pressing toward the use, within each organizational unit, of methods of promotion and selection designed to preserve routine rather than select leadership: seniority, competitive examination, and so on.[9] Yet every

[9] Since so much is said about the "civilization of capitalism," something should also be said about the flaccid civilization of trade-unionism. In this connection the author has found few fairer and more thorough statements

teacher will know that even competitive examination does not always reach the best minds, but often fosters instead an uncreative mediocrity intent upon cramming accepted prejudice rather than exploring new ideas (which might disturb the examiner's preconceptions). Thus within the modern organization the pressures, though fortunately still largely incipient, are toward routine conformity.

Intraorganizational problems, however, are still not overwhelming if there are *outside* competing independent units to which a man frustrated in one organization can transfer. But here, too, the emphasis on coordination and "cooperative" activity, inherent in the ideas of centralized planning and smooth routine, is increasingly cutting down on interorganizational competition and the in-

---

than that by Honor Croome, "Liberty, Equality and Full Employment," *Lloyd's Bank Review,* July, 1949, p. 14. The whole essay, especially its distinction between the "classless" state and the "one-class" state, is warmly recommended. But I wish only to quote the following (pp. 20–21): "The oppression-born, depression-fostered degeneracy of the wage earners' attitude to service . . . can, with some effort, be dismissed as a passing deformity of the social sense, certain of cure under the therapeutic influence of social justice. But there remains something more permanent; the profound dislike of the good trade-unionist, however public-spirited, for the free lance and his methods. Action should be collectively determined; benefits should be collectively assessed; the norm should be collectively established; and the individual's only business is to share—of course on a footing of democratic equality—in the taking of these decisions and loyally to co-operate in implementing them. Solidarity is the supreme working class virtue, and individualism is correspondingly open to condemnation in all its manifestations. Excellence is suspect; he who excels might constitute himself a pacemaker. Resourcefulness is suspect; it may lead to the cutting of collectively sanctioned corners. Imaginative innovation is suspect, no less because it is rarely the outcome of collective action than because it may threaten a vested interest in the obsolete. All must travel in convoy, at the pace of the slowest; whoever follows a privately charted course is, almost by definition, a pirate."

dependence of the separate units. The consequences of these two tendencies—seniority within the organization, tight control outside it—will, if pushed to an extreme, largely destroy the creative advance of our civilization.

For here we encounter a fundamental idea—the narrowing of the self-selecting noncompetitive group. All leaderships, it has often been observed, try to perpetuate themselves. The result is that, irrespective of the original innate endowment of a particular leadership, every dominant group or party, in the course of generations, is apt to develop an ever-increasing segment which is devoid of leadership qualities. Promotion increasingly goes to the "nice" boys rather than the able boys. Many historians, of whom recent analysts of the Nazis are only one instance, have pointed out that in a dictatorship vanity in its leaders and sycophancy in the followers tend to eliminate from the circle of the mighty those with courage to disagree with the voice of authority.[10] But is this only true of dictatorships? Here, I think, we reach the fundamental issue.

The question is: How, under any system, are the "minority," the "conceiving individuals," to be free to organize against leaders who adhere to outworn formulas if these individuals are open to stealthy economic reprisal? Trotsky, we must remember, said that under communism few would dare oppose the state because the state was the ultimate employer and transfer beyond its reach impossible.

We have seen that political freedom is underwritten not merely by votes but by votes buttressed by economic independence. And we have seen that this independence implies much more than mere security. If we want active, energetic, and adaptable leadership, we need a chance to *rise* on independent terms. Our basic

[10] As an example from our own discipline may I refer the reader to E. D. Domar, "The Varga Controversy," *American Economic Review,* March, 1950, p. 132.

point is well put in another connection by Mr. Huntingdon Cairns in "Composers Must Eat." [11]

> Both commercial and state patronage are defeated in the end by the same obstacle; the artist must establish his ability to the satisfaction of some authoritative jury. Neither business nor the state can afford to endow all who wish to follow an artistic career. There must be a selection of some kind. Inevitably the selection will be made by those regarded as most competent to judge—that is, by those who have already established their reputations in the field. But as a general rule it is the young and unestablished who support the innovations which appear in the life of art and without which it becomes stereotyped and sterile. What we may expect from official boards is typified by the French Academy—which, as has been remarked, is always half a generation behind the current practices. Molière, La Fontaine, Zola, Hugo, all were frowned upon by the Academy.
>
> At the same time organizations of that type foster standards which ought to be maintained. But since official boards will be composed of elderly specialists, it cannot be expected that the encouragement they will give to art will be of the kind that will foster *that anarchic element without which art ceases to grow.*

Cairns is talking of art, but the same thing is true of science, of business, and of every other form of endeavor. Growth and art come through change; change comes through independent minds.

I do not wish to give the impression, however, that the case for the competitive structure rests only on its value in helping toward a growing aggregate output. Far more deep-seated issues are at stake. We must consider not merely the output a society produces but also the lives of the men producing the output. Yet in this connection the modern drive toward routine security presents a basic inadequacy in its interpretation of the nature of

[11] Huntingdon Cairns, "Composers Must Eat," *Atlantic Monthly,* March, 1948.

man. Man is not merely artisan; he may also be artist. It is of the *nature* of many men to express themselves by introducing change. The artist paints a mural, and the businessman may build up a business or introduce some new product. There are, of course, immense differences between them. But both have the pride of work in creating novelty. Yet a certain number of people predisposed toward novelty-creating activity seem to appear in every generation. Set men free from the bonds of iron custom, and some of them will immediately start questioning *and* inventing. The creation of novelty is thus a concomitant of freedom. We cannot cut off one without deeply harming the other.[12] Perhaps the real class struggle is not "owner" versus "worker" but the struggle between the initiators of change and the lovers of routine.

The fundamental issue can be put very simply. Without *independent* competing units and lines of activity between which a man may shift when he finds his way blocked in one of them, the creative leader will have little chance. With comprehensive private monopoly or comprehensive public planning, we are not likely to have that "anarchic element" without which art or science or life itself ceases to grow.

Again without some backlog of competing opportunities the worker always risks the loss of genuine independence in his job. As the populations of Western Europe surrendered themselves to feudalism in the "dark ages" in return for protection from the barbarians, so the laboring population of the United States is permitting progressively greater inroads on its right to shift jobs in return for what it believes to be security from unemployment.[13]

The pressure of union action is not merely toward higher wages and shorter hours but also toward the splitting up of the labor

[12] Of course, I do not mean to deny the need for wartime and military-security secrecy measures. Yet even they raise a problem.

[13] It is not, of course, true that universal membership in a union necessarily protects a man, or even a country, from unemployment. Cf. Croome, *op. cit.* footnote 9.

market into a series of more and more watertight compartments. Seniority privileges, initiation fees, and so on, make transfer increasingly difficult and expensive *and to that extent* help to render the union less and less democratic.

Is Capitalism Democratic?

We must now apply our analysis more specifically to capitalism. Is it or is it not democratic, and if so, why or why not? The first problem we encountered was in the definition of democracy. We found at least three broad political definitions: majority rule no matter what; rule by a self-selecting *minority* in the "best interests" of the majority (this definition covers communism, fascism, and the so-called "good" dictatorships); and third, democracy as primarily the rule of justice and tolerance, by an act of faith, thought best obtained on average through elective government curbed by the people's conscience and a bill of rights.

Yet words like justice and tolerance require more specific definition, and we found that attempts to implement the idea of "economic democracy" have involved, in addition to the labor theory of value, which is not generally accepted, five other standards of economic democracy none of which are wholly harmonious with each other but each of which is in some degree accepted by representatives of *all* democratic groups of the Anglo-American tradition. These five standards were democracy of control, status, welfare, choice, and opportunity or aspiration. How does capitalism emerge when checked against this list?

It is clear that capitalism does not and cannot recognize labor's supposed "right" to the "whole product" of industry. But "labor" has no right to the "whole product," for it does not create the whole product. We shall discuss this problem in our next chapter.

Capitalism also does not give an absolutely literal application of the idea of democracy of control. Every voter can participate in the government, but every worker cannot vote in the management of his firm. If, therefore, we define democracy as the mere right to drop a ballot in a box when, for example, the question of purchasing more raw materials at the plant is involved or whenever we engage in any other activity, then capitalism is not democratic.[14]

But what of the other standards—democracy of status, welfare, choice, and opportunity. As far as democracy of status goes, capitalist incentives rule out literal equality. But both the Communists and the socialists have also been unable to eliminate inequality. The mistake often made here—as in so many social controversies—lies in the idea that, if we abolish the *particular* type of inequality with which we happen to be familiar, we thereby abolish *all* inequality. But as Hicks and Hart point out, what do we accomplish by diminishing inequality of income if at the same time we increase inequality of power.[15] And it must be remembered that power advantages no less than money advantages may be transmitted (however unofficially) from one generation to another. If we want to give a literally equal start, we should need to abolish, not just income differences or inheritance, but the family itself. For the commissar's son no less than the boss's nephew may get the "breaks." [16]

In short we do not have a choice between a world of equality and one of *in*equality. We have only a choice between different kinds of inequality. And it is by no means self-evident that the great inequalities of power which centralized planning inevitably implies are any better or any less easily transmitted than inequality of fortune.

[14] The author doubts if it is the mere fact of voting which matters so much as a certain feeling of intimacy—quite independent of whether there is union or employer control. See footnotes 5 and 9.

[15] See J. R. Hicks and A. G. Hart, *The Social Framework of the American Economy* (New York: Oxford University Press, 1945), p. 232.

[16] Could it be soberly maintained that a man named Joe Smith had an equal political start with a man named Taft or Roosevelt?

But perhaps the most searching answer to the "one man, one vote, one dollar" idea of democracy is that it defines "status" too narrowly. A man's status is not *only* his real income level but also his status as a (relatively) freely choosing and acting individual—the *pursuit* of happiness. The ante bellum Southerners frantically pointed out that the real income, or economic "welfare" level, of many slaves was higher than that of many workmen. And quite a number of modern writers, especially Marxists, have been quick to insist that they were right.[17] But the Civil War was fought just the same, and I should be surprised if there were many who regretted it.

The truth of the matter is that the problem can be handled only in terms of a "fair" chance. In other words democracy of status merges into democracy of choice and of aspiration. Here we have two opposing arguments. The socialist stresses the opportunities provided by socialism, through government services, to develop the health, education, and cultivation of the individual. But the capitalist points out that, though a man may acquire knowledge and health from state services under socialism (supposing the socialist economy to be adequately productive), a wealthy and developing capitalism can provide equally well for its poorer citizens. Still more important, he can show that, though the young socialist may learn certain skills from the state, it is by no means certain that he will be permitted either to learn the skills he *wishes* to learn or to *use* them in the way he wishes, after he has learned them. A mature socialism would, it is true, offer a man a chance to go up a preordained ladder of examination and seniority, but it would not offer a chance for an independent career. No new idea could be introduced without clearing through the state, and a

[17] The Marxist argument in this regard is, of course, that, since the slave owner has paid in advance for the full labor power of the slave instead of buying it piecemeal, he is thereby forced to give some thought to the "maintenance" of the individual. Thus mere self-interest would tend to make him more humane in action.

state administered with the high regard for routine security which socialism is likely to have is not likely to permit continued change and experiment.

The bias of many young radicals today is as understandable as it is tragic. They see only, at this stage of their lives, the fact that "government" is "giving" them their education. It will not be until they have become older that they will encounter government in another of its possible aspects—government as the agent of the "dead hand" of the past, forbidding independent exploration, thought, and adventure.[18] And while purely personal feeling may be out of place at this point, I cannot help saying that the pity of the whole thing to me lies in the fact that we *can* provide the opportunity-giving state services *without* involving the crushingly progressive taxation or the stultifying over-all planning which so many self-conscious "liberals" feel an inseparable part of the program. We can and we should spend more for schools and for health. But does this mean that we must wipe out incentive and let the pressure groups run riot in the name of "planning" for "security"? I do not think so. It is one of the glories of American capitalist democracy that from the start we began to spend on education to create opportunity.[19] As our incomes have grown, our expenditures have grown—and even faster. But take care lest uncritical policy destroy at once the growth and the opportunity—while education sinks into indoctrination.

[18] Needless to say I have pointed out only two of hundreds of possible aspects of government. I do not maintain that either of those given is conclusive.

[19] Under Jefferson's influence and before the curse of slavery had taken full hold, the Southern states were pioneers in public education. Thus the Universities of Georgia and North Carolina are the oldest state universities in the country. Also several of the Middle Western universities including Michigan trace back to Thomas Jefferson's insistence in the Northwest Territory ordinance that the five territories to be established set aside a certain amount of land for state universities. Jefferson, of course, also established the University of Virginia.

Is Capitalism More Productive?

Thus behind the problems of welfare and opportunity we find the problem of productivity, and it is necessary here to summarize the conclusions of our argument in so far as they concern the relative productivity of socialism or centralized planning on the one hand and capitalism on the other.

As a preface to such a summary it may help to define the capitalist *economic* organization a bit more specifically than we have done so far. Marxist writers have invariably asserted that capitalism must be considered not merely as an economic system but also as a culture or civilization, and in the preceding chapter we tacitly adopted that point of view. Nevertheless in so far as capitalism can be considered an economic system alone, the author has offered the following definition: "Capitalism is a system in which, on average, much the greater portion of economic life, and particularly of net new investment, is carried on by private (*i.e.*, non-government) units under conditions of active and substantially free competition, and avowedly, at least, under the incentive of a hope for profit." [20]

By adopting this definition we restrict our field in certain ways. Although the definition does not imply that capitalism survives only as long as "pure" or "perfect" competition survives (and this point must be treated in later chapters), nevertheless it does mean that, if capitalist or other pressure groups have log-rolled themselves into an industrial stalemate so that either there is no longer any *net* new investment or else full employment is maintained only by a permanent flow of government war or welfare expenditure, then such a system under our terminology can no more be called capitalist than socialist. In the remainder of this section we shall be discussing the pros and cons of a growth process which is still

[20] See D. McC. Wright, "The Prospects for Capitalism" in *A Survey of Contemporary Economics,* H. S. Ellis, ed. (Philadelphia: The Blakiston Company, 1948) p. 452.

taking place predominantly through "private" hands and within a competitive framework.

In comparing the productivity of such a process with that of the centrally planned or socialist economy two ancient proverbs may be invoked. One is: "A penny saved is a penny gained." The other is: "Penny wise, pound foolish." The crux of our argument has been that centrally coordinated planning, *if* the bureaucracy itself does not consume (in government costs) too large a proportion of resources, could conceivably give a more efficient or in any event more smoothly running economy than the capitalist one at a *fixed* income level. Thus from the point of thrift or tidy housekeeping—which is almost exclusively Veblen's standpoint—socialism gains. But on the other hand, substantial as the *short-run* gains from thrift or tidy allocation might be, over the long run the gains from *changing* technique, new invention, and venturesome investment far outshadow them. And it is therefore our contention that from the point of view of *continued* change and growth the competitive economy is far superior.

The crux of the matter lies in the "democracy of aspiration" and the right of transfer between independent units of which we have already spoken. The chance for an independent career is, we submit, one of the essential economic features which underwrite the superior productivity and inventiveness of capitalism. And it so happens that the institution which furnishes a degree of independent opportunity is also the institution which is one of the most important supplements to effective political democracy. That institution is the competitive market. Because of competition and the fact that industry is not organized under a single hierarchy of authorities, men have a chance to transfer from one line to another. This means that they are not forever at the mercy of a single directorate *or* group of associates. But also because of competition a man with a new idea or technical combination has a chance to get it introduced without asking the consent of all those already in power. Thus capitalism, while it is competitive, is likely to be over the long run both more productive and more democratic than a planned system. The planned system may give a more "rational" and more smooth-running application of a *given* set of techniques, but it will not make for comparable *continued* growth.

As pointed out in the Preface, *short-run* statistics of productivity do not furnish a conclusive basis for comparison.[21] There is first of all what I have called the idea of the "Imperial Age." When pressure groups run riot and the conflict of social philosophies becomes so great as to destroy effective cooperation, the "man on horseback" may be called in. Now whether such a leader professes to be implementing the "dictatorship of the proletariat," introducing a Nazi economy, or professing some other gospel, the fact remains that by the assertion of brute sovereignty he may break the particular groups obstructing the "general welfare" and reassert a more public point of view. Such a regime may at first be followed by a period of development, for example, the age of Augustus. But though the central bureaucracy may quell the subordinate pressure groups, it *itself* becomes in time a greater pressure group than any it supplanted. Over the years the narrowing of the self-perpetuating group will set in.[22]

Thus, for example, a centrally planned regime, operating in a backward country, may by bringing in a vast *known* technology give the appearance of rapid development. But once this country has caught up with more advanced ones, its institutional set-up may not be capable of generating any more growth on its own. The author feels that this fact plus the "parasitic" development mentioned in the Preface will explain all the known modern data.

[21] The existing, or rather the available, Russian statistics do not, I believe, furnish a reliable basis for comparison. Cf. Alexander Gerschenkron, "The Rate of Industrial Growth in Russia since 1885," *The Tasks of Economic History,* Supplement VII, 1947, to the *Journal of Economic History*. See also *The Review of Economic Statistics,* November, 1947.

[22] Cf. Domar, *op. cit.*

But a word of caution is necessary. As far as military superiority goes, it would be foolish to be complacent. A sufficiently centralized and ruthless regime may, as Hitler has shown, divert such a tremendous proportion of the resources into war goods as to build up an enormous short-run superiority over more decentralized and democratic countries. The superiority thus achieved could be fatal. On the other hand, if the initial thrust is withstood and public ideology is not too divided, the experience of the Nazis also shows clearly that the dictatorship's war tends to be a one-formula war. Less initially efficient but more independent people may thus over the long pull overtake and outwit them. Yet it would be foolish to court disaster by complacent inactivity. In this connection it may be worth while to quote some words of Oliver Wendell Holmes written in 1860: "Not by aggression, but by the naked fact of existence, we are an eternal danger and an unsleeping threat to any government that founds itself on anything but the will of the governed." [23]

[23] From Catherine Drinker Bowen, *Yankee from Olympus* (Boston: Little, Brown & Company, 1945) p. 160. I should also like to quote the following very apropos statement by Josef Stalin made in 1936 when *Germany* was the danger and the United States in high favor. See *Stalin on the New Soviet Constitution* (New York: International Publishers Co., 1936) p. 18:

"In one of his tales the great Russian writer, Schedrin, presents the type of an obstinate fool and bureaucrat, very narrow-minded and thick-headed but extremely self-assured and zealous.

"After this bureaucrat had restored 'peace and order' in a region 'entrusted' to him, by exterminating thousands of its inhabitants and burning scores of towns, he looked around on the horizon and caught sight of America, then a little known land, where it appeared there were certain liberties which bewilder people and where the state is administered by different methods. Catching sight of America the bureaucrat flew into a rage: 'What country was that? Where did it come from? What right had it to be there?'

"Of course it had been accidentally discovered several centuries ago and it could not be closed up again so that not a smell of it remained.

Final Word

From our conclusion, however, many problems arise, and we shall have to spend a large part of the remainder of this study exploring them. First of all, if our thesis is correct, there is a close connection between the independent "self-" selection of economic rulers displayed by the capitalist competitive market and the continued technical change of capitalist society. This conclusion is extremely disquieting for a society in which there is increasing clamor for the "rationalization" and routinization of selective methods.

Next, while capitalism may be more productive in the long run, it is, for the short run, very unstable. Can we stabilize the capitalist market without destroying that chance for independent access to the top on which, as we have seen, so much depends? Again, can we tax society generally in order to provide adequate services and an adequate chance for the less well-to-do without, again, destroying this chance for independent expansion and independent wealth?

Finally we have used the word "competition." But does this mean the "pure" competition of the textbooks?[24] Are we to try to help little ones get big or only to make big ones little? Until we have some answers to these questions, we are in a poor position to evaluate the future of capitalist society.

[But] desiring that end [to close it up] the bureaucrat wrote: 'Close up America.' "

I am indebted to Professor Z. C. Dickinson of the University of Michigan for this quotation.

[24] I have tried to give a comprehensive discussion of this knotty problem in "Toward Coherent Anti-trust," *Virginia Law Review,* October, 1949. See also Chap. 6, this book.

Part Two

The Problems of Capitalism

CHAPTER 5

Distribution and the Business Cycle

MANY PEOPLE who undertake to explain or to defend capitalism seem to feel that they can prove their point only by maintaining that the system is very nearly perfect and that it has no problems at all. Emphasis upon the self-adjusting qualities of the economy is likely—if we are not careful—to lead to the implication that there will never be any trouble about anything if we will only sit still and wait. To write in his manner is not only untrue but also futile. Most people of good sense realize how very far from perfect the world around us is, and they know how many problems we normally have to deal with. Accordingly, when they find a writer approaching the subject in this way, their inclination is simply to dismiss him as a fool. But the present book is far from denying the existence of problems under capitalism, and in our second part we shall turn our attention to the more seamy side of the system. Up to this point we have been discussing how the system works—to the extent that it does. Now we shall look at the other side and discuss the reasons why it sometimes does not work and what can be done about it. We want to deal with the various problems of capitalist organization, and of these the most important by far in the minds of many people is the business cycle.

We shall not dispute the importance of the cycle problem. We shall dispute instead only a single idea now generally accepted throughout the world. That idea is the notion that the business cycle is purely a capitalist phenomenon and that it would necessarily cease to exist under a generally planned economic system. We shall show that, on the contrary, a great many of the forces giving rise to cyclical movements, excess capacity, and so on are not necessarily the result of capitalism, capitalist organization, or mere lack of planning, but rather of certain basic values frequently taken to be inherent in the idea of a liberal economy. Furthermore, while absolute stability is impossible in any free system, cyclical movements can nevertheless be relatively stabilized under capitalism. And a truly liberal socialist system would have to use many of the *same* methods. The cycle problem far transcends mere capitalism.

Two general lines of argument are usually invoked by the left wing in the discussion of the business cycle. The first, as already implied, is that the business cycle is simply the outgrowth of lack of planning. But the second and perhaps the most important idea is the notion that the business cycle is due to certain peculiarities in the capitalist system of distribution. It is often maintained that the mere existence of profits, plus the urge to accumulate, is, standing alone, responsible for the cycle. We shall not maintain here, in this connection, either that there are no crashes or that the problems of profits or of planlessness have nothing to do with possible dislocation. What we shall argue is, rather, that the forces making for the cycle are in most cases the same forces which make for continued *growth* of the economic system. We shall maintain that without growth there would not be likely to be any cyclical movements and that profits, accumulation, and planlessness are alike largely guiltless except to the extent that they contribute to continued rapid growth.

Our discussion of distribution and the business cycle will be divided into several parts. The first part will discuss the nature of profits and their relation to growth and the business cycle. In this section we shall also spend some time upon the Marxian "labor theory" of value. The second part will explain and criticize some of the standard left-wing cycle theories. In the third part we shall tie our various threads together and ask whether it is planlessness alone which underlies cyclical movements.

Discussions of the nature and role of profits and of the labor theory of value must necessarily be more technical than most of the ground we have covered so far. Those readers, therefore, who are interested only in a fairly nontechnical description of the business cycle and its problems may skip to the second part of this chapter and leave profits and the labor theory to one side. But in view of the tremendous importance of profits and wages and the amount of confusion now existing regarding them, the author believes that anyone who really wants to understand, not merely a capitalist society, but any society should try to familiarize himself with the problem before going further.

Profits, Adjustment, and Growth

We want in this section to work out an analytical background for judging two important ideas: first, the notion that the search for profits and interest on the part of the capitalist is the main cause of the business cycle; second, the contention that profits, interest, and "rent" are "surplus value"—an unjustified and immoral exploitation of the "working class." In order to accomplish our aim we begin first by listing the various types of profit as they occur under capitalism and in a stationary state. Next we analyze the dynamic sources of profit—the profit which induces new investment. Finally, we sketch an over-all picture of distribution, generally, as it functions first under static and then under dynamic conditions. With the basic analysis thus worked out we then proceed to a brief analysis and evaluation of the Marxist labor theory of value and surplus value. Thus we first give a skeleton analysis of the working of the capitalist distribution scheme and next discuss its economic "morality."

The Types of "Profit." The first thing to remember in understanding the problem of profits is that a great deal of what is called "profit," even in fairly sophisticated accounting, is not really profit at all to the economist—or even in many cases to the more careful accountant or businessman. "Profit" is a sort of hodgepodge classification into which almost everything can be dumped, and clearness of thinking requires that we separate out its various components before we go further. We shall begin, therefore, with some examples of what might be called apparent profits—or profits which are, in fact, something quite different.

The first type of "profits" which are not really profits is called by economists "wages of management." If a man owns his own unincorporated business, he may under some circumstances believe that he is making a substantial profit when to the economist he is making no profit at all. Suppose, for example, that he clears, over and above all expenses, a net revenue for himself of, say, $7,000 a year. He may call this his profit, but in many cases it is really wages; for if the business, instead of being personally owned and unincorporated, was a corporation, it would have to hire a manager who might very well require at least $7,000 a year in order to work for that firm. Thus the apparent profits shown on the books are really only a sum equivalent to the money which the competitors of that particular businessman would perhaps be paying to their salaried managers. And just as more efficient managers may sometimes draw higher salaries than less efficient ones, so these wages of management may vary with the efficiency of the owner-manager.[1]

Looking at the matter from another standpoint the profits of an owner-manager may actually be losses. For example, if the

[1] Differences in the ability of individual managers create something of a problem both of definition and in reality. For in the real world a manager by no means always gets the whole return which he has in fact created. Thus a company may show a large return over its other costs *solely* because of especially fine management. But though the manager may get a high salary, this may be far from accounting for the whole return he makes possible. Something called "profit" may be left over.

Economists will recognize that we are touching here upon the "rent of ability" concept. Cf. Clare Griffin, *Enterprise in a Free Society* (Chicago:

individual who is operating his own business clears only about $7,000 a year when, in fact, he could make, say, $10,000 by hiring himself out as a manager, the enterprise is not really yielding him any profit at all. Of course he may count the moral satisfaction of being his own boss as worth the $3,000 less which he gets by running his own factory instead of working for someone else. In that case there is no loss, but equally there is no profit. Wages of management, we see, can, then, sometimes account for a great part of that which is reported as a profit by smaller firms.

Two other types of profit which are not really profit are frequently found in small enterprises with relatively crude bookkeeping. Examples are easily given. If a man owns his own store and therefore does not have to pay rent, he may believe that he is making profits, but in fact he may really only be earning money equal to the rent which his competitors are paying but which he does not have to pay since he owns his own store building. Again if a man is operating a business with his own money and does not have to borrow from anyone, he may be earning what he calls profits; yet in fact these so-called profits may only equal the interest which he would normally get had he chosen to invest his money in some other line. His competitors, for example, may not be so well situated as he is, and they may have had to borrow. The prices of the goods he deals in, therefore, may be pushed up high enough to cover the interest bill of his competitors. But the individual who operates on his own funds and does not have to pay interest will give the impression that he is making a special profit when, in fact, from an economic point of view, all that he is making is interest.

Richard D. Irwin, Inc., 1949), p. 124. The wages-of-management idea, modified to allow for differences in skill, merges into "rent of ability."

Professor Schumpeter speaks of the ease with which an entrepreneur may be deprived of his profit. Cf. J. A. Schumpeter, *The Theory of Economic Development* (Cambridge, Mass.: Harvard University Press, 1934), p. 155.

Each of the three types of apparent profit which we have named could exist in a perfectly quiet, perfectly stationary world.[2] But it is necessary to mention a fourth type of profit which, though it could also exist in a society that was on balance stationary, is identified with certain types of temporary disturbance. There are some businesses which, even if on average they are not expanding, are nevertheless so risky that they require a higher rate of profit in order to attract anyone willing to undergo the necessary anxiety and effort. Take, for example, the planting of rice or Sea Island cotton on the islands of the Georgia and South Carolina coasts in the 1790's. Simply tremendous profits were made in given years. There are many cases on record of planters who made as much as 200 or 300 per cent profit from a given crop. But there are also cases on record of staggering losses. The islands were very much exposed to hurricanes and to numerous other dangers. Accordingly, the 300 per cent profit of one year might well be wiped out by losses in the next two or three years. Risky lines of this sort may sometimes become associated with special "ways of life" which make them attractive to some people. Or since men are not always perfectly rational in estimating risks, the glitter of a few big prizes may wipe out the memory of many losses and keep men in the business even when the net return is low. But in a number of cases, as we have said, higher *average* net rates of profit may be needed to keep that line of business going. But even if a risky line earns a higher average rate of profit, such a net return is not exactly pure profit. Rather it is a special risk premium to take care of risks which are uninsurable and to induce a specially difficult kind of labor. Even if, on average, risky industry may be earning 10 per cent more than is earned in other lines, there may be no real profit. The difference may be simply a matter

[2] This is not, as far as the author personally is concerned, strictly correct. To the author, *interest* would not be likely to exist in the stationary state; therefore it could not be the source of illusory profits in that state. But see the discussion below, under the head of An Unchanging World.

of insurance against risk and compensation for special effort. The extra-high rate of return will have no effect in inducing the risky industry to expand, for the difference in profit may be only just enough to offset the unpleasant or hectic nature of that particular field.

So far we have mentioned only types of profit which might exist in a perfectly or almost perfectly stationary world. But in order to make a more complete list of illusory profits two other types must be mentioned. The first of these is the apparent profit created by an inflation. Rapid increases in the quantity of money may force up prices faster than costs are forced up, and for a time the businessman may think that he is making a very large profit. But once an inflation is well under way, costs are likely to rise even faster than prices, and the businessman who has made a large profit in depreciated dollars may often find that he cannot buy as much with his larger income, when he goes to replenish his stock, as he could buy with a much smaller money income at a lower price level. In order to see whether a business is really making money or not, we must not merely balance the books on the basis of *past* costs and *present* prices. We have also got to ask whether the businessman is going to be able to buy with the money he takes in at the inflationary price level as large a new stock of goods as he used to be able to buy at lower prices. When a major inflation gets under way, it is quite possible for a business to go completely bankrupt while making large money "profits" all the time! [3]

The final type of mistaken profits, or profits which are not really profits, is rather similar to the example we have just given. We have just seen that a business, if it is really to maintain its

[3] In other words, though the prices at which goods were sold were always higher than those at which they *had* been bought, by the time it was necessary to buy new inventory, prices had gone up so much *again* that a smaller and smaller number of goods could be bought at the end of each period even though the money income was larger and larger.

position, has got to be able to buy as large a new stock of goods from its profits as it bought before and that, when prices are going up very fast, the appearance of large money profits may be completely misleading. The same thing also occurs in connection with fixed plant. Even though it may be fifteen years before a business will have to rebuild its factory, nevertheless, if it does not provide for the slow deterioration of that factory during the intervening years, it will find itself at the end of fifteen years without resources to build a new factory. In the same way, even if the business is deducting depreciation before computing its profits, but if the depreciation is being figured on the basis of old costs which are no longer relevant owing to inflation, then profits may be very much overstated. For example, if the factory originally cost $100,000, and if depreciation is still being figured at a percentage of that amount, but if today it would cost $300,000 to replace that factory, then, obviously, depreciation figured on the old value will not be enough to meet the replacement costs when they come due and profits are being overstated by a proportionate amount. We must, however, also not forget that, just as profits may be overstated during an inflation, or if we fail to make adequate reserves for depreciation, so also profits can be understated during deflation when a smaller money profit may be very much more valuable in terms of real goods.

Total Profit versus Marginal Profit—Static versus Dynamic Theories of Distribution. Important as it may be to deal with profits in terms of the various types we have just given, such catalogues do not contain the really vital distinction which one needs in studying the business cycle. The really vital distinction is not so much the distinction between different kinds of profit as the distinction between what we shall call "total" profit—the profit which one is making on plant *already* built, operating at a figure *already* decided upon—and "marginal" or additional profit—the profit which one *expects* to make from building *another* plant or *increasing* the scale of output of the plant one already has. A full understanding of this point and its relation to Marxian literature and to the business cycle will require rather extended discussion. But so important is it that historians may well someday come to attribute the collapse of capitalism in large part to a failure of the general public to understand this point.[4]

An Unchanging World. Whether we wish merely to understand the functioning of a capitalist economy or to lay the groundwork for a more searching inquiry into the nature of economic "value," it is, in either case, necessary to begin with an examination of the distribution of income in a "stationary state," that is, a world which is neither growing nor changing. One important reason for approaching the problem in this way is that many radical theories of distribution, if taken merely as a *description* of the *results* of adjustment, do have a certain superficial validity if applied to a world that is neither growing nor changing.[5] When, however, we switch over to a growing, changing society, they may be entirely misleading. Accordingly it is necessary to get clearly in our heads the differences between the "dynamic" and the "static" principles of distribution. Such a procedure, of course, involves some "unrealistic" abstraction. But it is worth mentioning that nothing we shall attempt here will be any more (and generally less) abstract than the models used by the Marxians.[6]

Let us assume, then, that we are talking about a society in which the size of the population and its age distribution remain always the same. We assume, furthermore, that there are no new

[4] Since many left-wing demands which may, for the moment, seem to leave a "reasonable" amount of "total" profit will cut off all expectation of "marginal" profit and hence cut off growth, hence unemployment. This point will be developed at several places later on.

[5] Remember that approximate accuracy as description does not necessarily imply a valid theory of causation.

[6] Cf. Paul Sweezy, *The Theory of Capitalist Development* (New York: Oxford University Press, 1942), p. 11.

inventions, no changes in the type and amount of machines and equipment in use, and no changes in the styles and amounts of goods purchased by the people. The standard of living remains always the same. We assume in addition (though perhaps, as will be seen later, somewhat inconsistently) that there is private property, "pure" competition, no government planning, and a general use of money but no inflation.[7]

The first thing to notice about such a stationary state is that there will be no saving in it except what is needed to replace existing machinery and equipment as it wears out. In most cases under modern conditions this type of saving is taken care of by "depreciation" allowances. In other words an accountant, before figuring out the returns of a business, makes allowance for money needed to replace equipment, etc., which is being worn out. In the real world, of course, depreciation allowances do not necessarily correspond to the current demand for replacement and may often be greater than is really needed for replacement, but we omit complications of that sort. We assume that old machinery and equipment are wearing out in a steady stream and that depreciation allowances just capable of covering this replacement are being deducted before income is distributed, and spent to order new machinery in an equally steady stream. But would there be any profits in such an economy?

We have said that the really vital distinction is not so much between the various kinds of profit as between the profit being made on a plant *already* built, operating at the output *already*

[7] The possible "inconsistency" lies in the fact that if we establish free exchange, etc., it may be argued that these institutions, coupled with the creative instinct of man, will almost inevitably give rise to growth. A "free" stationary state might thus be argued to be virtually an impossibility. But the role of ideology described in Chap. 2 must not be forgotten. However, the effect of hostile ideology would probably be to end the "freedom" as well as the growth.

selected, and the "additional" or "marginal" profits which one would expect to make from building a *new* plant or from *increasing* output. But it follows from the way we have described our state that there could be no marginal profit in it. For marginal profit, as we have defined it, is an incentive to growth, and we have ruled out growth.[8] Yet here we soon come upon a basic and vital paradox. Even though there is no expectation of marginal profit, there may still be some incomes which an accountant might call profit. If we think a minute, this is no more than common sense. Just because a man is "making money" on the plant he already has does not mean that he would be bound to expect to make money from building *two* plants or from indefinitely increasing the output of the plant he has now. Vice versa, just because a man doesn't feel like risking the building of another plant doesn't mean that he is necessarily not making a profit on the one he already has.

We may describe the logic underlying calculations of this sort as follows: If a man were merely trying to figure whether or not to increase the output of a particular plant, he would first estimate how much money he would take in when he sold the increased output. In some cases the increased output could be sold only if prices were lowered. But in others his increased output might be so small compared with the total that it would have no effect on price. In either case, however, he would try to figure out what the total sales value of his additional output would be. Say that he produces 100 more goods and sells them at $10 each. This would mean that, if prices remained unchanged, his total gross income would go up by $1,000. But he would not just rush ahead blindly to increase output. A further calculation would be necessary in order to decide whether an increase was worth doing. Even though the plant had been making very large profits, it would be neces-

[8] This, of course, is proof by definition. But our whole method in this section is one of abstraction.

sary, before going ahead with a *further* increase, to compare the addition to *costs* involved in increasing output.[9]

Suppose that the additional cost of producing 100 more goods, in our example, is not $1,000 but $1,500. In that case the businessman would *lose* $500 by increasing output, and obviously, if his calculations are believed correct, he will not do so. On the other hand if the additional cost (overtime, extra repairs, more raw materials, etc.) was only $800, then he would have a $200 profit and might be tempted to go ahead. In an ideally rational system, the scale of output for each particular plant would be set, therefore, at the point at which *additional* cost of the extra output would just balance off the *additional* returns from the extra sales. When that is reached, the owner of the plant has carried output as far as will give him his maximum profit. If he goes beyond that point, he may not, indeed, be going "into the red" but he will be steadily reducing his *total* profit. Thus though he may be making total profit, he will not expect any marginal profit—and therefore will have no economic motive to expand.

We can't, however, stop with the profit calculations of the owner of any single plant. We have also to consider the calculations of other *potential* plant builders. Mr. X, for example, who has already built a plant, may for some reason be so favorably situated before there has been a general adjustment that he is making a very high profit, yet *he* may have no marginal profit

[9] There are at least two possible deterrents to expansion here: (1) A fall in price needed to sell increased output could offset any gain from increased sales; (2) a rise in costs, as output increased. Further complications are introduced in the real world by the fear of retaliation, etc., in "oligopolistic" situations. Economists will recognize this as a "short run" example. But see "Mr. X" in text above. Statistical studies made in the "lamentable thirties" indicated that at *that* time in many industries "marginal" costs would fall as output increased (increasing returns) or at least be constant over a considerable range. These studies, even assuming them to be accurate, do not furnish a fair picture of what normal "cost curves" might be under conditions of full employment and brisk demand for labor.

expectation from building another plant, for he personally might have his profits reduced by an expansion. Mr. Y, however, sees that X is earning unusually high profit, and Y may figure that he (Y) would like to "get in" on the high return. Y may therefore build the additional plant. But once Y builds a new plant, output may increase so much that prices will have to come down, and the expectation of a "marginal" profit may then be eliminated for everyone.

The question, however, must next be asked whether in a stationary, unchanging world there would be any *minimum* general level of "fair" "total" profit below which competition (in an ideally rational society) would not go. Speaking very broadly the answer is, for the most part, no. Since we are speaking of a purely routine society, the only type of service needed would be "managerial" ones.[10] These, to be sure, would have to be compensated, and there would, therefore, have to be "wages of management." Such wages, furthermore, would probably vary to some extent with the abilities of the individuals concerned. But whether in any given case the manager's income would appear on the books as "profit" or as "salary" would be a more or less arbitrary matter, depending largely, as we have already seen, on the organization of the firm and the sophistication of the accounting used.[11]

In the same way, special industries which were liable to uninsurable natural risks—hurricanes, etc.—would require certain "profits" in good years as risk offsets for probable bad ones and might in some cases require an average *net* return as a species of wage of management to offset the difficult and nerve-wracking nature of the work. Save for special cases like these, however, profits—both "total" and marginal, as distinguished from "rent" —would tend to disappear.

[10] For "managerial" services as distinguished from "entrepreneurial" ones see the distinction explained in Chap. 2.

[11] And as already explained (footnote 1), the bargaining skill of the manager.

The description we have given so far contains no more than a few rudimentary principles from the elaborate economic theory of distribution in a stationary state. Space is lacking in an "outline" like the present one to explore in detail the economic theory of allocation under stationary circumstances.[12] There are many descriptions available—perhaps the most vivid being the account of the "circular flow" in the first chapter of J. A. Schumpeter's *Theory of Economic Development*—and the reader is referred to it and to the others cited in the notes.[13] In order to complete our picture, however, we must give a brief summary of some of the relevant conclusions which static economic theory has reached.

Our analysis has shown that there would be no marginal profit and practically no "total" profit in a stationary state. And it can also easily be shown that in any kind of society the largest single share of income is likely to go to wages. This has certainly been the case under capitalism. But if we leave aside wages and profit, two further types of income still remain: "rent" and "interest." Payments between organizations, for example, money "put aside" for depreciation saving, may be disregarded when we consider the economy as a whole, for the "cost" of a new machine bought to replace an old one would itself, in turn, be broken down into wages, rent, and so on. The same thing may also be done with payments for raw or semifinished materials. Interest and rent are thus the only two elements left to mention.

Concerning the matter of interest there is a great deal of dis-

[12] In preparing a first draft of this chapter the author attempted to do just that. But it was soon discovered that nothing short of a complete "principles of economics" would suffice, and he has therefore been forced back upon a statement of results. But see the authorities cited below, footnote 13.

[13] See Schumpeter, *op. cit.;* J. B. Clark, *The Distribution of Wealth* (New York: The Macmillan Company, 1899); F. H. Knight, *Risk, Uncertainty and Profit* (Boston: Houghton Mifflin and Company, 1921); Eugen von Böhm-Bawerk, *Positive Theory of Capital,* W. Smart, trans. (London: Macmillan & Co., Ltd., 1891), Book IV, Chap. VIII, "The Law of Costs."

agreement among economists. Perhaps a majority of economists have maintained that the owners of machinery and equipment would have to be paid some interest in order to keep them from "using up" their capital. Putting the matter more concretely, they say that, if an owner has collected money for "depreciation"—in order to buy a new machine to replace an old one—but sees no chance of getting any interest on his investment, he will be likely to spend the money on immediate pleasure instead of buying another machine.[14] As a result machinery will begin to go to pieces and society will find itself getting poorer.

Another group, however, which includes the author feels that this idea would be wrong *in a stationary state*.[15] Replacement and depreciation would there be a quasi-automatic affair carried on as a matter of routine through bookkeeping deductions. We shall come back to this question later.

But if we assume for the moment, with the author, that interest would not be necessary in a stationary state such as we have defined, then we need consider only the remaining category of

[14] Cf. Böhm-Bawerk, *op. cit.*

[15] Among the economists who have not believed in the necessity of interest in a perfectly stationary state are Alfred Marshall, Taussig, Irving Fisher, Keynes, Schumpeter, and the author. For a discussion of this whole problem and the paradoxes involved in a zero interest rate, see D. McC. Wright, *The Economics of Disturbance* (New York: The Macmillan Company, 1947), Chap. IV, "A Right Proportion."

The basic point of our analysis could be just as well made, however, by assuming that there is some very low, minimum rate of interest needed in the stationary state to keep people from consuming their capital, but that dynamic development in the real world usually keeps the rate far above this minimum. I do not happen to believe in this necessary minimum, but if the formulation just given makes everybody happier, one need not insist upon other formulations—especially since, as will be shown later, the conditions needed to produce a *permanently* stationary state cannot, in the author's opinion, occur except as a result of drastic sociological changes. The heat engendered by the minimum-theory controversy far exceeds, therefore, its practical importance.

rent. Now by "rent," in the special sense we are using it here, we do not necessarily mean all of any actual rent one may be paying for a farm or an apartment. Such payments in the real world may include large elements of operating costs (for an apartment), depreciation on buildings or equipment, profits, interest, and so on. Again we do not mean by rent the modern economist's frequent technical meaning of "excess" income *wherever* found. What we shall primarily talk of here is "rent" in the sense of payment for types of space, "the original and indestructible powers of the soil" as the classical economist David Ricardo called it.[16] All economists are agreed that in a free-exchange economy the owners of certain types of land would under normal circumstances receive rent of this type. They are, furthermore, generally of the opinion that, *under* the circumstances we are assuming, rent of this type would not be a payment for any service but would merely be a payment needed to "ration" a commodity that nature has made inherently scarce relative to population and wants.[17]

It is time to summarize our discussion. Ruling out interest, as we have done for the moment, and assuming a perfectly stationary, purely competitive, routine society such as we have described, it can be shown that, under certain reasonable assumptions, the price of nearly all commodities would be set by their "marginal"

[16] We are skimming the surface of some of the most slippery problems in pure economic theory. For brevity's sake I speak only of "land." But *permanent, i.e.,* "everlasting," instruments could yield rent. See the discussion of rare works of art, etc., in the text. Alfred Marshall, *Principles of Economics* (London: Macmillan & Co., Ltd., 18th ed., 1936), pp. 415 *ff*. Speaking only of "land" omits, also, another case, the firm whose "profit" comes from an "under" paid manager.

[17] However, the income used to *pay* for the right to receive future land rents may have been validly earned, and therefore the income received, to the individual concerned, may be quite justified. In real life "pure" rent and other costs are so intermixed as to be virtually inseparable, practically speaking, most of the time.

cost and that this marginal cost would be almost exclusively "set" by wages.[18] There would be some wages of management which might or might not be called profit and some risk earnings, also called profit, needed to offset possible losses due to natural risks. There would in addition be a considerable amount of rent payments.[19] Finally, if we make our assumptions slightly more realistic, there might also be certain "monopoly" positions in which, for one reason or another, the leveling effects of competition might not be able to operate completely or might not be allowed to do so.

Now the significance of the (far too condensed) summary just given is that, as a statement of *results,* it differs hardly at all from the account which Marxian value theory would give of distribution under similar stationary circumstances. The preponderance of income goes to wages of various sorts, and in most cases prices are set equal to marginal labor costs. There is no marginal profit and virtually no "total" profit. But can we deduce from static descriptions like these the conclusion that labor is the sole *cause* of value? Has labor *caused* the value, or to put the matter very loosely, has the "value" induced the labor? Before we can discuss this problem, it is necessary to describe the principles of distribution for a dynamic changing world.

Dynamic Distribution. When we admit the possibility and desirability of growth, change, and opportunity, the whole distributive picture alters. The vital question to ask in such a growing world is: If there is no expectation of "marginal" profit in a stationary state, where does the expectation of profit on *increased* output come from in the world we live in? The answer is easily given.

[18] "Marginal" cost means the addition to total cost involved in increasing output by one more unit. Where "given" equipment is assumed, the addition may be almost wholly a matter of increased labor costs. But see the authorities cited in footnote 13. Also P. A. Samuelson, *Foundations of Economic Analysis* (Cambridge, Mass.: Harvard University Press, 1947).

[19] See Wright, *op. cit.,* regarding the paradoxes of valuing permanent rent payments without a rate of interest.

The source of expected marginal profits on additional investment is found in growth, change, and new inventions.[20] If the population is growing, additional goods will be demanded which may keep prices from falling or even raise them. This may cause a rise in the expectation of profit at the margin and will serve as an incentive to increase output. In the same way, if people's tastes change, profits will rise in the industry whose goods are wanted and fall in the industry which is no longer so popular. There may be an incentive toward net expansion. Finally, if new inventions are put to use, costs may be lowered while prices may remain for a time unchanged, and this too will give rise to an expectation of profit at the margin which will lead to an increase of output.

The basic point to remember, however, about these "marginal" profits is that, while they are *necessary* if output is to be increased in a capitalist society, still they do not indefinitely survive in any individual case. For when a new investment is made which yields a high profit, other people will immediately be attracted toward the same line, wages and other costs will probably rise while prices are forced down. Barring rare types of very strong monopoly, which will be discussed in the next chapter, the capitalist system tends sooner or later to eliminate both marginal and even total profit in each individual case. There are always businesses making money, but they are not necessarily the *same* businesses. The upper industrial brackets of a capitalist society have been compared to hotels which may, indeed, always be full—but filled with different people. There is always profit, but not profit on the same things. Here is one of the fundamental paradoxes of capitalism.

Let us try to get a comprehensive picture of distribution in a dynamic growing world, similar to the picture which we have attempted of distribution in the stationary state. The first thing to realize about such a growing society is that the amount of sav-

[20] For an elaborate discussion of this problem see Schumpeter, *op. cit.*, Chap. IV, "Entrepreneurial Profit."

ing is much larger than would be needed merely for replacement. In the same way the investment goods industries (steel, construction, etc.) are greater, too, than if their market were merely the replacement of the existing equipment of society. Many people have the idea that during a depression all we need to do is somehow pass out enough money to buy, let us say, all the goods on display in the stores in order automatically to have both full employment and security. This is a basic and a tragic mistake, nor is it hard to show where the error lies. *In addition* to the storekeepers and contractors who are busy making and building the things we need personally for ourselves and our families, there is a huge field of heavy industry or investment goods industry, and we cannot have full employment unless it is also kept busy. But the market of these investment industries is found in three main fields. Speaking very roughly, about half of investment goods output goes into replacement, the building of new plant, equipment, and so on, to take the place of that which is wearing out. Next about a fourth, on average, goes into simple expansion. Finally, the remaining margin is taken up by change and invention. This means that, if society stops growing and changing, about half of heavy industry will have to shut down. Everyone admits that, if a society wants to grow, it will have to do some saving, but we can also turn the matter around and say that, if a society does any saving beyond what is needed to replace equipment, it will also have to change or grow.

But the growth we are talking about is not automatic, nor is it induced merely by the existence of some "total" profit on factories already built, operating at a scale of output already selected. Growth is induced by the expectation of marginal profit—profit from building a *new* factory or *extending* the scale of output on an old one. Yet these profits are induced by constant expansion, growth, and change. In other words, the system cannot ever stand still. The capitalist system, in full employment, will thus exhibit three main types of industry. On one hand there will be new businesses just being introduced which will show high risks and high profits. Next will be old, established firms which are earning so-called "normal" profits but which are beginning to slip down toward a third class. This third class will be made up of dying firms, producing products which are no longer greatly in demand.

The presence of constant changes and constant new investments of the sort we have described has a profound effect upon the problem of distribution. In the first place when there is growth there must also be change and risk. The *risk* function of profits thus becomes very much greater. Their importance as the reward and compensation for running risks and initiating change becomes perhaps their most important aspect. The element of change also deprives "rent" of many of its static attributes, for the value of land will depend partly on the location of industry and other resources and also on the tastes of the consumer—all of which may be changing.

The most important repercussion, however, is on the nature of interest. When there is an expectation of a great deal of "marginal" profit, more people will try to borrow money than are saving it and it will become necessary for borrowers to pay something to those who are doing the lending. The problem, as we saw in Chap. 2, is not merely a matter of money. People who save from current income are leaving "free" a certain amount of men and resources which can be used to initiate *new* industries and new growth. People who borrow these money savings and invest them in new projects are putting the men thus left free to work. What the borrower really wants is not, in such a case, the money but *control over labor and materials*.[21] One of the oldest fallacies

[21] There is nothing non- or anti-Keynesian in this statement. We are talking of full employment. Cf. D. McC. Wright, "The Future of Keynesian Economics," *American Economic Review,* June, 1945, p. 284; D. H. Robertson, "What Has Happened to the Rate of Interest," *Three Banks Review,* March, 1949; D. McC. Wright, "Mr. Harrod and Growth Economics," *Review of Economics and Statistics,* November, 1949.

in economics is the idea that giving borrowers more *money* is all that is needed to get more factories built. For if the added money does not represent genuine saving, it will (under full employment) only cause an inflation, and although inflation, as we shall see later, may sometimes be used as a means of getting growth, it is not a very humane or a very just method of doing so.

Interest, then, in a dynamic world and under full employment has, we can now see, at least two functions: (1) It "rations" the supply of saving among the various people who want to borrow and invest; (2) it serves as a compensation to the lender for the risks of lending. There is, however, a third function. Looked at from a long-run point of view (say ten or fifteen years) interest also serves to some extent as an *incentive* for saving.[22] In the short run, say two or three years, it is probable that the rate of interest may have practically no effect on the volume of saving. But over the long run, in a dynamic world, both a rise and a fall in the rate of interest are likely, over the years, to have substantial repercussions on the incentive to save.[23]

In the last twenty years the theory of interest we are describing has been considerably extended and modified to take care of the case of unemployment and speculative changes in risks. During a period of unemployment, the risk function (to compensate lenders for the risk of losing their money) becomes temporarily the only one of the three functions of interest to survive. There may be a great deal of "hoarding," and it may help to get industry started if we both increase the amount of money and lower the rate of interest. But it should not be forgotten that this situation is temporary.[24] As soon as the system revives, real resources may

[22] See Robertson, *op. cit.*

[23] See also Roy Harrod, *Towards a Dynamic Economics* (London: Macmillan & Co., Ltd., 1948), Chap. II, "The Supply of Saving."

[24] In other words we may make a mistake if we try to liquidate the inducements to save, which will be needed in the next boom, for the sake of a short-run crisis. It is far better merely to offset their effects. See Chap. 7, this book.

once more become scarce and interest becomes once more something more than a matter of money or of risk. Few people were more conscious of that fact than Lord Keynes, but some of his disciples have difficulty in remembering it.[25]

Let us, however, summarize our general description once more. In a growing society there is a constant flow of net new investment. This flow is induced by the hope of profit on building new plants or increasing output from old ones. But these expected "marginal" profits are in their turn the outgrowth of change, invention, and expansion. Yet while, on average, a stable society will show a constant rate of investment, each individual project contains within it certain forces which will tend to eliminate the high profits that induced it in the first instance. There is, then, a constant turnover of enterprises. In addition to profit payments, one finds, as long as the desire to invest exceeds the desire to save, a number of payments called interest which represent among other things the price of a scarce commodity—saving. Under full employment, unless people can somehow be persuaded or forced to save, there can be no growth. But the crucial point of our whole discussion is that the distinctively capitalist incomes—profit on new investment and interest—are intimately linked with the phenomenon of change and growth. If it were not for change and growth, society would lapse into the stationary state in which we began. Profits would virtually disappear, and the existence of any interest at all would be highly debatable.

Thus in good Marxian fashion we find our two extremes meeting, for just as Marx maintained that the constant "revolutionizing of the means of production" was an absolute necessity for the continued existence of a capitalist system, so also we have come to substantially the same conclusion. Without change and expansion there would be no profitable net new investment, and without profitable net new investment a capitalism whose institutions and savings habits had become geared to growth would be

[25] See the articles cited in footnote 21.

forced into a condition of unemployment and insecurity which might well induce social revolution. But though our description of the process has much in common with the Marxian one, we draw an entirely different conclusion. For there is one fact concerning which Marx was glaringly and obviously mistaken. He thought of the "revolutionizing of the means of production" primarily as a means of keeping the worker's standard of living down to a "subsistence" level. He also spoke of a doctrine of increasing misery, whereby the level of well-being of the workers would fall so low and their conditions would become so intolerable that they would be forced to revolt. This doctrine of increasing misery has been entirely disproved by the record. The distribution of wealth between wages and salaries on one hand and rent, interest, and profits on the other hand has remained astonishingly stable. Labor on average has consistently taken something over 65 per cent of the total national income for as long as we have any record.[26] As a result the constant revolutionizing of the means of production, concerning which Marx talked, has not resulted in forcing down real wages. On the contrary the national income has gone up many times over. If the pie is getting larger and larger and each group gets a relatively unchanged share, each group must be better off. So far from having real wages fall and having the

[26] Great conflicts over definitions and classifications are found here. For the more recent (post First World War) data see the *Survey of Current Business,* July, 1949. Professor Knight argues that the standard definitions are too broad and that the income from ownership should be figured at only about 15 per cent of national income. On the left, the high salaries of executives are exposed to an opposite attack.

Dr. Simon Kuznets gives some interesting figures on distribution in general, as follows:

"1. The average income shares (income ex capital gains and before taxes) of upper income groups between the two World Wars were: top 1 per cent of the population, 15 per cent of income; top 5 per cent of population, 30 per cent of income.

"2. The shares of upper income groups were largest in the country-

worker left in a condition of increasing misery, as Marx predicted, we have had, on the contrary, a rapid rise in the level of real wages and a constant improvement in the average living standards of the worker. Those entrepreneurs who were lucky enough to succeed in their ventures have been rewarded, it is true, by high profits. But just as their service in carrying through a new combination is temporary, so also their unusual rewards have usually been temporary. Competition and change have followed them and gradually eliminated the greater portion of their unusual take.[27] Only if an individual or a family has managed to retain its energy and adaptability has it been able to retain commanding position in industrial life. By far the greater portion of the benefits of capitalist accumulation and capitalist revolutionizing of production has gone into rising living standards for the working population.

One problem, however, remains to be answered. Won't this process of expansion come to an end someday? Won't we reach a point at which we can no longer grow? The answer involves a

---

wide aggregate of dividends: the top 1 per cent of the population received on the average of 65 per cent of total dividends paid to individuals, the top 5 per cent received 77 per cent. Their shares were lowest in the countrywide total of employee compensation, amounting on the average to 6½ per cent for the top 1 per cent and 17 per cent for the top 5 per cent groups.

"3. The shares of upper income groups declined substantially from 1939 to 1944 or 1945, and by 1948 had recovered little. From 1939 to 1945 the share of the top 1 per cent group dropped from 13 to 9 per cent and the share of the top 5 per cent group dropped from 28 to 19 per cent. If capital gains and taxes are allowed for, the decline was even more marked—from 12 to 7 per cent for the top 1 and from 27 to 17 per cent for the top 5 per cent group.

From "New Facts on Business Cycles," *30th Annual Report of the National Bureau of Economic Research,* May, 1950, p. 49.

[27] It is important to realize that this process occurred for about a century *without* any trade-unionism of importance and with a rising trend of real wages.

certain amount of paradox. When laborers have completed a house, they tear down the scaffold they have used. In the same way when an author completes an explanation of a process, he may find that he can discard some of the assumptions he has made. The writer believes that *unless special sociological forces* (*e.g.*, pressure groups not merely of business but of workers, farmers, and so on) *are at work* stopping change, a stationary state is an impossibility. In other words we assume with the majority of economists that human wants are boundless and endlessly changeable[28] and that, if a society is kept relatively free, human ingenuity will constantly keep producing new methods and new discoveries. Thus stagnation, if it comes, will not be the result of any inexorable decree of nature but rather the result of changes in our government and our modes and values of life. Tendencies toward a stationary state, therefore, if they exist at all, are not "economic" but sociological.[29]

The Labor Theory of Value as an Account of the Origin of Wealth

The preceding sections have given us an outline of the analysis needed for evaluation of the Marxist "labor theory" of value. This theory can be looked at in at least three ways. First, it can be considered as a description of economic life which maintains that commodities do in fact actually exchange in accordance with the "socially desirable" labor time embodied in them. Marx him-

[28] Even Lewis Mumford admits that, while "vital" wants (whatever they are) are all necessarily "limited," the "necessities" of life *also* include "Song, story, music, painting, carving, idle play, drama." Can there be any fixed limit or pattern for these or for the amount of resources that could go into them? Cf. Lewis Mumford, *Technics and Civilization* (New York: Harcourt, Brace and Company, Inc., 1934), pp. 394, 395.

[29] Wright, *Economics of Disturbance,* Chap. IV; also "The Prospects for Capitalism" in *A Survey of Contemporary Economics,* H. S. Ellis, ed. (Philadelphia: The Blakiston Company, 1948), pp. 457, 459.

self did not accept this version of the theory. Next, one can take the theory as a vague and highly metaphysical doctrine concerning the origin of all wealth, namely, that labor is the sole "source" or "cause" of value. Finally, there is the idea frequently deduced from the second principle regarding the causation, or source, of wealth that, since "labor" creates all value, all payments other than wages—that is, all payments of rent, interest, or profits—are exploitation. We will discuss these ideas in turn.

The Labor Theory as Description. We have seen that in a stationary society, in which interest is ruled out, the relative values of most commodities will come tolerably close to approximating the Marxian rule that commodities would exchange in accordance with the "socially desirable" labor time (past and present) embodied in them. But this fact tells us nothing about the *causation* of the process—only its results.

On the other hand, in a dynamic world—which is the relevant world to use as a standard if a society values change, growth, and opportunity—the theory ceases to hold even as an approximate description. This Marx conceded, but it will help to be more specific.[30] The accepted economic theory of value is that price, in any given instance, is determined by the interaction of two quantities: the desirability of the good (its ability to satisfy human wants) and its "costs" of production. These two forces intermesh in a very complicated and subtle way. Diamonds cost more than bread, not because diamonds are more important, but because, *relative to the quantity desired,* it is more difficult (costs more) to produce them. If they could be produced as easily as bread, their price (barring monopoly) would soon fall. On the

[30] Cf. Sweezy, *op. cit.,* p. 19; *Socialism* (New York: McGraw-Hill Book Company, Inc., 1949), p. 139; Joan Robinson, *An Essay in Marxian Economics* (London: Macmillan & Co., Ltd., 1942), Chap. 3. See also E. von Böhm-Bawerk, *Karl Marx and the Close of His System,* R. Hilferding, *Böhm-Bawerk's Criticism of Marx,* P. M. Sweezy, ed. (New York: Augustus M. Kelly, 1949).

other hand, if people *ceased to want them* as badly as they have done (relative to their supply), the price would soon fall too.

But "costs of production," in the real dynamic world, contain many more elements than labor. There are interest, profits, and sometimes "rent." [31] Furthermore, neither interest nor profits necessarily appear in the *same proportions* in each good.[32] Thus the cost of one good may involve a great deal of interest and not much wages, while the price of another may be almost entirely made up of wages and very little interest. The same thing goes for profits. Relative labor time will thus not be an accurate indicator of relative price.

Again in any actual situation a number of goods have been already made (or found) which are more or less unique and very valuable, for example, a rare stone found by chance, an old master, and so on. These goods may *never* have exchanged in any specific ratio to labor time incurred concerning them. Yet they have "value." Finally, during the process of adjustment, price may far exceed costs of production. Only after competition has operated need the two begin to coincide.[33]

The Labor Theory as Causation. So much for the inadequacies of the theory as description. What about causation? Clearly, as

[31] I should explain for the benefit of economists that I assume rent may sometimes enter into price in the real world because discontinuities and scarcities may prevent perfect adjustment.

[32] And there are different rates of profit and interest proportionate to risk, etc. Whatever the ultimate origin of interest, it is, as we actually find it operating, a payment for time, and some goods have more *time* in them than others.

[33] Marx attempts to answer the difficulty caused by variation in the proportion of fixed capital used and hence in the degree in which interest, profits, etc., may appear in the cost of a given commodity, by setting up a table wherein "values" are "transformed into prices." Cf. Böhm-Bawerk, *op. cit.*, pp. 22–23.

Roughly his contention is that, while "competition" redistributes the "surplus value" as between individual commodities so that they no longer

Marx conceded, mere labor does not make a thing valuable. I may work hard on a book (or a chair), but unless people want it, it has no value. Furthermore it may not even have any use value, for "labor" *as such* cannot even be guaranteed to produce that. Thus the labor has to be directed in the "right" channels. But as soon as we recognize that fact, as Marx did, and say "socially desirable" or "socially necessary" labor, we get into the problem of determining what *is* socially necessary, and this may lead to all sorts of circular reasoning. For example, Marx was immediately confronted by the problem that labor was not "homogeneous." Some labor gets more (is more valuable) than other labor. He solved this problem by reducing everything to an hour's work of "common labor." If a common laborer gets $3 an hour and a scientist gets $30 an hour, the scientist-hour would count as ten basic hours. But why should one man's hour be worth more than another's? Not necessarily because the more expensive man has "cost" more to train. It may simply be because the public *wants* the product or service he produces more than it wants other services—superior *desirability* has affected *relative* labor values. Perhaps, to be sure, in a very long-run *stationary* world most of these differences in wages would reduce to mere differences in the costs of rearing and training different men. (Remem-

---

exchange in accordance with the socially desirable labor time, yet the total *aggregate* "surplus value" is the same as would be obtained under "primitive conditions."

This demonstration, however, is an interesting example of proof by definition. Marx's table is mere arithmetic. If, indeed, it could be proved (other than by assumption) that the results yielded in an ultimate equilibrium by the competitive leveling and shifting would be precisely the same (so far as "surplus value" goes) as those previously existing in a hypothetical "primitive" state, Marx's reconciliation would have some claim to independent intellectual respectability. But the process in real life would be chemical, not mechanical. It is virtually impossible to suppose the transformation carried through, in fact, without involving changes in the wage rate, capital stock, and so on, and hence in the final result.

ber that in a dynamic world even these costs would include other costs besides labor and such other costs would not necessarily be present in the same proportion with labor for each good.) Furthermore and more important, there would be some types of labor whose value *never* could be reduced to costs. Two artists, for example, working equally hard (equal labor time) and with equally expensive training might yet receive entirely different prices for their pictures because the public *liked* one more than the other—likewise two doctors, and so on.

Some adherents of the labor theory, at this point, finding themselves defeated in other arguments, will take refuge in a broad general statement that economic goods seldom come into existence without someone's having done (or not done) something regarding them. This statement is of course more or less, though not entirely, true, and by equating "labor" with any human act, thought, nonact, feeling, or decision might seem to furnish the basis for some sort of proof "by definition" that "labor" is the main source of value. But even on its own terms such an approach runs up against three facts: (1) even so broadly defined, labor cannot create anything valuable unless the thing is "wanted"; (2) even under such a definition goods might not exchange in the "proper" ratio; (3) such a definition does not prove that interest, profits, etc., are "exploitation." This leads us to the final point—the theory of surplus value.

Surplus Value. The aspect of the labor theory of greatest interest to many people today is the notion of profits, etc., as "surplus value." Dr. Paul Sweezy writes:

> We assume that the capitalist buys labor power [the use of the worker's labor for a given period] at its value, that is to say, pays the worker a wage equal to the worker's means of subsistence. Let us say, for the sake of illustration, that this value is the product of six hours' labor. After production has proceeded for six hours the worker has produced enough value to cover his wages. If the process were to break off at this point, the cap-

> italist would just come out even . . . but the capitalist has bought the worker [sic] for a day. [Assume he works ten hours.] Then in the last four hours the worker continues to add value over and above his wages, and it is this which constitutes the *surplus value* in which the capitalist is interested.[34]

The first thing to say about Sweezy's passage is that names, as such, are not very important. If Sweezy (following Marx) chooses to give the name "surplus value" to what in most cases we would call the "rewards of capital and entrepreneurship," the mere choice of a different name does not prove anything *in itself*. The real question is: Is this payment of surplus value justified, or is it really "exploitation"? Is the search for it the main cause of the business cycle?

Business cycles will be discussed in the next section. What we are interested in deciding here is whether or not the extra four (or two or one) hours' labor constitutes "robbery" and "exploitation." Now in deciding this question the vital thing to ask is: How was the laborer able to earn his "subsistence" in only six hours? In many primitive societies he might have had to work twelve or fourteen hours barely to stay alive. It should be noted that Sweezy, in using the word "subsistence," is employing a "loaded" adjective with all the overtones of "bare" minimum, "iron law of wages," etc., which go with it. What he should have said instead of subsistence was "real wages" or "standard of living." We have, however, seen that the worker's standard of living has been rising rapidly ever since the beginning of the capitalist era and that we certainly cannot relate the present level of real wages to any *minimum* "cost of production" theory for raising children. Of course one can, *by definition,* say the "cost" of raising children has risen, but this would be only another way of saying the *standard of living* has risen. There is certainly nothing "minimum" about it. If one wishes merely to stay alive, Professor Paul

[34] Sweezy, *Socialism,* p. 142.

Samuelson of Massachusetts Institute of Technology points out that $57 *a year* will suffice for food.[35] And the author suggests that similar expense for heat, clothes, and shelter—an old barrel(?)—would not run the total up to more than $300 *a year.*

Accordingly we ask once more: Why could the laborer earn the high modern American standard of living in, say, six hours (as Sweezy suggests) when earlier generations have toiled twelve or fourteen hours for no more than could keep them alive? Does the answer lie merely in the strength of the American worker or in his *personal* skill? Obviously not. Put him back in the technical environment of his ancestors, and he would in the first instance produce little more than they did. The worker earns his high living standard *because he is working in partnership with the best machinery mankind has ever known. Without* that machinery he would do little more than the cave man. If he did better, it would be almost entirely because someone succeeded in recreating new machinery.

But now we ask: Where did the machinery come from? Is it the product *merely* of the manual labor that went into making it? Certainly not. Is it the product *merely* even of manual labor plus the labor of the engineer who designed it? Certainly not. It is *also* the product of the *not-consuming* by some people which enabled men to keep working on machine tools rather than satisfying immediate wants. It is also the product of the *risk bearing* of others who took the chances which starting a new idea implies at some point. It is also the product of the *entrepreneurial* energy and the managerial genius of someone who "put across" the *idea* embodied in the machine.[36]

[35] P. A. Samuelson, *Economics: An Introductory Analysis* (New York: McGraw-Hill Book Company, Inc., 1948), p. 206. (These figures are based on 1944 prices.)

[36] Attempts to deny the analysis given in this paragraph all refer either to brief periods in the business cycle or to transitional conditions in a dying

Thus Dr. Sweezy's four "surplus" hours might go to (1) depreciation (offsetting wear and tear on the machine); [37] (2) interest, rewarding the man whose not-consuming made possible the investment; (3) profits, the risk premium and compensation for the entrepreneur.

To be sure, as we have explained earlier, if we *stop* the process of growth and change and lapse into changeless routine, then most risks disappear and there will be no need to compensate entrepreneurial ability, for change will not be wanted. Also replacement saving (not-consuming) might become automatic. All this would be reflected in the distributional scheme by the disappearance of interest and most "profit," but only because we had decided we *did not want to raise our standard of living.* While we want growth, while we want to call forth the effort needed to make a *better* machine under the most productive circumstances, then the so-called "surplus" payments detailed in our example become

---

system. If pressure groups, etc., make growth increasingly difficult, then, indeed, investment may not be enough to offset saving, while attempts at saving may *for a while* continue without reward. But the basic cause of the trouble is that we have shut off growth. One cannot found a true "general" theory on the peculiarities of a transition. See Chaps. 2 and 3 of this book, especially the discussion of incentives.

But our reference to the *idea* embodied in the machine gives a clue to the question often asked: Is capital "merely" "canned labor"? The answer depends on the circumstances. In a routine state all costs and efforts have been adjusted and a given machine is merely a repetition of the same set of fixed ideas on which the whole system is organized. Consequently we may forget about the idea and reduce the value of the machine merely to the labor in it. But if it is a new *type* of machine, then the mere labor going into making it combined with the *new idea* may have, at first, an independent value creating quality. Growth does not come through mere energy or foot-pounds. It is the product also, among other things, of mind and personality—mind and personality conceiving novelty as possibility.

[37] In some places Sweezy admits the legitimacy of depreciation allowances. Cf. Sweezy, *Socialism,* p. 143.

necessary.[38] It is not, of course, maintained that *all* actual profit, interest, etc., are always justified any more than one could say that every wage earner was always receiving no more than his due. But Marxian theory does not turn on accidental overpayments, "frictions of adjustment," "monopolies," or "rents." It says that *all* profit, interest, and so on, are surplus and exploitation. This idea is clearly and demonstrably false.

Left-wing Theories of the Cycle

Our study of profits and of the labor theory of value leaves us with the conclusion that a capitalist system is a changing and growing system and in order to survive must continue to be so. The next step in our analysis is the realization that a changing and growing system is almost bound to be a cyclically disturbed system. But there is more in the problem than mere growth. In the preceding chapter we conceded that in the short run it would be possible for a centralized planning board to arrange growth and change in such a way as to produce a smooth, constant expansion. We did maintain that such an institutional framework would result in a slow smothering of the creative and growth impulses so as to induce eventual social stagnation. But it was admitted that in the short run—say over a period of perhaps as much as one or two generations—[39] it would be possible to plan growth and change

[38] It could be argued that it might not be necessary to make some of these payments under socialism. But note our qualification "under the most productive circumstances," and compare our argument (Chap. 4 of this book) for the superior productivity of private property. Furthermore, as a matter of bare fact, even Russia pays some interest to savers, and requires some profit of its enterprises.

[39] Clare Griffin objects here that my allowance of "one or two generations" is far too generous. He says that before 1939 Britain's rate of progress in man-hour productivity was only about 1.3 per cent and has been about zero since then while in the United States before 1939 it was 2.5 per cent and has been about 3.5 per cent for the last few years.

so as to produce a smooth aggregate without stopping *all* expansion. Admitting then that in the *short run* a central planning board can plan smooth growth and change, we are still left with the question: Could the board plan smooth growth and change and still give the consumer *what* he wants *when* he wants it?

Left-wing theories of the business cycle seldom consider this problem in its full complexity and nearly always imply two basic assumptions. First of all, it is usually supposed, though seldom explicitly stated, that the activity of spending money is a more or less homogeneous one. In other words, the consumer is often thought of as spending money on a certain given "bundle" of consumers' goods. This bundle is supposed to remain more or less the same in make-up. And it is frequently supposed that the consumption of all commodities goes up in the same proportion. We have already seen that expansion does not behave that way. Yet the Marxians frequently write as if there were never any changes in taste under capitalism except those induced by the businessman. Their assumption might perhaps be reasonably true in a stationary state. But we have seen that, once expansion is well under way, simple growth in and of itself induces disproportionate and unexpected changes in consumption patterns.[40]

A second cyclical assumption often made by left-wing writers and Marxists alike is the idea that for each given level of consumption society requires only a fixed and definite stock of capital equipment bearing a fixed definite ratio to the amount of spending. Thus Dr. Paul Sweezy writes,[41]

[40] The process—like most processes—is one of *mutual* interaction. To give an example we might say that, when society is getting richer, people are like holiday travelers getting off a boat. They are in a "spending mood" and almost bound to buy something. *What* they buy may depend on what the vendors happen to bring to the pier that day. But conversely, over a longer pull, what the vendors have brought is partly determined by their experience and expectation as to what they think the tourists will want.

[41] All these quotations here given from Sweezy come from p. 182 of his *The Theory of Capitalist Development*.

> We see that a definite relation must exist between the mass of means of production (assuming, it will be remembered, that they are fully utilized) and the output of consumers' goods. Moreover, this definite relation must similarly exist between changes in the stock of means of production (investment) and changes in the output of consumption goods.

Sweezy, to be sure, does go on to add,

> These relations are ultimately determined by the technical characteristics of production and accordingly can vary with the progressive development of the methods of production.

But he continues,

> Such evidence as we have, however, strongly suggests a remarkably high degree of stability for a reasonably well developed capitalist economy. In other words, it appears that *over long periods* [italics added] a given percentage increase in the stock of means of production will generally be accompanied by approximately the same percentage increase in output. On this basis we are justified in making the assumption that the technically determined relation between the stock of means of production and output of consumption goods remains constant.

Thus though Sweezy does admit the possibility of some *short-run* variation, he nevertheless lays it down as a basic law that the ratio of investment goods to the consumption level is practically a (long-run?) constant. As he puts it himself, "The ratio of the rate of growth in the output of consumption goods to the rate of growth of means of production remains a constant." The practical implication of Sweezy's idea is that, once the number of plants has reached the "definite" ratio (whatever that may be), construction of any more plant will mean a loss—unless consumption is rising too.

When we study not merely the Marxian but also many labor-union and other left-wing theories of the cycle, we shall find that this assumption of fixed limits to investment is a basic one for nearly all of them. The matter can be put in a more homely and popular manner as follows: Suppose we consider a given commodity—say beer—and use it as a sort of indicator of general behavior. The Marxists and many labor unionists would tend to say that, on average, nobody would ever build another beer brewery unless the consumption of beer was increasing. In other words, they would suppose that there was a fairly fixed technical relationship between the level of consumption of beer and the number of beer factories, also between increases in beer consumption and increases in the number of beer factories. But this idea is clearly wrong. There is not, in the short run, *any* close or mechanical association between changes in the level of consumption and changes in the demand for machinery and equipment. To use our beer example, there are at least three ways in which it might pay an individual to build another brewery even if the consumption of beer were declining. First of all, a man may have invented a new kind of beer which the public would like very much. It would then pay him to build another kind of brewery, even though *general* beer demand were falling. Second, he might have invented a newer and more efficient method of brewing which would be so much cheaper that, even though total demand was falling, he would nevertheless make a profit on *his* plant by installing it. *His* costs would be falling faster than general prices. Third, he might feel that the demand for beer, even though it was low or declining at that time, was going to rise within a few months or perhaps a year, and under those circumstances he might go ahead and build the factory. And in some cases the very fact that he has the courage to build the factory may justify that courage.[42] The increased outlay on the new beer factory might raise *general* income and confidence and give rise to a demand for more beer. In two of these cases the ratio of capital to consumption could be varied

[42] In making this statement we do not, of course, commit ourselves to any literal adherence to "Say's law" that "supply *always* creates its own demand." But we do say that it *frequently* does.

considerably without any change or even without any maintenance of the level of consumption, and even the third case involves no *immediate* change in consumption.

One often hears that a "mature" economy cannot use as much investment as a developing one. Of course we can *define* "mature" in such a way as to make this statement true. But definitions are not reality. Speaking more accurately one should rather say that an *unchanging* society will absorb less investment than a changing one. No matter how wealthy a society may be, it can always use more capital *if* its patterns of tastes and techniques are changing sufficiently. The question of limits therefore cannot possibly be discussed in mechanical terms. There may sometimes be *temporary* gluts. But if the long-run trends in the growth of consumption and in inventive activity are permitted to continue, no permanent glut need be expected. As already pointed out, to explain permanent glut we must bring in some new sociological or institutional factor *preventing* further activity.

We are now in a position to explain and evaluate the most usual left-wing idea of the business cycle. It is based on the assumption of a supposed lag in the rate of consumption. According to Lord Keynes, who was not exactly a left-wing author but whose theories are often quoted by left-wingers including the Marxists, the normal law of consumers' behavior is as follows: As income increases, consumption increases but not so much. In other words, as a man gets richer, he may buy more beer, but his *proportionate* consumption of beer will not keep pace with his income. In other words, if we take beer as a sort of index of his general consumption (we could equally well take clothes or any other good), his *proportionate* amount of spending is falling—so his proportionate amount of saving is rising. Another view which comes to much the same thing is that the distribution of wealth alters in an expansion and that there is a shift to profit. Since the theory supposes that profit takers, being wealthier than the rest of society, consume less and save more than other people, it is assumed that in this case, too, the *proportion* of consumption will fall.

Now if one supposes such a lag in the *proportionate* increase of consumption as we have been describing, and if one also adopts the Marxian assumption that the stock of equipment is rigidly linked to the consumption level, then it is easy to see how the "lag" can cause trouble. Everybody agrees that, in order to have full employment, it is necessary for saving to be offset by investment. But the total usable amount of equipment under the left-wing and Marxian view is very closely and immediately geared to the level of consumption. Now if we are investing (building new plant and equipment) faster and faster but consumption is rising more and more slowly, there will obviously soon be a glut.

Putting the matter once more in terms of beer, if the consumption of beer is not *rising* very fast—let us say if it increased 10 per cent last month and only 5 per cent this month and will increase only 2 per cent next month, and if at the same time the construction of breweries is proceeding at an ever faster rate—10 per cent last month, 20 per cent this month, and 30 per cent next month—then obviously we are headed for a state of affairs in which there will be too many breweries and the prosperity of the beer business will collapse. Most left-wing and Marxian cycle theorists of the cycle, therefore, assume that, because consumption does not keep pace with output, the capitalist desire to accumulate is eventually frustrated by a failure to disburse "adequate proportionate purchasing power" to the "masses" or, alternatively, a failure of the "well-to-do" to spend fast enough themselves.

There are many objections which might be made to this theory, and we shall detail some of them shortly. But its fundamental weakness is that it tries to combine a *long-run* theory of capital with a *short-run* theory of consumption. If we are going to use some short-run data, we ought to use *all* short-run data. If we are going to use some long-run data, we should use *all* long-run data. Sweezy's idea that the amount of capital (equipment, etc.) bears a fixed ratio to consumption is based on long-run calculations. But Dr. Duesenberry, Dr. Fellner, and numerous others have pointed out that, if we consider *long-run* consumption trends, consumption *also* rises proportionately and spontaneously with income.[43] There may be some short-run lags, but these lags are eventually overcome, and we do not even know enough, as yet, to be able to say just when they will occur. Furthermore, there is no iron necessity that a consumption lag *has* to turn into a depression.

Putting the matter once more in terms of beer, if aggregate beer consumption is not rising, for the moment, as fast as it has been, and if this spending lag is pretty widespread, the Marxians and many labor unionists would tend to say that there would be bound to be a slump. But suppose that, just at the time a short-run lag in consumption occurs, some new invention or new industry begins or something else happens to raise the demand for investment. In that case the temporary lag in consumption may be offset by an increase in investment. *General* expansion and prosperity continue unabated.

Thus the business cycle cannot be studied in the mechanical terms in which the Marxians and many left-wingers like to write. We have to think of the whole matter in terms of overlapping *rates of change*. Some businesses may be rising; others falling. Consumption and investment may both be shifting and often quite independently of each other. There could be sometimes and undoubtedly have been depressions brought on by a consumption lag. But there have also been other cases in which a con-

[43] See A. H. Hansen, *Fiscal Policy and Business Cycles* (New York: W. W. Norton & Company, 1941), p. 233; P. A. Samuelson, "Full Employment after the War" in *Postwar Economic Problems*, S. E. Harris, ed. (New York: McGraw-Hill Book Company, Inc., 1943); W. J. Fellner, *Monetary Policy and Full Employment* (Berkeley: University of California Press, 1946); J. S. Duesenberry, *Income, Saving, and the Theory of Consumer Behavior* (Cambridge, Mass.: Harvard University Press, 1949).

sumption lag did not cause a depression and yet other cases in which a depression was caused by something quite different. Indeed, as we shall see in the last section of this chapter, depressions can be caused by *too much* purchasing power or too *equal* distribution.

"Planlessness" and the Business Cycle

From what we have seen, it will be clear that it would be quite miraculous if the total of individual movements in output and in demand always added up to continuous, smooth full employment. But there is one more problem which we must deal with before we can go further. Some left-wingers who do not accept the mechanical consumption-lag theories which we have just given nevertheless take refuge in a general accusation that it is planlessness alone which is responsible for the failure of society always to experience a smooth expansion. This allegation, we have seen, is correct in the sense that undoubtedly in the short run a planning board could plan a smooth expansion. But again we are left with the vital question: Would planning for smooth expansion be possible if we attempted always to give the consumer *what* he wanted *when* he wanted it? In other words is the occasional failure of the total of change to add up to full employment merely the result of lack of planning and the search of businessmen for "surplus value," or can unevennesses in economic expansion also arise from some deeper cause? Can we ensure smooth constant expansion without using rationing? The author believes that we cannot, and it is time to examine this question in greater detail.

Let us take a very favorable case. Suppose the United States is governed by a politically omnipotent and economically omniscient planning board, possessed of every moral virtue. Assume that there is no failure of consumption to keep pace with consumers' goods output and that there are no monopolies, no pressure groups, no price lags, no hoarding, no need of foreign trade or foreign investment. But suppose further that such an economy is confronted with the same problem with which we have been confronted since the war: a large, newly released labor force, considerable deferred demand, a huge potential rise in the output of consumers' goods. Does not the way seem open, then, for peaceful and uninterrupted expansion? Unfortunately, one further question remains: How *fast* shall consumers' demand be satisfied?

It can be shown that even in such an ideal state it will be impossible to increase the output of consumers' goods rapidly without running a risk of distorting the structure of industry, "overbuilding" the durable goods industries, and eventually entailing "waste" or unemployment. Take housing as an example. Suppose that the population is increasing fairly evenly. The chances would be that about the same number of additional houses would be needed every year. If we wanted a really stable housing industry, we should have to gear it to this steady demand, and fluctuations in either direction would be most undesirable. Say that the normal output for a given general situation and distribution of wealth would be 10,000 units per year. But now suppose that for four or five years—during, say, a war—no houses are built and a "backlog" of accumulated demand piles up. In our example, this comes to about 50,000 houses. Or we can use the example of a "front-log" created by a new invention which people are rushing to buy. Can the planning board, using careful advance planning alone, satisfy the backlog (or front-log) promptly and still stabilize the private industry? Unfortunately under the circumstances we have given it cannot. The task is impossible, no matter what the form of government.

Suppose we decide to satisfy this housing demand right away. Thousands of young architects, foremen, and skilled workers are trained. A huge increase in plant is undertaken. The industry suddenly raises its capacity from 10,000 units a year to 50,000 units. The backlog is satisfied. But then will come the tragedy: We may not want 50,000 new houses *every* year. We may only want 50,000 houses *now.* Once the backlog is satisfied, demand may drop to the old level of 10,000, and about four-fifths of the men whom we have induced to go into the housing business are out of jobs. Yet there has been no "overproduction." Not one house "too many" has been built. It is simply that (from the point of view of stability) we have built them "too fast." The planners face a well-nigh insoluble conflict between giving people what they want when they want it and stabilizing the industry.[44]

The full realization of this dilemma is tremendously important. For if we really follow through the left-wing criticisms of capitalism and of management, it will be found that they often cancel out and conflict. For example, if the steel industry, for the sake of future stability, acts like a socialist state trust and does *not* expand its output rapidly, then the cry is raised of "monopolist." But if on the other hand there were a rapid expansion and later on demand falls (as could also be the case under planning), then the very people who most violently attack the industry for a failure to expand will be the first to blame it for unemployment. They will maintain that, if only there had been comprehensive planning, all would have been well. What they should say is rather that, if only we had kept consumers waiting *even longer,* all would have been well.

One of the outstanding authorities on socialism, Professor Abram Bergson of Columbia, has lately conceded that socialism, or comprehensive planning, could not in itself avoid excess capacity in the durable industries under the circumstances just outlined.[45] However, he argues that this would not be "waste" in any economic sense. The author would quite agree. But his reply would be that, if it ought not to be called waste under socialism, neither

[44] For a more detailed formulation of this problem see Wright, *The Economics of Disturbance,* Chap. VI, "The Planned Business Cycle."

[45] The author should explain, however, that to the best of his knowledge Dr. Bergson is not a socialist.

ought it to be called waste under capitalism. You cannot eat your cake and have it too.[46]

Distribution, Purchasing Power, and the Business Cycle

Before we conclude our account of the cycle, we have to relate it a bit more specifically to problems of income distribution and social organization. We need, first, to compare our account with Marx's theory of the "industrial reserve army" and, second, to explain the statement made in the preceding section—which must sound so paradoxical to many people—that a depression can *sometimes* be caused by too *much* purchasing power or by attempting too *equal* a distribution of wealth.

Our analysis so far has shown that save in a few cases to be detailed at the end of this section the *fundamental* cause of the business cycle is the failure of changes in taste and technique to occur at rates which smoothly offset one another.[47] If the total of individual changes did occur in a smoothly offsetting manner, there would be no reason why we could not have continued expansion and the continued payment of "surplus value," that is, the continued payment of rewards to enterprise and saving, plus a continued rise in the standard of living of society as a whole, including the worker. And we have seen, in addition, that the

[46] Abram Bergson, "Socialist Economics" in *A Survey of Contemporary Economics,* H. S. Ellis, ed. (Philadelphia: The Blakiston Company, 1948), pp. 416, 438. Professor Bergson's idea, however, that I consider "large-scale" unemployment inevitable under socialism is quite incorrect. As I point out repeatedly in *The Economics of Disturbance* (see, for example, the end of Chap. VI), fiscal policy—under either socialism or capitalism—could greatly mitigate the impact of the problem. See Chap. 7 of this book.

[47] A few special cases will be described later. Excessive taxation and excessive wage demands could under some circumstances both stop invest ment and precipitate a crisis.

long-run shares of labor and capital and the long-run ratios of consumption to income do actually move in a fairly stable manner.

But in the short run both the movements of innovation and of new investment plus the spontaneous changes of consumer wants do not always occur at just the proper offsetting rates. This is the *fundamental* cause of most business declines. But once a crash does occur, then many *secondary* features develop which, again as a matter of *description,* do give plausibility to certain Marxian ideas but which, again, are not valid as theories of fundamental *causation.* This is especially the case with Marx's idea of the industrial reserve army.

Marx, we have seen, felt that the rewards of the capitalist could be maintained only if wages were somehow kept from taking up the whole income of society. But he developed not one but at least two theories as to why this did not occur. The first, we have already seen, was simply that profits, etc., were maintained by the effect of technical change and of expansion. But he had another, though closely related, idea, namely, that the "profits" of the "bourgeois" were maintained by unemployment, and from this he developed a second theory of the cycle—the theory of the "industrial reserve army." [48]

After a crash has occurred, Marx maintained, there will be many unemployed. Consequently labor will be willing to work for low wages. "As a result" profit expectations become more favorable and a general expansion begins. But as output expands and more and more workers are employed, wages rise, profit margins are cut down, and soon (though Marx did not express it in these terms) the expectation of "marginal" profit disappears, investment is cut off, and a slump begins. After the slump is started, unemployment rises, wages again fall, the industrial reserve army again increases, and so on. Thus the backlog difficulty expounded in the previous section could be viewed as a result of the industrial

[48] Cf. Sweezy, *Socialism,* p. 146.

reserve army. For it might be maintained that without "slack" in the system, rapid expansion *to satisfy wants* (the three words italicized being left unstressed by radical theorists) and to make up the backlog (or front-log) would be impossible.

Our previous analysis, however, enables us to see Marx's theory in proper light. Unquestionably, *once* a cycle begins, repeated unemployment and deflation tend to make it worse. But the reserve-army theory does not explain how the *first* depression got started. And we have already seen that the rewards of the capitalist are not necessarily related to any unemployment at all. It is also worth mentioning that the Marxian industrial reserve-army theory and the shift-to-profit theory mentioned earlier cannot possibly *both* be true at the same time. One says the slump comes because profits are too low; the other, because they are too high. However, the contradiction does not stop some radical theorists from referring to them indiscriminately.

In any case, the attempt to relate the backlog to the reserve army is especially vulnerable. The author, in his *Economics of Disturbance,* has given a number of cases in which slumps could occur without there having been *any* preceding general "boom" or "overexpansion" whatever.[49] But perhaps the most interesting case, because most likely to be forgotten today, is the case of overexpansion induced by *too much* purchasing power. This is more apt to concern the front-log than the backlog.

Suppose that some new invention comes in which greatly increases the expectation of "marginal" profits. People are clamoring for the new good, and businessmen are anxious to build new plants to satisfy this demand. But the amount of saving which people would voluntarily do would not set "free" enough labor and resources to build the new plants as fast as they are wanted. In such a case businessmen may persuade the banks to lend them newly "created" funds which increase the money supply, and they may use this new money to "raid" the labor supply of the con-

[49] Cf. Wright, *The Economics of Disturbance,* Chap. V.

sumers' goods industries.[50] Workers, let us say in a bakery, are persuaded by offers of specially high wages to shift to construction work. The effect is twofold. At one and the same time the *supply* of goods for personal enjoyment is cut down and the amount of money for spending is increased. Inflationary pressure is almost inevitable. The same thing can happen in an inflationary war boom.

But as long as the investment industries can keep on borrowing from the banks, there will be no trouble in carrying out *their* construction program. No matter how much higher prices and wages may go in the rest of the economic system, the investment industries with special access to bank funds may offer higher still. The process of inflation can continue until one of three things occurs: (1) The banks run out of funds; (2) the backlog (or front-log) is exhausted; (3) investors find that costs have become so high that profit expectations are no longer favorable and therefore they stop further investment. And though consumption may still be rising, the collapse of investment may be so sudden and severe as to start a *general* decline. *After* the smash an increase in purchasing power may help to keep things from getting worse. But before the boom got out of hand, it might well have been the case that *more* saving, *less* consumption, and less bank lending would have made possible a smoother and more stable expansion than actually occurred. It is worth remarking in this regard, however, that precisely the same sort of investment-through-inflation was practiced in Soviet Russia and in the supposedly model economy of Sweden after the Second World War.[51]

[50] It is important for the layman to realize that the banks not merely are the custodians of savings but also may, *if* sufficient borrowers are available, create new funds. Any standard textbook on economics or money and banking will describe the process.

[51] Cf. Bertil Ohlin, *The Problem of Employment Policy* (New York: Columbia University Press, 1949), pp. 86, 87. Anyone believing in the omnipotence of planning would do well to read this passage.

In Russia the only thing that stopped it was the threatened reduction of the ruble to worthlessness.

Two other distributive aspects of the business cycle must be briefly mentioned. First of all, if we refer back to the major left-wing theory of a "consumption lag," with which we began, this cannot be overcome, when (or if) it exists, by a mere permanent shift in the distribution of wealth. For the thing which is supposed to cause the consumption lag is not the average amount of consumption but the lag in its *rate* of increase—the failure of people to form new wants *fast* enough. And rich or poor the speed of formation of *new* wants may yet be variable.[52]

Our second point concerns the much debated subject of whether or not an increase in money wages and in taxes *could* sometimes cause a depression. Most people think that the sole cause of depressions is "lack of purchasing power," and they suppose that raising money wages, on the one hand, will increase spending, while "soaking the rich" (taxing saving), on the other hand, will do the same thing. With such a double dose of purchasing power, they would maintain, we should have no need to fear depression.

Unfortunately this policy can sometimes prove to be entirely wrong; the two factors forgotten are (1) the difference between "total" and "marginal" profit, (2) the need for *new* investment in *growth and change* if we are to have full employment. Raising labor costs may indeed increase buying. But if the expectation of profit on building *additional* plant is at the same time cut off, investment may be forced into a slump by the very measures which were taken to prevent one. We shall discuss this problem in more detail in our section on labor in the next chapter. I do not, however, wish to give the impression that all wage increases or tax

[52] Cf. D. McC. Wright, *The Creation of Purchasing Power* (Cambridge, Mass.: Harvard University Press, 1942), Chap. III, "Redistribution and Purchasing Power Creation"; also *The Economics of Disturbance,* Chap. III.

increases must cause a depression—far from it. It is only if they are so excessive or so badly planned that they cut off the legitimate expectation of marginal profit that they will do so. If wages rise as productivity rises but not faster, no crisis—Marxian or otherwise—need ensue.

Summary

It is time to put together the various points which we have made thus far and to indicate the attitude toward the business cycle which will be followed throughout the remainder of this book. We have seen that Karl Marx maintained that a constant "revolutionizing of the means of production" was an indispensable condition for the existence of capitalism. We agreed with the Marxians that this statement was correct, but we gave it an even broader meaning. We said that the constant revolutionizing of the means of production was an indispensable accompaniment of *any* growing system. Thus it is not merely capitalism but *growth* which depends upon constant change, and one of the most important value judgments which we have to make, in deciding whether or not we shall favor capitalism, is whether or not we consider a rising standard of living to be a good thing. But a further value judgment was also necessary before we could decide between capitalism and socialism, and that was whether or not we wished to give the consumer approximately what he wanted when he wanted it. If one accepts the two values—first, that growth is desirable and, second, that it is desirable to try to meet the consumers' wants with tolerable promptness—then the likelihood of instability and insecurity in a growing world is overwhelming regardless of the social institutions within which the growth process occurs.

Many Marxians, we have seen, tend to suppose that there are no changes in taste except those emanating from the businessman. But this is incorrect in a growing society. The mere fact of growth, in and of itself, gives rise to asymmetrical and unpredictable changes in the pattern of consumers' wants. And this would be the case even though everybody received an equal and an equally growing income.

But there is another point which must be discussed. Theoretically the spontaneous pattern of change could operate so that there was always a smooth aggregate. Theoretically every time a business began to decline, some *other* business would be expanding. Every time people stopped increasing their spending on one commodity, they would switch the extra money to some other commodity. In a pure and a frictionless market it is conceivable that things would really behave in just this way. But unfortunately a frictionless market is impossible. In the real world we cannot always have a spontaneously smooth and perfectly balanced expansion. The Marxists tend to claim that this failure to have a perfectly balanced expansion is due to lack of planning. But again their claim is incorrect. The trouble lies, among other things, in which might be called the backlog problem. The rate of output which would be necessary in order to make up quickly a backlog of demand for a particular good is much larger than the rate of output which society will want once the backlog has been made up. Furthermore, the term "backlog" is misleading. One could just as well speak of a front-log. By this we mean that a new invention will create the same problem of building up an appropriate *stock* of *new* goods, followed by a drop to simply maintaining or slightly increasing the supply of those goods. It is *durability* of equipment plus asymmetrical *changeability* of wants plus inevitable frictions plus *consumer sovereignty* which produces the business cycle.

Once we encounter this fundamental jerkiness and unevenness of expansion, which is inherent in the nature of the process itself, then a number of other forces supervene which are sometimes themselves blamed for the crisis. For example, "swings of optimism and pessimism" may be held to be at fault, or changes in prices relative to wages, and so on. These forces undoubtedly may contribute to some extent to the violence of the movement. But they are not the fundamental root cause. The fundamental cause is the changeability of consumer wants during an expansion coupled with the backlog problem. An example is well given in the 1929 crash. There you have a rise in profits which, according to the conservative doctrine, should have led to increased prosperity rather than to a slump. And you also have most of the time a fairly constant trend of increase in consumption which directly contradicts the radical doctrine. There was some consumption lag at the last. But it would appear that, on the basis of available statistics, the weakest spot in the 1929 situation was the housing cycle. The housing market had been glutted. The First World War housing backlog had been made up by 1928, and there did not happen to be, at that time, any other domestic source of investment capable of taking its place.

We are not yet in a position to discuss contracyclical policy in detail. It is enough to realize that any growing society which wants to meet the pattern of consumer spending will inevitably suffer certain instabilities and insecurities. These instabilities are not the mere result of lack of plannng but on the contrary spring from the nature of the changes in consumers' wants themselves. Yet we must be careful not to be too pessimistic in the conclusions which we draw. The long-run trend of consumption seems to parallel output very closely. The long-run tendency of the capitalist social framework to produce technical change is at least as well marked a uniformity as any of the economic quantitative data that we have. Accordingly, it is submitted that, if the system is not forced into stagnation by unwise remedies during a slump, new sources of activity and growth will soon be forthcoming. Our task therefore in depression is indeed to keep national income from falling too far, but the task is also to maintain national income in such a way as not to produce an ossification of the growth-making incentives and growth-making characteristics of society.

In the remainder of this book we shall discuss first the mistaken and second the valid methods by which a capitalist system can deal with the insecurity inherent in its creativity and its freedom. We begin first with mistaken notions of stabilization, and our next chapter will deal with monopoly—right-wing and left-wing.

CHAPTER 6

Monopoly--Right-Wing and Left-Wing

TO RESPOND effectively to a social force we must not merely oppose it, we must also understand it. But it is exceedingly difficult at the present time to get a balanced insight into the "monopoly" problem. In the first place the word has come to bear a quite one-sided meaning in the folkways. That is to say that certain acts deemed "monopolistic" by one group and correspondingly condemned are considered quite all right in others and even applauded. We shall try to take a broader point of view in this chapter, and, for example, we shall not restrict the word "monopoly" to the acts of business groups alone.

But perhaps the principal barrier to a scientific approach to monopoly today is our tendency to treat it as a theological rather than an economic problem. The word "monopoly" has come to be as highly charged with emotion as it is vague in meaning. Monopoly to many people is the equivalent of economic sin, and monopolistic action by such a view can only be the outgrowth of a warped morality, greed, or stupidity. Unfortunately, the danger and the tragedy of the situation go far deeper than that. Monopoly is not necessarily the result of bad intentions. It may be the result of quite good intentions. As a result the theological approach is unfortunate for two reasons. First of all, it may encourage an attitude of embittered partisanship which makes careful thought almost impossible. But second, if a man starts out with the idea that monopoly is not so much undesirable as morally wrong, he may decide, when he discovers that the objections to the system are not necessarily rooted in greed, that monopoly is all right. Yet as a matter of fact, the undesirable effects of monopolistic restriction are just as undesirable whether they spring from lofty motives or from greedy ones. Our task in this chapter will be to deal with the problem from a more dispassionate point of view, in both its right-wing and left-wing manifestations.

The attitude toward capitalism taken in this book is simply that, as long as most people accept its basic requirements, it is on balance the most workable method of getting continued growth, change, opportunity, and democracy in a relatively peaceful manner. We are not trying to maintain that the system is perfect, and our aim throughout is to show where the weak spots lie. Following out this general approach, we shall begin by showing the inadequacies of a pure market. Before one can discuss policy, one has to have some idea of standards. Many economists have the feeling that, if only there were "pure" competition, there would quite literally be almost no trouble of any kind. This point of view is extraordinarily naïve, and it will be necessary for us to go much more deeply into the problem than it permits.[1]

The Inadequacies of "Pure" Competition

The most important assumptions of any branch of knowledge, or of any culture, are apt to go largely unstated. The author has found it difficult to find a satisfactory account in nontechnical language of the assumptions behind the standard theoretical economic approach to monopoly and the antitrust law. However, a fair summary might run as follows: The economic model of

[1] This chapter is taken in considerable part from the author's "Toward Coherent Anti-trust," *Virginia Law Review,* October, 1949, p. 665. See also his *Democracy and Progress* (New York: The Macmillan Company, 1948), Chap. VII; "The Problem of Competition"; and *The Economics of Disturbance* (New York: The Macmillan Company, 1947), Chap. VII, Sec. 2. "Speed Growth and Cutthroat Competition."

a "purely" competitive society furnishes our most valid social ideal. Our aim therefore should be to get us as near that ideal as possible.

Mathematical economists of what is known as the "welfare" school go further. They have believed that they could prove, by the joint use of mathematics and "psychology," that even in the case of "pure" competition the total of "satisfaction" would be greater if an elaborate program of rearrangement and redistribution were carried out. Accordingly, monopoly policy survives for them, if at all, only as a subordinate part in a general scheme of paternal reallocation involving the full tax and control powers of the state.

The author feels that this entire theoretical economic approach is seriously inadequate.[2] Whether we discuss only the purely competitive adjustment or deal further with the various mathematical

[2] Basic criticisms here will concern the purely competitive ideal as such, but it might be well, before going further, to explain for the benefit of readers who might be intimidated by mathematics the basic inadequacies of the standards used by the "welfare" economists. As originally worked out, mathematical welfare economics included a more or less explicit general assumption that people had substantially similar tastes and capacities for enjoyment. On that basis it was possible to prove "scientifically" that subsidizing certain industries and penalizing others, taking money from Peter and paying Paul, if done according to certain rules, would give greater total "satisfaction." But it was soon found out that we cannot *scientifically* compare the "satisfactions" of particular individuals; for since people have different tastes, money and everything else may mean different things subjectively to different persons. About all that is left of the theory now, therefore, as a *scientific* proposition is that, if one man is made better off without anyone else being worse off, total "welfare" has (probably) increased. But still worse, in full employment we cannot subsidize Peter without taxing Paul directly or by inflation. So the theory further reduces itself merely to a statement that, if the national output grows in such a way as to permit a gain to both Paul and Peter at neither's expense, it will (probably) be a good thing—and we scarcely needed mathematics to guess that.

standards of rearrangement and redistribution, the same deficiencies appear. Fortunately the basic issues do not primarily concern the more esoteric regions of mathematical economics. What economic policy must deal with is the evolution of permissible standards of business *policy* in a world of *growth* and *change*. But the general fundamental model of economic theory, even leaving aside mathematical rearrangements, usually deals with a businessman operating under circumstances in which he has almost no real scope for a personal business policy and in a world which is stationary. This cleavage in approach is only just now being overcome.

Increasingly today economists are distinguishing between the "economics of allocation" on the one hand and what might be called the "economics of growth" on the other hand.[3] The first type takes a "given" output and asks how it will be divided up under various circumstances. The second concerns itself with the way in which output can be made *larger* and the consequences of such an increase upon social stability. The first type lies at the base of modern economic "theory." The second is most explicitly developed in the study of unemployment, business cycles, pressure groups, and so on. An ideal economics and antitrust law would, of course, combine both, but the introduction of the problem of growth greatly complicates the analysis.[4] For undoubtedly if we spend too much time disputing how we shall divide up what we have, we may ruin valuable chances for getting more to divide; but, on the other hand, if we care only about the size of output or the number of jobs, rather than some degree of efficiency or quality, vast quantities of energy may be wasted.

Now the problem is that the theory of monopoly, as it has existed until recently, concerned itself almost entirely with models

[3] Compare Roy Harrod, *Towards a Dynamic Economics* (London: Macmillan & Co., Ltd., 1948); Wright, *The Economics of Disturbance.*

[4] Compare D. McC. Wright, "Mr. Harrod and Growth Economics," *Review of Economics and Statistics,* November, 1950.

taken from a stationary society. Worse yet, the theories of monopoly and competition were not only static, they were also *mechanical.* The courts, for example, deal with a world of developing organisms all striving to stay alive. But the theoretical economic ideal has largely been, and to some extent still is, a world of minute mechanical units each so helpless that all major decisions on price and output are solely the work of the "impersonal forces of supply and demand." Such a world would have appealed to Montesquieu, but its inadequacies as a description of reality are glaring. Nor is it necessarily true that we would want such a world if we could get it. To understand why this is so it will be necessary to make a basic terminological distinction.

"Pure" and "Perfect" Competition. "Pure" competition, as defined by Professor Edward Chamberlin of Harvard, means a world in which each individual firm thinks that *acting by itself* it has no significant influence on its prices or output.[5] This definition reflects two requirements: (1) The product is more or less standardized, and consumers are therefore entirely (or almost entirely) indifferent between sellers. (2) There are a sufficiently large number of sellers in the field for each unit to *feel* itself virtually without influence on the general market, acting alone.[6] It should be noted that this definition is subjective and that we cannot state flatly that ten producers are not "pure" competition but twenty are. On the contrary, as businessmen are

[5] See Edward H. Chamberlin, *The Theory of Monopolistic Competition* (Cambridge, Mass.: Harvard University Press, 5th ed., 1946).

[6] The symmetry, though by no means the usefulness, of Professor Chamberlin's definitions has been somewhat impaired by the recent work of Professor Alfred Nicols. Professor Nicols shows that in some special cases results resembling a pure market can be found even when there is considerable specialization, advertising, etc. Cf. Nicols, "The Rehabilitation of Pure Competition," *Quarterly Journal of Economics* (Vol. 62, 1947); "The Development of Monopolistic Competition and the Monopoly Problem," *Review of Economics and Statistics,* May, 1949. But see Professor Chamberlin's comments in the same issue.

more and more "educated" by trade institutes to be more and more conscious of the effects of their acts on the general market and more conscious of the danger of reprisal, it takes a larger and larger number of competitors to produce a "purely competitive" market. As we shall see later, this subjective aspect of competitive action is one of the major problems of "monopoly" control.

The implications of Chamberlin's definition are exceedingly drastic. Under pure competition, as defined by him, there would be no private advertising, for it would not pay anyone to advertise. A trade association, applying the insurance principle of sharing the risk, might do so, but no single unit. Next, the function of the businessman would be very narrowly limited. Business "strategy" as usually understood would be almost eliminated. The businessman would be doing only two things: First, he would be trying to forecast the movements of an impersonal market whose functioning, to be sure, he might understand but which he would feel himself unable to influence acting alone. Second, he would be trying to "maximize" his profits by producing, in the most efficient manner, the output which he thinks *will* be salable in the light of his *forecasts* of future economic activity. I have formulated this account of "purely competitive" behavior rather differently from most in order to bring into focus the problem of perfect forecasting and perfect knowledge. The purely competitive producer is *not* simply an efficiency expert motivated solely by the "instinct of workmanship" as some romantic lawyers, sociologists, and economists have implied. He is also a forecaster, and if his forecasts are pessimistic, he may produce *less* rather than more than the "monopolist." [7] This problem of forecasting brings us up against the definition of "perfect competition."

Infinite confusion, both in theory and in policy, has resulted

[7] *I.e.*, risks may be greater and therefore output less. I state this simply as a fact, not as an argument for monopoly. There is much more to the problem than that.

from the identification of "pure" competition, as defined above, with a superficially similar but fundamentally quite different concept of perfect competition. Perfect competition, again following Chamberlin's terminology, means two things: (1) a complete absence of "frictional" obstacles to change (everyone can be everywhere at once; all men can change professions instantaneously and so on), (2) absolutely "perfect knowledge" (everybody knows all the relevant facts past, present, and future relating to the market).[8] It is not hard to see that this definition implies an impossibility. For one thing, what *I* do may depend on what *you* do, and vice versa. The situation does not become determinate until someone acts. Yet by a curious logical naïveté it often is thought that, if only we have *enough* competitors in a field, there would be an approximation to perfect competition in this sense of perfect knowledge and perfect adjustability. Accordingly, in the terminology much favored by English writers, "perfect" competition simply means large numbers of competitors while its opposite, "imperfect" competition, is thought only to mean a small number of competitors.

Now the really crucial point is that, while we might (if we wanted to pay the price) get very close to a state of *pure* competition by pulverizing industry through antitrust and related policies, no power under Heaven would ever give us *perfect* competition in the sense of a "frictionless" world. The modern English writers, therefore, by wrapping up the concept of automatic *smooth adjustment* in the same word with the idea of *large numbers,* have done very great harm. We can never have a world of pure *and* perfect competition. The most we can have is a world of pure *but imperfect* competition. Yet a world of pure but imperfect competition may be "imperfect" in more than terminology. And until we realize what the shortcomings of such a system can be,

[8] Chamberlin, *op. cit.* It should be pointed out that these two terms, "pure" and "perfect," overlap. That is, a "perfect" market must be "pure," but a "pure" market need not be "perfect."

we shall not properly understand the considerations necessary for a more realistic competitive standard.

The principal disadvantages of a world of pure but imperfect competition—in other words, of a world in which all industries are pulverized into small homogeneous units but in which there are still frictions of adjustments—may be given under four heads. First of all, the pure but imperfectly competitive world would not necessarily be a stable one. Mere purity of competition, as we shall shortly see, would not prevent the oscillations of the business cycle. Second, it is at least doubtful that the world of pure but imperfect competition would always give the best environment for social growth.[9] We shall have to explain this in some detail. Third, the world of pure but imperfect competition would have in it a great deal of waste of natural resources and might also have a number of other disagreeable features which the competitive market could not remedy. Finally, the world of pure *but imperfect* competition could have a great deal of unnecessary bankruptcy and suffering. We shall discuss each of these points in turn.

A Self-adjusting Society. The statement that a world of pure competition would probably be unstable and subject to deep cyclical swings runs directly counter to many influential schools of economic and legal thought. Even today, perhaps a third of the economic profession would say that in a world of pure competition there would be no unemployment and no business cycle.

The fundamental confusion here, however, lies in the scrambling together of "pure" and "perfect" competition. Space is lacking to repeat the business-cycle analysis of the previous chapter. All that is necessary, however, is to remember that the discontinuous, unsymmetrical changes in consumer preferences; the durability of equipment and consequent backlog problems; the necessary lacks of perfect knowledge, etc., on which we based our cycle theory are all of them *imperfections* of competition

[9] Compare J. A. Schumpeter, *Capitalism, Socialism and Democracy* (New York: Harper & Brothers, 2d ed., 1947), Chap. VIII.

rather than the result of "impurities" or "monopoly" elements. Purity of competition, for example, does not mean *predictability* of expansion.

It follows that a growing but "purely" competitive system—which would, of course, have to contain "imperfections"—would be bound to experience fluctuations in output, employment, and prices. The mathematical economists have, it is true, established that "by definition," "sooner or later," wage and price reduction would bring such a decline to a stop, and pure competition would undoubtedly make for greater price flexibility. But whether the "eventual" halting of the depression would come *soon* enough or before the national output had fallen more than was socially tolerable has not been established. Furthermore, it is not enough merely to *stop* a decline. In order to have full employment and growth we have got to get new investment started. The whole monopoly-versus-competition problem must be judged in relation to economic growth.[10] We shall discuss this problem in more detail in our next chapter.

Incentives for Growth—Low Prices, Low Profits, and Full Employment. Yet once we admit the need of incentives for growth, we come to one of the key difficulties of the monopoly-antitrust problem—the question of profits. Many writers talk as if the aim of the antitrust laws were to keep prices and profits *always* low. Such an outlook considers high profits as an unfailing index

[10] The full impact of this point has not, in the author's opinion, ever been fully evaluated. Most treatments of the problem (even to a certain extent the Keynesian one) discuss the matter as if it were one of fitting a certain number of men to a *given, existing* equipment. But I submit that the effectiveness of wage and/or price reduction should be judged instead by the degree to which it creates *an atmosphere favorable to the launching of new ventures and expansion of existing plant.* This complicates the matter greatly. But the author submits that, if we want to stop the progress of a violent deflation, our conclusion leads at once, in most cases, to at least equal emphasis on fiscal policy remedies rather than mere price flexibility. See the discussion in Chap. 8 of this book.

of monopoly. But if we are not careful, ideas of this sort can be used to throw society into a permanent stagnation.

Remember that we cannot get either full employment or further increases in the standard of living unless we create a social environment in which corporations or individuals will be willing to risk money in constructing new permanent plant, houses, and equipment. But under capitalism, a necessary part of such an environment is the *expectation* of a high rate of profit on *new* ventures. It is almost universally conceded, for example, by Mrs. Joan Robinson, one of the leading left-wing English neo-Keynesian and almost Marxian economists, that the rate of return which is needed merely to keep a business alive, and functioning in an unchanging round, is much *less* than the rate of return needed to induce it to start a new method or build a new plant. But much of our modern competitive literature reads as if high profit were in itself an index of monopoly and ought to be eliminated. In fact, a high profit may be the sign of real competition (not necessarily, to be sure, of "pure" competition) and the thing which induces rapid expansion.

Confusions of this type are frequently derived from the mathematical economic models of pure competition and spring from a confusion of the *results* of competition with the *forces* which induce it. According to orthodox economists from the time of Adam Smith on down, if a particular industry shows unusual profits, many people will come into the field and by increasing output bring down the price and eliminate unusual profit returns. Nobody disputes this analysis in so far as there is any real degree of competition and freedom of access to the particular field. The trouble, however, with a good deal of the modern literature on the subject is that it overlooks one vital step in the process. The *increase* in supply, which results from the entry into the industry of a large number of new units, is not induced by *low* profits. Quite the contrary. It is *high* profit that induces the very increase in investment in the industry which eventually gives low profit. In other words the sequence of events over time would be as follows: High profit would induce increased investment, which in turn would induce a fall in prices, which in turn would reduce profits to normal. But the question almost never asked is this: What would happen if, by operation of law or trade-unionism, we eliminated the high profit *before* we got the additional investment? In that case it is probable that an increase in output never would spontaneously occur.

The hope of *supernormal* profits is the thing which induces the investment which eventually gives us normal profits. If we do not allow some hope of high profits in order to cover the special risks of expansion, we shall never get the increased output which will eventually give us low profits. Low profits are the *result* of increased output and not its cause. A fundamental paradox of our system is that it runs by stimulating hopes which it is the business of the system *eventually* to frustrate in any particular case.[11]

The usual textbook exposition of "pure" competition, however, is apt to consider only a final state of adjustment or "equilibrium" where supernormal profits have been eliminated. From this it is an easy jump to the conclusion that there will not be high profits under "pure" competition. In fact this idea is quite untrue. An industry (for example, agriculture before the AAA and in one of its boom periods) may be "purely" competitive and still be earning very high profits.[12]

The basic confusion here traces back to the distinction between "pure" and "perfect" competition which we spoke of earlier. Pure competition by itself does not give a frictionless world. Now as long as there is a minimum of friction, that is, as long as it takes time for businessmen to see new opportunities and to form

[11] On all these points see Schumpeter, *loc. cit.*

[12] During the inflation following the Second World War, prices have risen much higher in agriculture (in percentage terms) than in more "monopolistically" competitive industries.

plans concerning them or as long as it takes time to organize or build new plant, just so long there may be high profits even in a purely competitive field. And there may also be some limitations on supply, etc., which can *never* be removed. Pure competition, therefore, does not necessarily mean low profits. Quite the contrary. As a matter of fact, the idea of "reasonable" profit was originally associated with monopoly regulation in the sense of public utilities or other legally recognized single sellers. From the point of view of dynamic economic theory, the 100 per cent profit of a new and rapidly expanding firm, in a risky field, may be far more justified than the 5 per cent profit of the stationary legal monopoly which is merely operating in a fixed groove.

One final point must be mentioned in this connection, and that is the notion which has been very much pushed in recent years—for example, by Dr. Nourse, former chairman of the Council of Economic Advisors—that, if only big business, or monopoly, would reduce its prices at the right time (whenever that is), we should be able to avoid an impending depression or at any rate to keep it within a relatively narrow range. No very great knowledge of economic theory is needed to show that this hypothesis must rest on two assumptions of fact, both of which would frequently be untrue. First, if we consider only established businesses, then Dr. Nourse must be implying that businessmen would always and of necessity find that sales would increase so largely in response to price reduction that output could be maintained. In other words, there is an assumed proportionate response of sales to price reduction which has to be of a very special nature. But particularly in the case of durable goods such as houses, automobiles, and so on, this is well known not always to be true. Next, if we consider new business and remember that the constant founding of new businesses is essential to full employment, we must assume that the best time in which to get new businesses started is a time of general price reduction. Surely this is a questionable doctrine. I do not mean to say that price reduction may not often be a useful and desirable business policy and that it may not sometimes help to ameliorate a depression. But it is ridiculous to suppose that it will always stabilize output sufficiently.

Waste, Conservation, and Value Standards. In dealing with purely economic problems, we must not forget that in the last analysis the market mechanism will not give us much more than is put into it. In other words, although the market mechanism may satisfy consumers' choices, it will not by itself improve consumers' choices. Therefore, even in a purely competitive world, if one has a number of ugly or vulgar consumers' choices, the competitive production of goods may be, in Ruskin's term, the competitive production of "illth." This is one of the most important inadequacies of the pure market.

We can only mention such problems of aesthetic and moral standards, although they form the true and vital "framework of the pricing system." We must, instead, pass on to more specifically "economic" inadequacies regarding social waste and the destruction of natural resources. There are numerous costs which for one reason or another do not show up in the business balance sheet even under pure competition but yet must be borne by the community. In a world regulated only by pure competition, for example, individual producers would be able to pour smoke and soot into the air, polluting the homes and destroying the health of an entire community. Yet this cost, which should be borne by those who are really at fault or should at least be deliberately apportioned by the community, is shifted over willy-nilly to the budgets of hundreds of innocent people most of whom have no direct connection with the industry, many of whom furthermore are quite unable to meet it and consequently live in disease and dirt. The "purest" of "pure" competition could not overcome this evil.

Again in the case of many natural resources, such as commercial fishing, unregulated pure competition gives great encouragement to complete destruction. If our descendants are to eat, say, salmon, the salmon must be allowed to spawn sufficiently.

But a small producer—alone among thousands—has no motive for self-restraint. Suppose a single producer thinks the rivers are being "fished out" and decides not to catch as many. Will he help the fish or only make an unnecessary present to his competitors? Conditions being what they are, there is nothing for him to do but go on fishing, whether he thinks it unwise or not.

"Cutthroat" Competition. Closely allied with those inadequacies of pure competition which deal with the exhaustion of natural resources, we have the difficulty of "cutthroat" competition.[13] Cutthroat competition may be most charitably and respectably defined as sales below the *long-run real* costs of production. In time of prosperity price reduction *may* increase sales and even make for larger profits. But in a depression—though there are some circumstances in which price reduction can help—the chances are that, once income has begun to fall rapidly, price cutting within the range of possibility will increase profits or turnover very little if at all. Furthermore, no one can tell when panic price cuts, once begun, will stop, and the small producer alone among a crowd of similar competitors is peculiarly vulnerable. Individual businessmen may know that things are going too far, but they can do nothing. As in the case of a small fish-packing plant, refusal to follow the crowd will not remedy the basic evil—it will only give temporary help to competitors.

The chances are, therefore, that in a more or less purely competitive field price cuts during a depression may be carried beyond reason. Prices will sink to a level far below long-run costs of production, and in order to salvage something from the wreck the owner of the business may keep it in operation as long as minimum payroll and other day-by-day expenses can be met—even though depreciation, profit, interest, all are in default. Continued operation is possible in the case of industry, particularly just after a boom, because a quantity of durable new equipment has been freshly installed, and hence, even though creditors take over the

[13] See Wright, *Democracy and Progress; The Economics of Disturbance.*

plant and prices are exceedingly low, the factory can still be kept going. In agriculture, on the other hand, production is maintained by exhausting, or "mining," the soil. No adequate fertilization or conservation can be managed, but the starved land continues to yield crops of a sort.

Conditions like these may justly be called "cutthroat" competition, and though businessmen constantly used the expression as a smear word against anyone who ever reduced a price, no one who remembers what happened after 1929 should deny that the phrase can sometimes describe both a real and an important problem. Nor can it be entirely confined to depression. Whenever we find the combination of a great deal of durable equipment and a product whose sales do not react quickly to price reductions, pure competition is likely to be unstable and may be disastrous. It should be noted, however, that, save in the case of occasional suicidal competitive frenzy, *both* slow sales response and durable equipment are necessary for a disastrous price war. For if price reduction brought a quick increase in sales, there would be no need for wholesale cutting, and if a price war began at a time in which there was a great deal of plant about to wear out, firms with decrepit equipment would simply shut down. Supply would then be cut, and (barring general depression) prices would soon rise or stabilize themselves. Nevertheless we have here a paradox: The competitive order, precisely because it is competitive, tends to rush ahead to satisfy demand. But in so doing it produces a jerky installation of durable plant which may start both depressions and unwise price cutting.[14] We find ourselves in the vicious circle not unfairly satirized by a student of the author who remarked that competition was bad—because it gave rise to monopoly!

Here is the core of the monopoly problem. It is not so much superior technical efficiency that furnishes the drive to "monopoly." Technical efficiency only furnishes a drive to large-scale business—and that, as we shall shortly see, is quite a different

[14] Compare the discussion of the "backlog" difficulty in Chap. 5.

thing. The real "advantage" of monopolistic restriction to the individuals involved, as far at least as survival is concerned, is its power to steady the market during a deflation, enabling the industry to prevent or minimize cutthroat competition. Whenever it is proposed to decentralize an industry by antitrust action, the cry is always raised that decentralization will lead to cutthroat conditions, and no defense of the competitive order which overlooks this problem can have any real validity.

We shall discuss the question of standards shortly. But before going farther we must stop and summarize our problem. From what has been said we can see that pure but imperfect competition—which is the nearest one ever gets to the academic ideals of economic theory—has many important shortcomings and cannot be used uncritically as a standard for industrial organization. It need not stabilize society adequately. It sometimes does not permit adequate growth incentives. It does not guarantee beauty, health, or morals. It may permit vast waste of natural resources. It often involves needless suffering and insolvency. Any workable concept of competition must be far more carefully thought out and more complicated than a simple splitting up of all fields among swarms of competitors. Let us try to see what we can evolve instead.

The Inadequacies of Monopoly and of "Cooperative" Planning

Before we can discuss the inadequacies of monopoly, we have got to make our terms clear. The word "monopoly" has traditionally been associated with greedy, immoral, and generally antisocial conduct. But the problems with which we will be dealing are of far wider scope than simple piggishness. It is, accordingly, necessary to find words which will indicate the required distinctions.

It will help, we believe, to restrict the word "monopoly" to the precise evil with which it has been historically associated and which has earned it such constant condemnation. Monopoly in the remainder of this section will therefore mean only those cases in which an individual or corporation deliberately restricts output, raises prices, or withholds supply from a desire for *unreasonably* high profit.[15] The word used in this sense would apply to behavior resembling Jay Gould's Black Friday corner of the gold market in the 1870's or the inordinate profits derived from the legal monopolies of the Elizabethan courtiers or the East India Company of Adam Smith's time.

But though the exploitations of the historic monopolies were usually linked with large size or with the exclusion of competitors, it does not always follow that either large size or the exclusion of competitors will always result in reduction of output or inordinate profit. What we have to deal with in this section is a much more subtle problem—the problem of individuals (or corporations) who (or which) feel that on the whole an industry would be more stable and better planned if it were brought under substantially centralized direction but who disavow any intent to make inordinate profits or exploit the public—in other words the problem of what might be called "good" combinations.

[15] This definition is very carefully worded because of the number of ambiguities inherent in the concept of competition. Even a *purely* competitive producer "restricts" output in the sense that he does not produce indiscriminately no matter what the loss. In theory anyhow, he stops at the intersection of "marginal cost" and marginal revenue, though often he could go further without losing money in the sense of "going in the red."

We are left with the question of what is a "reasonable" profit. To this there is no mechanical answer. The reasonableness of a profit depends on the circumstances surrounding the investment—high risk, for example, justifies high profit. One might clarify matters somewhat by saying that a profit is unreasonable if it is greater than would be necessary to bring forth the effort it compensates. But since the "necessary" size of the reward is often a matter of individual temperament, we are still left a long way from an objective definition.

Another form which historic monopoly took was the getting together in an agreement of all the individuals or corporations in an industry to raise prices to monopoly figures and share in the resulting gains. Conspiracies of this sort have been frowned upon by lawyers and economists alike for the past two hundred years at least. But just as forming a single large company need not result in high prices, inordinate profits, or restriction of output, so also the getting together of the firms which make up an industry, in order to plan output, *need* not be accompanied by high prices, inordinate profits, or restricted output—at least not in the first instance anyhow. Often the motives are of the highest and not merely hypocritically so. Just as in the case of the single seller, it may be believed that on the whole a planned direction of the industry would be the best for all concerned.

Now when "good" mergers and "good" conspiracies of the sort we have been describing are attacked, they always reply, "Look, we are giving good service; we are not charging unreasonable prices; we are not withholding products; our profits are not out of line. What is wrong with what we are doing?" And indeed, in order to form a proper judgment of the case, it will be necessary to go far beyond many of the standards usually invoked in academic economic theory.

The truth of the matter is that the basic ideals and aims underlying many business "monopolies," so-called, or business "conspiracies" are much the same as the aims and ideals underlying the cry for economic planning. However paradoxical it may sound to say so, much modern so-called monopoly is motivated not by greed but by the same static instinct of workmanship which also animates the disciples of Thorstein Veblen. The ideals which underlie plans and mergers of this sort are a love of uninterrupted routine, a desire for security, a desire for the "rational" and economic organization of a particular industry. And precisely in this point lies the danger, for it is exceedingly easy for the believer in "good" combinations and the ardent planner to get together on a practical footing. But in order to understand why this tendency cannot be allowed to go too far, we have got to remember a number of problems and sociological questions which are usually shoved to one side in the textbooks.

Yet before we go further, we need to make our terminology still clearer. We have already defined monopoly; let us try, next, to get some other name for "good" monopoly. The force which we will be discussing in the remainder of this section can best be described as "restrictionism for stability or security." In other words the *greedy* restrictionism which is traditionally associated with the word "monopoly" is a relatively rare phenomenon in modern American business life. We have to deal instead with restrictionism initiated by business, government, farm, or labor groups for stability or "rationalization" rather than (in the first instance anyhow) for greed. More and more today the question is not whether or not there should be restrictionism for stability but simply who is going to do the restricting.

The argument against restrictionism for security or stability falls under two main heads—political and economic—and the basic analysis underlying our point of view has already been given in an earlier chapter. As far as political liberty goes, we have argued that, without competing leaders and without separate and alternative *independent* employment opportunities, the effectiveness of political democracy will rapidly decline.[16] In the same way we said many of the same forces which underlie political freedom also

[16] One of the many hidden ambiguities in the word "competition" is the argument which confuses competition with "multiple ownership." Thus when various cartel or fair-trade schemes are proposed, they are often justified as "maintaining competition." What is meant is, of course, merely maintaining multiple ownership. If *policy* is centralized, then decentralization of "ownership" is a secondary factor—except in so far as continuance of multiple ownership preserves a potentiality of revolt which may serve as a restraining feature.

underlie technological creativeness. For without the presence of alternative employment opportunities it is not likely that the man with a new idea will be able to put his point over, especially if his idea is of a type which seriously disturbs many existing occupational vested interests.[17]

The economic objections to restrictionism have a similar dynamic base. Essentially the basic trouble is that entrenched groups nearly always tend to underestimate the size of their demand. They nearly always assume that reductions in price would have no effect in stimulating income or sales, and they tend to suppose that very little more than the amount which they now have could be sold under any circumstances. As Judge Learned Hand put the matter in the Aluminum decision,[18]

> It is no excuse for monopolizing a market that the monopoly has not been used to extract from the consumer more than a fair profit. The act has wider purposes. Many people believe that possession of unchallenged economic power deadens initiative, discourages thrift, and depresses energy, that immunity from competition is a narcotic, and rivalry is a stimulant to industrial progress, that the spur of constant stress is necessary to counteract an inevitable disposition to let well enough alone.

We are confronted here, as so often in economic life, with a problem which does not have any perfect solution. On the one hand Say's law that "supply creates its own demand" is clearly

17 Professor Schumpeter has argued in terms of the "obsolescence of the entrepreneurial function." The author believes that, had Schumpeter had greater firsthand experience with the working of large-scale business or government organizations, he would probably have been less positive. Always, in the author's opinion, there is some *individual* somewhere in the organization who is "spark-plugging" its achievements. "Personality and will power" still count immensely. But see Schumpeter, *op. cit.*, p. 131.

18 *United States v. Aluminum Company of America,* 148 F. 2d 416, 427 (1945).

untrue in the short run. We can never guarantee that the total of individual industrial movements will *always* add up to a smooth, steady flow. But on the other hand it is easy to jump from a realization that supply does not *always* create its own demand to a belief that it *never* creates its own demand. And this attitude is dangerous in the extreme; for if we can state positively that supply will not *always* create its own demand, we can also state with equal positiveness that, if everyone is too afraid to take a chance, then we shall all cut our own throats and keep ourselves in self-imposed poverty. We thus know, without any doubt whatever, that, if all groups hold back production in order to avoid the possibility of unexpected declines, we may be perfectly certain that the growth of national output will be stopped. The assurance of short-run stability thus easily leads to long-run stagnation.

Toward Workable Standards of Competition

From all that has been said so far in this chapter, it will be seen that our standard of competition cannot be "perfect" competition, for that is impossible. Nor should it be "pure but imperfect" competition, for that is frequently undesirable. We are left, therefore, with the problem of working out some compromise solution. In this connection it is important to separate certain romantic or noneconomic aims from others which relate more directly to the problems of democracy and growth. Some people feel that we should aim at a world of compulsory small businesses. Now it cannot be said that this ideal is wrong if one feels as a matter of deep cultural conviction that the village economy is the most humane method of association for the human race. But such schemes should not be treated as having anything to do with capitalism. Often such plans for "obtaining competition" are really methods of smuggling in comprehensive planning by the back door. For when a little businessman borrows the money from the government to buy his plant under terms which require him to fit his price policy, his wage policy, and his output policy into some form of government cooperative planning, such a little businessman is not the industrial pioneer of a developing capitalism but only the foreman or hired manager of the government who is allowed to flatter himself by saying that he "owns" his plant. Perhaps such a "phalangist" form of social organization is the most humane variety of socialism, but it must not be confused with the maintenance of capitalist competition.[19]

Since all that the economic model of competition requires is not small size but large numbers, it is necessary for us before we decide whether a given large business is either a "monopoly" or an undesirable restriction to ask how many competitors it has and over how wide an area does it trade. The village mill, for example, might have had a fairly tight control of the market because there was almost no effective competition within the range of the economic area which it served, whereas a very large flour-milling concern may be much more competitive because it has a great deal of competition in the large area over which it trades.

Again in determining whether a given business is a "monopoly" or an undesirable restriction we have to consider interproduct competition. For example, the United Mine Workers have organized practically all the coal mines of the country, but still there remain the oil producers, and until the mine workers can bring the oil producers within their control, they do not have a tight monopoly—fortunately for the country. Interproduct competition is frequently much more active than legal standards would lead one to suppose.[20]

Another problem raised in determining what is monopoly or undesirable restriction is the monopolist-in-spite-of-himself. Under

[19] David Lilienthal seems to the author to be inclined to confuse mere geographical decentralization of units or of some property rights with real competition and decentralization of policy. See David Lilienthal, *This I Do Believe* (New York: Harper & Brothers, 1949).

[20] Cf. "Monopolistic Practices," in Schumpeter, *op. cit.*

many economic definitions of "monopoly" a monopolist would be any man who produced a more or less unique product.[21] Now under such a broad definition the man who is promoting a new product would, of course, be a monopolist. Thus by a curious inversion of language, we find ourselves applying the term monopoly to precisely the form of industrial pioneering which is, in fact, most associated with competition. Perhaps the best solution to this difficulty would be to consider the element of time. It is not likely under normal conditions that a man would continue to be in sole possession of an unusually profitable field for an indefinite length of time without its being discovered that he was doing something more than merely being efficient. In the ordinary course of events other substitute products are almost certain to arise, and if they fail to do so, some overt step toward the maintenance of a private restricted market is almost certain to be found. Thus, in determining whether or not a business is a "monopoly" or an undesirable restriction we have to consider first the size of the market and the number of competitors in the market. In some cases this involves considering the whole world. Next we have to consider the question of interproduct competition—the competition of other products and other metals or other fuels, for example. Finally we have to consider the element of time. Has there been time yet for competitors to spring up? It is only when all these three elements have been evaluated that we can begin to talk about competition, restriction, or monopoly in any economic sense. A standard of competition which wishes to force a world of small units should be judged rather in terms of cultural revolution than in terms of economic competition.

[21] Cf. Paul A. Samuelson, *Economics: An Introductory Analysis* (New York: McGraw-Hill Book Company, Inc., 1948), "A monopolist is not a fat greasy man with a big mustache and cigar who goes around violating the law. If he were we could put him in jail. *He is anyone important enough to affect the prices of the things that he sells and buys.*" But compare Nicols, *op. cit.*

The most difficult problems of the monopoly question, however, involve two special cases. First there is the single large seller surrounded by many other smaller competitors. This we shall call "megapoly." It is perhaps exemplified in the case of the United States Steel Corporation. Next there is the case of a few sellers of about equal size. Here we find a tolerable example in the tobacco industry. The first case is called "megapoly," the second "oligopoly." These two cases furnish the most difficult aspects of the monopoly problem.

We cannot here go into a general discussion of antitrust weapons. The author wishes to suggest merely that our motto here as in most cases should be "some but not too much." In the case of the United States Steel Corporation, for example, one has an inherently unstable industry, an industry which would be unstable even in a planned economy that wanted rapid growth and a minimum of rationing, and which is peculiarly open to potential cutthroat competition. Under such circumstances the presence of the stabilizing influence of a price leader does not seem necessarily evil. In the same way the presence of certain oligopolistic influences which lead producers to exercise discretion in price cutting seems also to be on balance not wholly evil.[22] But we cannot let these forms of industry become too stable. The author would suggest that an *un*easy preeminence is the most that can be tolerated. In other words it is necessary to see to it that no stabilization schemes or elements of oligopoly are carried to such an extent that new competitors with new ideas will have no opportunity to get ahead.

Our concepts of competition, it is therefore submitted, should run in terms of turnover and of a fair chance. We do not merely want to keep business little. The little business which we want is the little business which has a chance to develop into big business. In order to have such a system it will, of course, be neces-

[22] Compare John Maurice Clark, "Toward a Concept of Workable Competition," *American Economic Review,* June, 1940, p. 242.

sary to prevent industry from becoming too centralized. But if we are honest, we shall realize that a concept of competition running in terms of a fair chance must require consideration of many factors other than those of business concentration. In particular, the problems of government restriction, unwise equalitarian taxation, and labor planning must be considered. As we have already seen in an earlier chapter, taxation to redistribute income may have the effect of immensely stimulating monopoly. Income taxation bears with tremendous and disproportionate weight upon the new man and the new firm and also upon the risky venture as opposed to the stable one. If the American people really want real competition in the sense of opportunity for small businesses to become large, then they will have to revise their tax laws.

The second feature which is not usually considered is the problem of credit facilities. If the banks are allowed to form a single rationalized coalition, then the impetus to monopoly or restriction for security is greatly increased, for the use of credit is one of the main forces which make it possible for the individual who is not a capitalist to rise under capitalism. We should therefore consider the repercussions of some of our credit policies, for example, that which frowns upon capital loans, if we are to get a true evaluation of the monopoly problem. But before we can give a final summary, we need to consider the labor movement and labor restrictionism. To that we shall now turn our attention.

Monopoly by Labor

In the preceding sections we have mentioned many of the shortcomings of monopoly for good intentions or, more accurately, of restrictionism for stability. But we have not stressed enough what is perhaps the most important feature of the case, namely, that restrictive measures, undertaken with whatever good intentions and however reasonably at the time, have a tendency to be misused so that over the years they may become increasingly repressive and an increasing barrier to the growth of national output. And just as this is the case with restrictionism by business, so also we find it in many of the motives underlying the labor-union movement.

Many people are drawn to the union movement because of semantic associations linking the idea of "union" with the idea of "lack of conflict." It is often supposed that, if all industry were organized in such a way that the business was controlled by the workers, there would be no conflict. We have already seen in our first chapter on the "withering away of the state" and again in our chapter on the problems of democracy and planning that the idea that worker participation would eliminate conflict is very largely mistaken. Change would still entail the possibility of fierce debates over the status of individual members. A system which attempts to guarantee every man security in his routine cannot possibly permit of very rapid or indeed any economic growth. We may repeat our quotation from Krech and Crutchfield:[23]

> Technological changes in and of themselves . . . frequently operate so as to balk the expression of many important needs of the worker on the job. . . . The worker whose painfully acquired skill has suddenly become useless and meaningless by some new invention or improvement in production method finds himself facing very serious psychological problems. Not only must he learn new skills and routines in work, but his feeling of personal worth and self-esteem, based in many instances on his mastery of the now obsolescent skill, is threatened. Technological development has resulted in the frustration of strong needs formerly expressed upon the job and *best expressed* on the job.

Although much can be done by consultation and tact to improve and mitigate conditions in this regard, it seems impossible alto-

[23] See David Krech and R. S. Crutchfield, *Theory and Problems of Social Psychology* (New York: McGraw-Hill Book Company, Inc., 1948), p. 539.

gether to avoid this basic friction of technological progress. It is one of the most fundamental issues raised by technical development in the modern world.

Again it is sometimes said that the labor union may help to overcome the feeling of loneliness or sociological "anomie" which many men have in a large organization. But this, too, can be overstressed. As Krech and Crutchfield also say:[24]

> Labor unions *deepen the depersonalization of worker-management contacts*—induced in the first instance by the nature of capitalistic economy and technological growth. The union member no longer even seeks for personal contact with management when he wishes to discuss grievances, wage increases, or better working conditions. This is done for him by his union leader or grievance committees and through regularized channels. Frequently even the recognition that a grievance exists or determination of what is a just and adequate remedy for the grievance is not determined by the needs and beliefs of the worker concerned. The majority vote of the union membership or the decisions of the top union leadership may determine these matters for the individual.

Again, regarding the feeling of identification and exaltation which union membership sometimes furnishes, Krech and Crutchfield say:[25]

> Some unions whose battles are in the far past no longer offer their members an exultant sense of progress toward an increasing share in controlling the conditions of their work. A number of unions are dictatorial in their procedures and are not adverse to using violence and goon squads to silence their members who would participate in free speech. Other unions operate under a tight bureaucracy and opportunities for leadership are limited to a selected and self-perpetuating few.

[24] *Ibid.*, p. 537.
[25] *Ibid.*, p. 549.

A most interesting suggestion regarding the possible origin of labor strife has been made concerning the opportunities to rise which unionism now furnishes. Mr. G. Watson pointed out in 1942 as follows:[26]

> The average young man or woman from a working class home once had two avenues open. One was through rising to the top in the business hierarchy, a ladder which has now been largely blocked off for those youths without college training or family position. The second has been the ladder of politics, but elections, too, are expensive nowadays. The labor movement now offers another full line of promotion.

While the author would not subscribe unreservedly to everything in the passage quoted, nevertheless it is true that we have here an important source of possible conflict. Its origin, however, is not so much to be found in an increasing snobbishness or social class division in our society as in the increasing demands for *technological* training which are made upon the business executive. In other words, there is not in many cases a straight line of promotion from the workbench to the management. It may be necessary to acquire a number of skills which cannot be attained in the job alone. This problem, however, cannot entirely be overcome even by free, general education, for it would remain true that the workman on the bench, even if his brother has been able to go through college, would nevertheless feel himself at a disadvantage because he did not have the technical skills which his brother had acquired. In other words, there may be a growing tendency to develop a loop or kink in the path to promotion, a loop leading through training in some institution rather than through simple performance in the mill. This fact is an outgrowth of technology itself rather than of capitalism but may nevertheless be an important contributing factor to social unrest.

We have mentioned these psychological bases of union restric-

[26] *Ibid.*, p. 548.

tivism because it is impossible to deal with a force unless one understands the basic factors underlying it. Nevertheless, despite the fact that many of the motives underlying unionism are in themselves understandable and often admirable, the fact remains that they are often in conflict with *other* motives often held by labor and that union organization, like business organization, is capable of tremendous distortion for antisocial purposes. Antisocial union action can take at least three forms: First there is the obstruction of technical change already spoken of. Next there is the deliberate adoption by the union of a philosophy of slowing down for stability. This either may be adopted as a matter of union policy or may be imposed upon the whole industry by the union as Mr. John L. Lewis has attempted to do in the case of the miners. Finally there is action regarding wage rates which either serves indirectly to foster monopoly or acts directly to cut off the opportunities of some of the weaker, unorganized laborers or in some cases to stop the entire economy from its development.

Whether the planned slowdown is initiated by labor or by business, it is subject to the same criticisms, and we shall not repeat what we have said earlier in reference to business. But the question of excessive wage demands is much more complicated. We are not denying that the union by asking for money wage increases which parallel the spontaneous increases of productivity in a society may perform a valuable and desirable service for the whole community.[27] But this is not the same thing as saying, as many people do, that *any* money wage increase is necessarily good and that every conflict between the union and management is inevitably a conflict between an angelic union and a diabolic business interest (or, for that matter, vice versa).

[27] However, here, too, we run into the problem of incentives already spoken of regarding monopoly (see pp. 165, 166 of this chapter). If demands for higher wages come so immediately upon the installation of new methods as to destroy the incentive for risk taking, technical progress may be considerably retarded.

Space is lacking in an outline of this sort to elaborate the academic theory of marginal productivity. In recent years there has been a flood of literature designed to show that the union can raise the real wages of its members under some circumstances. While by no means always incorrect such articles are for the most part masterpieces of question begging.[28] No one could deny that the union can surround a given piece of durable equipment with a barbwire entanglement of restrictions and thereby capture for itself nearly the whole, or perhaps the entire, return which

[28] Of course, wages may be below the marginal product, and in such cases the union by forcing an adjustment may be doing no more than remedying injustices. This point is conceded even by such stringent critics as Professor Henry Simons. See Henry Simons, "Some Reflections on Syndicalism" in *Economic Policy for a Free Society* (Chicago: University of Chicago Press, 1948).

We must also realize (see footnote 27) that in a dynamic world marginal cost and marginal revenue are not always equal—simply because the entrepreneur may not have had time to equate them. In a static equilibrium any wage increase above the intersection of *MR* and *MC* will reduce employment and output as well as profit. But in a dynamic world the effect of a change in cost functions induced by technological change may be to lower the cost curve—both marginal and average. In such a case an increase in wage rates, even though it raises the curves again, may not *reduce* employment. *Ceteris paribus,* however, it will reduce the incentive for further expansion.

One final point of great importance which may be mentioned, though it is probably impossible to explain it to anyone not trained in economic theory, concerns the effect of wage increases on prices in times of inflation. It is often thought that if when wage rates go up 10 per cent, profits rise by, say, 15 per cent, some "monopoly" element is indicated. It should be realized, however, that an absolute increase in wage rates may affect the *marginal* cost curve more than the average, *i.e.* make it steeper in slope. If that is the case, and if the public wants the same output, a purely competitive industry would still have to raise its prices more than proportionately. The public, however, will always think that a businessman always "first" calculates his costs and then "adds" a (10 per cent, let us say) margin, and they will always ask, "Why could not he add only a 5 per cent one?"

that particular plant yields. But what academic theory says is that excessive wage demands are likely to result in one of the following *consequences*:[29] First, the growth of the economy may be hampered. Second, the opportunities of nonunion men to find jobs may be restricted. Third, in some extreme cases the owners of the given instrument of production may refuse to replace it or even to operate it. Finally, action of this sort is likely to give rise to an artificial demand for laborsaving devices. If, in spite of all these things, we sometimes find an increase in real wages, the question must still be asked: Might not the same or an even larger increase have taken place in spite of union action? In other words, the mere statistical showing that real wages in a given industry have increased following unionization does not tell us anything as to whether (*a*) the increase was really the result of the union or (*b*) the increase has taken place at the expense of the opportunities of other people who, but for excessive union demands, might have been able to find jobs in the new plants which might have been built but now will not be.

In this connection it may help to remember once more the distinction which we insisted upon in the preceding chapter between total profit and marginal profit. Everyone has heard, for example, a great deal during the last few months about the huge profits of the steel industry. When labor was pressing for increased steel output, a great deal was said about the "monopoly" action of the steel industry in not expanding more rapidly. But very little was ever heard about the tremendous increase which had simultaneously occurred in steel construction costs. Merely because the steel industry reports a large profit in depreciated dollars, we cannot jump to the idea that this return is unwarranted or that another wage increase could be granted by the steel companies without affecting the incentive for expansion. It is not money profit on old plant or old costs that counts. What matters is the

[29] See Wright, *Democracy and Progress,* Chap. VIII, "Coöperation Unlimited."

expectation of net profit on *new* plant built at *new* costs. When we consider the risks of backlog saturation and of demand change which are inevitably involved in an expansion endeavoring to satisfy the consumer, and when we consider the great increase in construction costs which has occurred since the war, it might well be argued that steel profits were *too low* for adequate expansion, and still more may this be the case in some other industries.

The idea of marginal profit and of *new* construction costs gives us the final clue needed to understand how increased money wages can sometimes *increase* unemployment or *stop* growth rather than help it. An increase in money wage rates cuts both ways. It may raise an expectation of greater sales which, other things being equal, should stimulate output. But on the other hand it also creates an expectation of higher costs, especially of higher *additional* costs, if output is increased or new construction begun. These two sets of expectations, favorable and unfavorable, may completely cancel each other out. Worse yet, they may on balance be *unfavorable*. Not only may there be no increase in the actual total money income paid labor, there may even be a drop. For labor, like business, can price itself out of the market and, by demanding too high money wages, may stop growth, greatly stimulate technological unemployment, and reduce the job opportunities of thousands who do not happen already to belong to some well-entrenched union.

For present purposes it is enough to realize that, once a union becomes well entrenched, it may exhibit all the antisocial tendencies of private business and of private monopoly. Ruthless interunion competition, a vehicle for the will to power of individuals, may have the effect of cutting off industrial expansion. The union may adopt all the restrictive tendencies, and more, of monopolistic business. Finally the union may adopt policies of discriminating monopoly, imposing higher rates upon one firm than upon another, and thus force an amalgamation of industrial units which would not otherwise have taken place.

Summary. We have said enough now to be able to see how labor's antiprofits policy may sometimes have results quite similar to those of monopoly or restrictive action by business and with equally disastrous effects upon the growth of national output. It will not be necessary to develop the way in which union wage policies frequently operate to foster business concentration. The point has been made over and over again in recent years that, simply because a given *industry* is making high profits, we cannot jump to the conclusion that every firm in it is making high profits or can afford a raise in wages. The problem is fundamentally an individual one unless the union is to embark upon a policy of deliberately destroying the weaker and newer firms. We must return instead to the tendency toward planning of industry under labor direction.

It will be remembered that we began our discussion by pointing out that it was quite mistaken to attribute all "monopoly" action or restriction to economic sin or moral turpitude. The urge underlying much security restriction, both by labor and by business, is not so much one of greed as the desire for perfect security and uninterrupted routine. As long as we fix our minds only on the goal of planning for routine, planned slowdowns of the type often advocated by business and labor seem quite reasonable. But as we have already shown, continued social growth is impossible if the vested interest of every individual is to be respected, and by vested interest is meant not merely the vested interest of the businessman but also the vested interest of the bureaucrat in his job and the laborer in his skills.

But the cry always is, "Why not let the various groups get together to plan growth? Why not put together all the available statistics and see if we cannot, from them, derive a plan of growth which will give us a smooth, general aggregate?" This idea is deceptively simple, but it has at least one basic economic weakness in addition to the political danger mentioned in Chap. 4. The trouble is that individual groups nearly always underestimate their demands. Backlogs are not mechanical things, and if each individual group refuses to expand for fear that it may glut its market, all groups may find themselves becoming relatively impoverished. An advanced industrial economy is a highly specialized and highly integrated machine. Each man's work depends upon the work of those who perform complementary tasks. In such a society the pace of production and the choice between more leisure and more goods and services tend to be determined by the *least* ambitious occupational group strong enough to make its wishes felt. If the steelworkers, for example, are not willing to work an adequate length of time or cut off their market by demanding too high a price, all the rest of society suffers. In the same way if the coal miners refuse to do enough work in order to stabilize what they conceive to be the demand for their goods, and if they raise their prices to inordinate lengths, they will stop the steelworkers from working, and so on. During the last ten years a great deal of ridicule—and much of it justified—has been heaped on those orthodox economists who said that "supply always creates its own demand." But it must equally well be realized that the left wing tends to an opposite fallacy—that "demand creates its own supply."

Nothing that we have said so far is to be construed as an attack upon the institution of unionism itself. No one in his senses would maintain that labor always got everything that it should. No one should deny that the role of the union in pressing for higher wages may sometimes be a socially useful one. But by a parity of reasoning we could equally well make out a very good case for leaving business absolutely free to combine. We might literally apply Adam Smith's doctrine of the invisible hand and say that every man working for his own selfish interest will be led by an invisible hand to promote the public good. Many labor leaders do talk as if the doctrine of the invisible hand had received a new incarnation and every *union* working in its own selfish interest was led by an invisible hand to promote the public good. But the clear-headed student of social affairs has to make a more intelligent distinction. Just as the American people long ago decided that business enterprise needed to be kept from becoming too powerful and needed to be subordinated to certain considerations of the public good, so also in the same way it is necessary for us to realize that the union cannot be allowed to become too powerful and that it, too, must be subordinated to certain standards of public welfare. A pressure group is a pressure group, no matter what its name.

Conclusion

We have now come to a point at which we can offer certain suggestions regarding antimonopoly policy. As already stated it is impossible to go into the technical details of antitrust law enforcement. What we want to do here is merely to give a general summary.

The first thing necessary to grasp is that the matter cannot be handled by cut-and-dried formulas—at least not if we want a growing and capitalist world. A passion for mental tidiness may be one of the most oustanding attributes of economic theorists, but that does not prove that it is necessarily admirable. Clear headedness is often confused with accuracy. But the monopoly problem, like the definition of democracy, requires us to strike a commonsense balance among many standards none of which are ever wholly harmonious. The result must always be somewhat blurred.

In the matter of industrial control there are, to be sure, two sets of apparently precise slogans which many people seem to find intellectually satisfying. The first of these is "plan everything." The second is "get as near pure competition as possible." Now the intellectual tidiness of the first slogan is clearly a delusion. One of the main points we have tried to make in this book is that the word "planning" is almost wholly indeterminate. In so far, however, as planning is taken to mean an advance over-all budgeting and licensing of social growth and net new investment by a central board, we have sought to show that it is not consistent, over the long pull, either with social growth and development or with democratic political organization. From the value standards suggested in this study these objections ought to be conclusive.

Many lawyers and economists, however, who would agree in rejecting the over-all planning standards, find it much harder to question the purely competitive one. At least the purely competitive slogan has more real context than the "planning" one in that it is less indeterminate. But the very precision which gives it its appeal also constitutes one of its main weaknesses. Attention is focused upon getting "maximum" or "optimum" output in a "given" set of conditions and usually from a "given" amount of equipment. But add growth with its resulting disturbances plus the effects of social costs which the market does not register, and the purely competitive case becomes far less convincing.

As far as social costs are concerned, the author would argue that it was not necessary save in the most extreme cases to handle the matter of conservation either by government ownership on the one hand or by private monopoly on the other hand. Reasonably impartial regulations, "closed seasons," and so on *could* handle the problem without inducing too much centralization and routine. I am not so naïve as to think the problem easy, but I am also not so pessimistic as to think it impossible of a workable solution.

It is in the matter of growth and stabilization, however, that we find the major difficulties. Some "imperfections" and impurities, as Schumpeter has shown, are not merely inevitable but also desirable. Many of the more extreme Robinson-Patman Act interpretations come close to ending real competition. "Competition," we have said in this chapter, is not mere multiple "ownership" of small-size units but genuine variation of policy in a world of adequate "turnover" rather than of equal size.

Applying our standards more concretely I submit that our aim should be one of "workable" competition, which involves a recognition of many so-called "monopolistic" elements. I refer the reader to Professor J. M. Clark's admirable article for elaboration of this point.[30] But given "workable" competition of the sort suggested, then the author believes that proper fiscal policy designed to keep general deflation within bounds would reduce the dilemma of cutthroat competition sufficiently for us to treat the "cutthroat" argument on the same basis as, say, the infant industry argument for tariffs. That is, we should consider it as an analytically valid point but not important enough, practically speaking, to keep us from trying to have a fairly competitive market.

We are left with the problem of numbers, and here, too, we are caught with a conflict of standards not easily reconciled. We say that we want antitrust enforcement aimed at keeping any one firm from having too large a proportion of the market. This point of view is justified as desirable to keep business "on its toes." Yet no one really conversant with the facts ought to deny that in some cases the fear of antitrust action acts as a deterrent to efficiency. I have in mind the case of those large corporations which are really afraid to operate with full efficiency because they fear they would thus obtain too large a proportion of the field and invite public condemnation and antitrust suits.

Until recently at least the Supreme Court has been so impressed with the "monopolist in spite of oneself" or "through efficiency" argument that it has made a very generous proportional allowance regarding the upper limit—about two-thirds as nearly as one can tell. Many writers have also suggested that the law should limit itself to evolving codes of *behavior* for large units (proportionately large, that is) rather than splitting them up. The idea is that, if the large units are not allowed to "throw their weight around" too arbitrarily, the little fellow will still have a chance. This view is frought with many Hegelian paradoxes,

[30] Clark, *op. cit.*

some of which have been explored by Dr. Adelman and which cannot be elaborated here.

The author feels, however, that antitrust action should to some extent be along both lines. In other words one must realize that setting a proportional limit does in the short run deter certain of the larger firms from expanding as much as they might. But on the other hand a two-thirds limit, if there is really that much control, seems to me likely to be so high as to allow a degree of influence almost impossible of dislodgment. And a firm thus securely placed, though initially very efficient, would have a tendency to run down. The narrowing of the noncompeting group, we saw, was not confined to government.

In summary then *if* we have allowed for all the other factors—*if* we have considered the size of the market, the interproduct competition, the length of time a given firm has been in operation, and so on, and *then* find a proportional control running more than 40 or 50 per cent—I believe some reduction in proportional size would be desirable because of the long-run advantages of decentralization and multiple policy determination.

But the antitrust laws can at best ensure only oligopoly rather than monopoly. If we really want vigorous growth, competition, and turnover, our approach must consider a much wider field than mere legal action. We need to consider other and more important barriers to the development of new independent businesses.

Such barriers come under three main heads: (1) the general "security" attitude and resulting government and private schemes of "cooperative" restriction, (2) the frequent effects of labor union action, (3) excessive income taxation. As shown in the author's *Democracy and Progress* and again in Chap. 3. of this book, the income tax—especially the highly progressive income tax—is easily converted into a heavy tax on *opportunity*. For the absolute size of the income of a new and an old firm may be much the same. Yet the old firm already has many of its trade contacts and reserves, while a new one needs to spend much more in order to catch up. But they will be taxed at much the same rate, and so it is easier for the older firm to save—a fact concerning which I believe there is considerable evidence. Yet in any event the corporate income tax tends to be a tax upon opportunity and growth. One must indeed admire recent proposals to deal with inflation by removing the excise taxes on luxuries and taxing instead the corporate saving and investment through which so much growth takes place.

In mentioning these problems of taxation, labor action, and restrictions for security we do no more than call attention to a group of problems often slurred over by modern equalitarian bias. But it is important that the reader should realize that it is in this area that we must look for the major sources and major remedies of the "monopoly" problem.

CHAPTER 7

Can We Stabilize Capitalism?

CLEARLY NOT—if by "stability" we mean perfect stability. But on the other hand we could not stabilize a growing socialism either—if by stability we mean perfect stability. Accordingly, the question to ask under any growing system, be it capitalist or socialist, is not whether we can stabilize perfectly but whether we can keep social disturbance within tolerable bounds.

In dealing with the problem on these terms it will help to run over once more the basic dilemma which we have been exploring. We have seen that a growing national income will induce spontaneous and unsymmetrical changes in the pattern of consumers' wants in *any* society which allows some leeway for free choice to the consumer. It also will induce periodic revision of the technological methods of production, even leaving aside new inventions. It follows, therefore, that the mere fact of growth in and of itself must necessitate constant revision of skills, of work teams, of regional and industrial prosperity, and of the general pattern of social resources. No matter what our social system, if we continue to want growth, we cannot prevent this reorganization—all we can do is to put a floor under the risks which the reorganization entails for individuals. The problem furthermore would exist even if there were no business cycle at all, for a continuous *general* expansion, even under socialism, still implies reorganization and hence individual insecurity.

Space is lacking in an outline like the present one to elaborate the mechanism of social security, state-financed old-age pensions, unemployment compensation, and so on.[1] These palliatives of

[1] I say state-financed old-age pensions because pension plans for individual businesses may constitute a very heavy burden on the individual

change are relatively easy to grasp as far as general principles go and furnish one of the most important fields for continued social betterment. It must be pointed out, however, that they are subject to at least two fundamental limitations. We cannot do so good a job of protecting the individual from insecurity that he would just as soon not work. Also we cannot tax the investor so heavily that he will cease to invest. If we do that, we begin to undermine the whole structure of incentives upon which a rising living standard depends. But short of these upper limits, there is no reason why we cannot continue to expand and develop our social services and our unemployment programs, especially as our productive standards rise.[2]

But the type of unemployment best handled by "social security," etc., is "frictional" unemployment. Unemployment allowances, etc., do not adequately cope with the far more formidable problems of stabilizing the cycle or overcoming long-run trends toward either inflation or stagnation.[3] Such problems involve not merely economic but political problems of the utmost difficulty. Unques-

---

firm especially in time of depression. The individual industrial corporation is not immortal, nor can it be made so without setting up a regime of cartelized routine, and we have seen the disadvantages of schemes of that sort. But in addition the individual corporation does not have access to the taxing or, still more important, the credit-creating power of the government; hence, the ability of the individual corporation to guarantee pensions is much more limited.

In addition to the burden on the firm, the pension plan which is privately financed often comes to tie the worker to a given job (and union) almost as effectively as a serf was tied to the land. For the man who moves may lose his "accumulation."

[2] We must also remember that, unless there is a great deal of investment, pension plans are in reality mere levies on current consumption. This is true, for example, of the social-security "reserve" of the Federal government.

[3] *Government*-financed plans may, of course, have important stabilizing effects, since they may help "automatically" to balance and unbalance the budget in a countercyclical manner.

tionably there is no single patent cure-all, but also there is no overwhelming and inherent necessity for hopeless pessimism.

A physical scientist of the author's acquaintance once declared that economists were useless because they "didn't know how to end the business cycle." "Not at all," I replied, "if ending the cycle is *all* you want I can easily tell you how to do it." "How?" said he. "Put everybody in jail."

This may seem a flippant as well as trite reply, but it carries a vital truth: We cannot discuss economic policy intelligently unless we first agree upon value standards. It *is* true that the quickest, easiest way to end the business cycle would be to put everyone in jail. It *is* true that many forms of security could most easily be granted under slavery. The inadequacies of economic policy are not so much the result of the failures of "scientific" economics as the outgrowth of conflicts of value or else the outgrowth of certain of the values themselves. Accordingly before we begin to outline a stabilization policy, we must summarize once more the value standards which we wish to follow.

Value Standards for Economic Policy

As one looks over the field of modern political and economic thought, two widespread, basic, and closely connected mistakes regarding the nature of democracy are soon evident. The paternal conservative attitude is that democracy consists *merely* in being "kind" to the lower income groups. This attitude appears to be the essence of the "responsible" conservatism recently lauded by Dr. A. M. Schlesinger, Jr.[4] On the other side the left wing appears to feel that we attain democracy if we move a *single* group of poor boys into power or wealth. Practically no attention

[4] See A. M. Schlesinger, Jr., *The Vital Center* (Boston: Houghton Mifflin Company, 1949). I do not mean to minimize the achievements of *noblesse oblige,* but can one rely entirely upon *oblige* without creating a *noblesse*?

is paid to the problem of getting *continued* infiltration of new blood on independent terms.

Economically speaking, these two mistaken concepts very easily merge into general advocacy of a regime of strict, centralized, paternalistic planning. Many paternal (and other) conservatives are inclined to think that capitalism survives as long as most claims to property are still nominally lodged in the hands of people called businessmen. To such men capitalism exists as long as they "own" their factories and other people whom they know and regard as businessmen own "their" factories. The fact that there may be a great deal of planning by industry or government may not seem to be so important; indeed if it helps to cut down "unfair" competition, it may be a "good" thing. Yet on the left the ardent planner and adherent of the welfare state may be equally as indifferent toward the survival of *some* property rights as the conservative is toward *some* planning. The two groups can therefore get together on the following terms: No property will be confiscated outright or in full. The structure of management will remain largely unimpaired. But the direction of all *new* growth will be planned by a single central board made up of representatives of business, "government," and labor. This seems to be the essential ideal of both the Tory (conservative) and the Labour (socialist) party in England. The only points of difference surviving then become questions of degree as to the *amount* of labor "participation," the *amount* of soak-the-rich taxation, and the *amount* of welfare subsidy. Independence, opportunity, growth, change, and competition seem equally repugnant to right and left.

The widespread appeal of such schemes is due to the fact that superficially they appear so very reasonable to all concerned. We have already pointed out, however, many vital defects. In the first place regimes of "cooperative" regulation are likely to result in a "You scratch my back, I'll scratch yours" attitude in which all the vested interests of labor, business, and government combine to choke off growth and its inevitable insecurities. Furthermore, choking off growth is likely to lead to a second main defect—continued unemployment—for remember that we cannot have continuous full employment in our society unless *new* business and *new* equipment are constantly being built or unless we cut off all savings. The NIRA attitude, therefore, is likely either to prolong unemployment instead of ending it or else to lead to immense government outlay to "fill in the gap." This outlay can, it is true, take the form of welfare expenditures. But it can equally well take the form of vast military outlay or of *social* conspicuous waste—ornate stadiums, monuments, etc. Or the government, having helped to cut off private growth, may next build a new industrial plant parallel to the old and thus gradually socialize the economy. Waste, however, is the most likely solution as anyone with political experience will soon learn.

It is not necessary to repeat here the economic analysis underlying the points just given. What we want to do, before going further, is to analyze the basic *social* weaknesses of the type of planning we have discussed in its left-wing and right-wing manifestations. The defects of the right-wing gospel will probably seem fairly obvious. But the full extent of the betrayal of the left is scarcely yet appreciated. Let us try to understand it more clearly.

Our analysis implies no necessary stupidity or moral treachery. The tendency to reason from one's own experience to general laws is perfectly natural, universal, and often valuable. It is, in fact, as understandable as it can be dangerous. What happens is this: A man who has *himself* achieved power or perquisites (and often wealth) by advocating, say, planning or the extension of government or union control comes to identify the institution, through whose extension *he* rose, with *permanent* opportunity in general for *everybody*. To him, then (say, John L. Lewis), unions *in general,* or in other cases a big bureaucracy *in general,* become synonymous with opportunity for poor people because he—a poor boy, or one without influence—rose through their establishment.

But when one analyzes the circumstances more closely, it will be seen that it was not the particular institution itself that furnished opportunity so much as the fact that it was a new institution in *process* of being created. Those *inaugurating* socialism or fighting for it have an opportunity for thrilling, independent careers. They seldom stop to think that, had they been fighting for the reestablishment of the Holy Roman Empire, they would have received much the same opportunities and satisfactions. It is not so much the "cause" or the institution per se but the process of "putting over" that cause that gave them their chance.

What the mature and honest thinker has to ask is not, "Have I, a poor or obscure person, got powerful or rich by *setting up* a method of ruling society?" but "What chance will the poor or obscure boys who come *after me* have of building up independent careers in the new society I am creating?" The test of the democracy of a social system comes, then, not in the first but in the third generation. Thus in Russia great efforts at first were made to give a parity of opportunity between the children of the manual workers and the children of the intellectuals and bureaucrats. But now, according to some authorities, scarcity forces the imposition of high tuition fees which only the children of well-salaried people can meet.[5] True, there are doubtless scholarships. But when one considers the great program of public education in the United States and the opportunities available (in Keynes' words) to any one "of capacity at all exceeding the average," it is by no means clear that Soviet Communism really gives as great democracy of opportunity.

However, we must not confine our thoughts only to actual discriminations which could be conceived of as eliminated in an ideal state. Even in the pure model of the highly centralized state there is a vital defect. No room is left for *independent* advancement. Some people do rise in even the most highly despotic and

[5] Arthur Koestler, *The Yogi and the Commissar* (New York: The Macmillan Company, 1945), p. 150.

centralized society, and sometimes they have been able and patriotic. But the means of their advancement have usually been degrading. Men and women who have literally prostituted minds or bodies cannot as a rule be depended upon suddenly to develop virtue and character when in power—especially if continued power often depends on continued prostitution. And even if the means to power are honorable enough—passing examinations—they still may not permit of originality.

The essential advantage of *competitive* capitalism, while it is competitive, is that it is so decentralized that it admits of a great deal of independent turnover and originality. The essential weakness of the centralized planned state, whether it is Tory conservative or Labourite socialist, is that it tremendously discourages independent activity. The centralized welfare state may, indeed, train a promising poor boy to be a physicist. But what if thereafter his science is reduced to being—as Aldous Huxley put it—a mere "cookery book." [6] He can learn to use the accepted recipes. But woe to the man who tries to think up a new one!

In this matter of opportunity we also find the vital weakness of the regime of cooperative planned control from the conservative point of view. The Achilles heel lies precisely in the problem of selection and promotion. The capitalist, especially the second- or third-generation possessor of *inherited* power and wealth, gets a bad attack of social "conscience" or jitters (the first being often closely allied with the second). And he will say: "These people want security and routine. Well, let Bill and Joe and me get together and plan the output of our respective factories, and we can see that things will run smoothly. We will let the government in on the deal and some of the labor leaders, and then the left-wingers won't have any ground for complaint."

Over the long pull, however, such plans are a delusion. It will not be long before people will begin to ask just why Mr. X con-

[6] Aldous Huxley, *Brave New World* (New York: Doubleday & Company, Inc. 1932), Chap. XVI.

tinues to sit on the board of directors and to enjoy wealth. He cannot *then* appeal to the capitalist sanction of competitive opportunity, for he has himself helped to abolish that. Nor—unlike the left-wingers—can he appeal to the new socialist sanction of selection by government. We have here a basic point which the author has often stressed. The reconciliation of the people to some authority is one of the principal requirements of civilization. The capitalist myth is: Every man working for his own selfish interest is led by an invisible hand to promote the public good. And it of course is not literally true. The planning myth is: Every man working for the government is led by an invisible hand to promote the public good. And *it* is not literally true either. But at least the decentralized competition of capitalism does permit of opportunity and growth. And at least the routinized bureaucracy of socialism does give people the alleged emotional satisfaction of "working for the state." But the "conservative" planned state ("guided capitalism," Professor Schumpeter called it) has neither the productivity of the one nor the emotional satisfaction of the other. Equality, we must realize, forever eludes us. But some degree of independent opportunity we may well hope to attain. A nation, while it remains saturated in the democratic ethos, cannot achieve stable political organization on a basis which denies both.

Outlines of Stabilization Policy

Depression. Having summarized our basic values we are now in a position to discuss specific policy. We shall first take up depression and unemployment and next deal with the problems of inflation.

In regard to depression there sometimes seem to be almost as many policies as there are people thinking about the subject. But a more careful examination will show a general tendency to fall into two main groups: On the one hand there are those who favor wage or price reductions and "adjustments" of various sorts, and on the other hand the adherents of a policy of "offsetting" deflation by "creating purchasing power," etc.

It may be said at once that no one policy has universal validity. In order to decide what should be done about a depression we have first got to have some idea of why the depression occurred. But depressions may be started in many different ways. A business cycle, if we may talk about it in medical terms, is like a high fever. It is not a single disease in itself but may be the result of many different diseases—measles, mumps, smallpox, influenza, and what have you. And the remedy that might cure one disease may kill the patient if applied in another—so also it may be in economic policy.

We can, however, help things somewhat by making a tentative distinction between those sources of depression which are inherent *in* the system and those which arise from attacks *upon* the system or from uncritical or mistaken attempts to reform it. Our attitude toward policy may differ considerably depending upon which type of crisis we are discussing.

The general cycle analysis given in Chap. 6 of this book deals primarily with those causes which are inherent in the system. We have seen, first of all, that full employment and growth alike require the constant starting of new plants and new enterprises which will keep busy the margin of growth and hence the investment goods industries. But we have also seen that the process of growth in itself induces all sorts of unsymmetrical changes in the pattern of wants, of techniques, and of the general level of consumption. Add to these the likelihood of backlog (or frontlog) difficulties and of the discontinuous and spasmodic introduction of new inventions, and it is clear that occasional failure of the total mass of changes to occur at smoothly offsetting rates is not to be wondered at.

But if a depression occurs which is due to the reasons just named, a policy of general wage and/or price reduction seems to the author an unnecessarily harsh and disturbing remedy. Especially is this the case if wage and price reduction are to be our *sole* dependence. Even Professor Schumpeter has admitted that deflations so treated can go far beyond the point of usefulness and entail much needless suffering. The essential "cause" of such a depression as we are discussing here is that investment has slacked off—either because the *rate* of consumption has temporarily declined or because the rate of *change* of the pattern of consumption or technique has suddenly altered. Some businesses are declining more rapidly than others can offset them, or new wants and new techniques are not being introduced in a sufficient quantity. But if the economy can be kept from a violent collapse *without* the use of unduly restrictive measures, then this temporary discontinuity will soon be overcome. The prime aim should be, first, to maintain consumption *and,* second, to stimulate investment. The trouble with most modern theories on the subject is that they try one or the other of these two requirements but seldom both. Yet *both* are essential.

The conservative policy of wage reduction may conceivably operate to stimulate new investment. But except in very favorable cases (where deliberate policy is probably not necessary anyhow) the favorable effects upon "confidence" or business "expectations" may be entirely offset by the discouraging effect of decreased sales from lower money wages. Again, price reduction may stimulate sales *if* income is not falling so fast as prices, but it is, on balance, more likely to discourage new investment than the reverse.[7] "By definition," of course, a deflation must stop somewhere, but there is no guarantee that the "bottom" will be reached either in a

[7] The fundamental inadequacy of much orthodox theory, as the author sees it, lies in the fact that too much emphasis is placed on fitting more men to a *given* set of equipment or a given demand curve. Likewise the left wing is too much concerned with increasing "consumption" under the impression that consumption is all that is needed. The real question, however, should be: What price and fiscal policy will contribute most to the *growth* of capital equipment and the organization of *new business units?*

tolerable length of time or before the national income has fallen far more than is necessary. With luck the conservative policy may work without entailing an exorbitant price in human suffering and social dislocation. But it cannot be relied upon to do so.

The left-wing policy on the other hand is equally unsatisfactory. If the conservatives neglect demand, the left wing neglects investment. But *investment* is the basic problem. Measures to stabilize consumption (public works, unbalanced budgets, etc.) may indeed keep the slump from getting worse. But they are after all mere first aid, that is, if we are not just trying to smuggle socialism in by the back door. Until growth once more gets under way and with it new investment, there cannot be a spontaneous recovery of the private economy.

Unfortunately, however, the left-wing policy of maintaining demand is usually accompanied by all sorts of policies which strike at the incentives for social growth and private investment. The very words "creating purchasing power" are ambiguous; for if all one wishes to do is to get people to try to *buy* more, then purchasing power can be created almost as much by transferring money from those who would normally save (and, in depression, hoard) to those who will spend as by increasing the total of money payments.

The first decision we have to make in selecting policy, therefore, is to decide whether or not saving is on balance useful. In other words, is the American propensity to save over the long pull excessive, and are we really in danger of what is called "secular stagnation"? Of course *at the moment* during a depression savings may not be being invested. But we cannot just stop

---

For the organization of new business units still forms the vital margin of investment.

Wage reduction as explained in our last chapter may, of course, give rise to profit expectation and "confidence." But if they occur at a time when the national income is falling rapidly, their stimulatory effect may be completely offset.

there. We must ask why. There are in this connection two theories of secular stagnation. The first of these assumes a fairly fixed definite relationship between the stock of capital and the level of consumption. It implies that, unless population is growing or consumption is expanding in rigid correspondence with output, there will be no adequate demand for investment. The second theory runs in terms of ideology. It does not say that there is any close, necessary connection between consumption and the stock of capital but rather maintains that, because of hostile ideology, it may become impossible to make the necessary changes which would give rise to continued growth. The author repudiates the first of these theories. He by no means denies the possibility of a stagnation brought on by the forces outlined in the second. In other words, it may quite possibly happen that hostility to change will become so great as to cut off investment outlets, and this is particularly the case if the investment outlets are abroad. But we must be careful how far we go in our analysis in this direction. For the idea of secular stagnation can easily become a self-verifying prediction. In other words, secular stagnation may be used as an excuse for adopting certain restrictive measures that in themselves may produce the hostile ideology which will finally give us the restraint of change on which the theory depends. Our task in depression, as I see it, is, indeed, to prevent continued deflation but to prevent it in such a way as *not* to stop the fundamental forces which would lead to further change and development.[8]

It is hard to believe that anyone who honestly studies the figures on world consumption and world production can possibly deny

[8] See D. McC. Wright, "The Prospects for Capitalism" in *A Survey of Contemporary Economics,* H. S. Ellis, ed. (Philadelphia: The Blakiston Company, 1948). In my *Democracy and Progress* I sum up our problem in the following formula:

"From freedom and science came rapid growth and change.
From rapid growth and change came insecurity.
From insecurity came demands which ended growth and change.
Ending growth and change ended science and freedom."

that there is today throughout the world a tremendous need for investment and, if we want to prevent inflation, for saving. Even within the continental United States alone, at the present time, it may well be true that we are still underequipped and that we still need large-scale investment. Accordingly we submit that a depression policy should be based on the assumption that the depression will be temporary and that the growth impulses of society will reassert themselves. Unquestionably it requires a great deal of faith to maintain in the depths of a depression that, if the system is not made too rigid by a mistaken policy, new wants and new methods will soon appear. But if we consider the historical record of capitalism over the last 150 years, its technological creativeness would seem quite as stable a basis for prediction as the Keynesian "normal" law of consumers' behavior. Indeed it is probably more so. Therefore we must not allow ourselves to be stampeded into an uncritical pessimism any more than we should permit ourselves to be stampeded into an uncritical optimism.

The left wing, however, is seldom willing to make a favorable assessment of long-run needs. Either they assume gratuitously that saving will "never" be needed again, or else they consider nothing at all except the immediate fact that for the moment money is being "hoarded." But attacks on incentives to save are nearly always also attacks on incentives to *invest*.[9] Yet lack of investment is the crucial problem.

The author has frequently used a simile in connection with left-wing policies as follows: By creating purchasing power through deficit finance we do indeed put "oil" in the machinery. But if, when we pour in the oil, we also fill it with sand and monkey wrenches, we are not likely to be improving the situation. The conservative mistake is to blame the results of the monkey

[9] See D. McC. Wright, "Income Redistribution Reconsidered" in *Income Employment and Public Policy: Essays in Honor of Alvin Hansen* (New York: W. W. Norton & Company, 1948).

wrenches on the oil. But the left-wing mistake is to put in no oil unless a due quota of monkey wrenches and sand is also added.

The principal policies discouraging investment which are likely to be used in connection with a policy of creating purchasing power are as follows: First of all there is the idea of centralized "cooperative" planning and "guided" capitalism—the NIRA. Many right-wing interests, we have seen, will work for this as well as people on the left. The many inadequacies of this policy have already been discussed. Next comes a more radical policy of having the state parallel private investment by government-owned plants. *If* we want a freely competitive society, this policy is most undesirable except in cases in which for some reason of general long-run (noncyclical) policy a specific decision has been taken once and for all to socialize that field. *Unless* such a definite decision has been taken, we must realize that for every dollar put into "circulation" by a government plant, five or six dollars of potential private investment may be frightened out of it. Government can ideally be a fair competitor. Practically speaking, it seldom is.

The next two policies are increased soak-the-rich taxation and increased money wage rates. The weakness of both is the failure to consider "marginal" or "additional" profit expectations, such as we analyzed in Chap. 5, and the margin of growth. When we consider all the bad effects of highly progressive income taxes upon the inducement to invest, upon opportunity, and upon the competitive market mentioned in Chap. 3, it will be seen that these taxes are in themselves extraordinarily powerful as an inducement toward stagnation. The author does not, therefore, favor the redistribution of wealth as a means of raising the secular propensity to consume. And if we are to consider not the long-run but merely the cyclical problem, then in so far as it has any relationship to the level of consumption, it is to its rate of change rather than to its absolute level. But as we saw in our business cycle chapter, a change in the distribution of wealth is not likely to affect the *rate of change* of consumption quickly enough to be a very effective means of cyclical stabilization.

Still more important, however, is the argument that we should raise money wages in a slump in order to "increase purchasing power." Many people, both outside the labor movement and in it, are apt to think that, if only we manage somehow to pass out enough money to buy, let us say, all the goods which are at one time on display in the stores, we shall automatically have full employment and security. This idea is entirely wrong, but it is so widespread that we must once more point out its weakness. In addition to the storekeepers and contractors who are busy making and building the things we need personally for ourselves and our families, there is a huge field of heavy industry or investment goods industry, and we cannot have full employment unless it also is kept busy. But the market for these investments goods industries is not automatic. Perhaps half of their output is absorbed in replacement, which might be thought of as quasi-automatic, and a certain other proportion is taken up in the profitless, semi-automatic investment of established large firms. There remains, however, the margin of growth and change which requires special incentives and which furnishes what might be called the setscrew of economic activity. If it is active, the rest is active. When it is depressed, the rest of business is soon apt to become depressed also. The crucial market, then, of heavy industry, the market which determines at once whether we shall have growth and whether we shall have full employment, comes from change and from expansion. This means that, though we can enable people to spend more merely by passing out more money, we cannot get either full employment or a steady increase in production unless we also create *a social environment in which individuals or corporations will be willing to risk money in constructing new permanent plant and equipment.*

Those of us, however, who think mostly about purchasing power are apt to suppose—if we think about the matter at all—

that an increase in spending or in consumption will automatically bring about new investment. More spending, it is said, will create more markets. More markets will call for more investment. But it is just here that one touches on the vital link. *Unless* there is also created adequate "marginal" or "additional" inducement of profit, increased spending on the part of the public in an enterprise system will not produce any increase in investment but will, instead, merely waste itself in higher prices. It must be remembered that the expectation of profit which will serve to keep a business going in a steady routine is usually very much less than the expectation needed before we get growth and change. Full employment means growth, growth means change, change means risk, and risk demands especially high profits to offset it.

It is against the background of this analysis that we must consider the high-wage argument. Money wage increases *may* raise the total money expenditure of society in a depression, although even that need not necessarily occur.[10] But will the increased money spending of the consumer, supposing that it actually occurs, necessarily result in increased activity of business and in increased investment outlay? The answer is: Not necessarily. Only if the expectation of profit on new plant—or what we have called "marginal" profit—rises will there be a flow of increased investment.

The trouble with money wage increases is that, at the same time in which they may increase spending, they also increase costs, especially the marginal costs of increased output. Two sets of expectations, we have seen, are put into motion. On the one hand there may be the expectation of more money being spent and of more sales. This will be favorable. But on the other hand there will be the expectation of higher costs, especially higher additional costs, and this will be unfavorable. These two types of

[10] For so many men may be dismissed that even the higher wage *rates* of those still employed may not give so large a total income as was being received before.

expectation may cancel out, and indeed it is quite possible that the pessimistic expectations raised by a money wage increase may offset the favorable ones, so that no rise in total spending may take place. Furthermore, even if some rise in total spending takes place, and even though there may be some moderate increase in consumption from existing plants, the increase in costs, especially the increased additional costs in the vulnerable investment goods industry, may have the effect of cutting off the margin of growth of additional plants upon which continued full employment depends. Accordingly, the author follows Lord Keynes in believing that the best policy for money wages in a depression is to keep them constant. And it may be the case that in some industries it would be better *to reduce* money wages.[11] If these arguments seem to sound strangely un-Keyneslike, it may be of interest to quote his own words. He said: "When we enter on a period of weakening effective demand a sudden large reduction of money wages to a level so low that no one believes in its indefinite continuance would be the event most favorable to a strengthening of effective demand." [12] Also: "I do not want to see money wages forever soaring upward to a level to which real wages cannot follow. It is one of the chief tasks ahead of our statesmanship to find a way to prevent this." [13] And again: "I am now of the opinion that the maintenance of a stable general level of money

[11] We must remember the problems of single industries as well as those of the economy as a whole. A reduction in wages and prices in a single industry, say coal mining, may result in a larger total income for all concerned in that industry. Nor need we suppose that this gain is necessarily all at the expense of other sellers. *Total* production and income may be increased. Just as the orthodox nineteenth-century economists made the mistake of thinking of a fixed "wages fund," so also the modern radical and trade-unionist tend mistakenly to think of a fixed "expenditure fund."

[12] J. M. Keynes, *The General Theory of Employment, Interest and Money* (New York: Harcourt, Brace and Company, Inc., 1936), p. 265.

[13] J. M. Keynes, "Keynes v. Hayek on a Commodity Reserve Currency: Reply," *The Economic Journal,* December, 1944, p. 430.

wages is on a balance of considerations the most advisable policy." [14]

In summary, the author would in most cases favor deficit finance in a depression. But it should be deficit finance accompanied by two things: (1) a stable money wage rate and in some cases and under some circumstances a reduction in money wages; and (2) lower taxes all along the line, *especially* in the *upper* income brackets, because it is there that the venture considerations are most important.[15] Reducing taxes on the lower income group increases only consumption. It may have no effect on increasing the inducement to invest, and it must be remembered that both aspects of the case have to be considered. The policy described is in a sense "planning." But if by planning we mean *any* collective action to improve or stabilize society, then we are all of us planners anyhow whether we know it or not. But the policy does not mean the setting up of a centralized board to plan the flow of net new investment. It is not necessarily inconsistent with a dynamic competitive capitalism.

Die-hard conservatives and Communists, in a surprising unanimity of opinion, have, alike, one final argument. They say that without the "club" of a fear of unemployment the unions cannot be kept from making such unreasonable wage demands as to bring on a depression. This returns us once more to one of the fundamental problems of democracy. Of course if we believe with the Communists that the system is basically a swindle, then it does follow that only ignorance and force can serve to "keep

[14] Keynes, *General Theory,* p. 270.

[15] It should be remembered that these high progressive rates have almost no *revenue* significance. They yield only a pittance compared with other taxes and the size of government budgets. They are merely the reflection of an "ethical" prejudice. The author submits, however, that they tend (1) to reduce *opportunity,* and (2) to reduce investment. But see Wright, "Income Redistribution Reconsidered."

the worker down" and that mass unemployment is the most potent type of force. But if, on the other hand, the system is not basically unfair—and we have argued that case in Chap. 5—then a statement that unemployment is necessary to keep wage demands from going too high must mean that the majority of people are such jealous fools that they cannot be trusted to see the general welfare or so selfish that they are unwilling to give way to it. The die-hard, of course, often believes just that. But if it is true, it is difficult to see how democracy can be relied upon in any field.

Shall our major reliance be on force, then, or persuasion? Difficult as it may seem to talk of persuasion at this time of predatory and militant trade-union monopolies—"men of iron wills and wooden heads" as Mr. Koestler puts it—it does not seem to me that the democratic ethic admits of any doubt concerning the answer. Some discipline and some force may be necessary from time to time under a democracy to protect the basic public welfare, but persuasion should be the major weapon whenever possible. Indeed, whatever we think, if there comes such a failure of communication and values between large groups of people that it is no longer possible to persuade, democracy will probably blow up anyhow. The man on horseback will be called in to restore order among the struggling pressure groups and reassert in however crude a form some emphasis on the "general" welfare.

But accepting the standard of persuasion rather than force, what policy is most likely to succeed as a starting point for persuasion? Shall we tell the worker that the system is inherently unstable (because of its virtues to be sure, but still *inherently* unstable) *and* that *nothing* can be done about it except general and disturbing wage cuts, wage cuts furthermore which *may* succeed in stopping the deflation in a reasonable time perhaps but which again may not? Or shall we tell them that some insecurity and some instability are an inseparable part of growth, of opportunity, and of social freedom but that we can guarantee to keep major deflation within bounds? That furthermore if *they* in turn do not themselves stop the wheels with selfish and irrational demands, growth and rising living standards will soon begin once more? Which idea do you think is more likely to succeed?

In the author's experience, at any rate, the force which most hampers anyone endeavoring to suggest that there may be certain merits in capitalist society after all is the notion that such a system inevitably involves constant repetition and risk of years similar to the tragic era between 1929 and 1933. It is the ceaseless endeavor of the trade-unionists, socialists, and Communists to stamp in on the public mind the belief that a "free" pricing system must mean unlimited insecurity. Yet the orthodox, conservative, die-hard policy of the *always* balanced budget fosters and encourages the left-wing attack. What a difference it would make if a candidate believing in competitive capitalism got up and said, as he could easily do, "We will not allow a major deflation." Could a more effective prelude to argument be imagined? Can there indeed today be *any* effective belief in capitalism on any lower terms?

The author, however, must not be misunderstood. It is not indiscriminate deficit finance and public works which we are advocating. In the first place deficit finance under conditions of inflation or expansion will only make matters worse. In the second place our analysis shows clearly that deficit finance, like aspirin, can be misused to give immediate temporary relief while the basic dislocation becomes worse. While not all depressions or even many of them (up to now at least) may be the result of extravagant wage demands, it is clear that such demands could be a source of depression. And again, even if not the source of the original collapse, bad policies could serve to prolong it indefinitely. Deficit finance and public works, under these conditions, could serve to keep things just tolerable enough to prevent a general outbreak and yet be accompanied by such foolish measures as never to permit of a real recovery. This is the real danger of the unbalanced budget—not the "spend-ourselves-into-ruin" arguments of the ultraconservatives.[16]

Once more, however, we are brought back to the basic problem of whether a democracy ever can act wisely and whether government by persuasion and education is ever possible. Perhaps it will help in this connection to read the misgivings of some of the liberal thinkers at the beginning of the modern era of popular democracy. Thus Lord Macaulay, the English historian, wrote in 1857 concerning the United States: [17]

> It is quite plain that your Government will never be able to restrain a distressed and discontented majority. For with you the majority is the Government, and has the rich, who are always a minority, absolutely at its mercy. The day will come when in the State of New York a multitude of people, none of whom has had more than half a breakfast, or expects to have more than half a dinner, will choose a Legislature. Is it possible to doubt what sort of Legislature will be chosen? On one side is a statesman preaching patience, respect for vested rights, strict observance of public faith. On the other is a demagogue ranting about the tyranny of capitalists and usurers, and asking why any body should be permitted to drink Champagne and to ride in a carriage, while thousands of honest folks are in want of necessaries. Which of the two candidates is likely to be preferred by a working-man who hears his children cry for more bread? I seriously apprehend that you will, in some such season of adversity as I have described, *do things which will prevent prosperity from returning*; that you will act like people who should in a year of scarcity devour all the seed-corn, and thus make the next a

[16] On this point see D. McC. Wright, *The Creation of Purchasing Power* (Cambridge, Mass.: Harvard University Press, 1942), Chap. VII, Sec. B, "Is There an Economic Limit and an Economic Burden to an Internally Held National Debt?"

[17] Letter from Macaulay to H. S. Randall, May 23, 1857. G. O. Trevelyan, *The Life and Letters of Lord Macaulay* (New York: Harper & Brothers, 1875) Appendix to Vol. II.

> year not of scarcity, but of absolute famine. There will be, I fear, spoliation. The spoliation will increase the distress. The distress will produce fresh spoliation. There is nothing to stop you. [Italics supplied.]

I do not, however, insert this letter to breed pessimism or to indicate the deficiencies of the left. It presents, it seems to me, an equal challenge to the right. For why should we permit *needless* suffering? There could, of course, be dislocations and unemployment brought on by an actual scarcity of food and equipment. But crises of this sort, so far at least, are not likely in our country save in war. In the usual downswing, for instance, 1930–1931, it could have been perfectly possible to stop the major decline had we wished. Let us do that, and *then* we can point out that the gain from redistribution would be trivial compared with the gains from the renewed social growth of a productive capitalism.

Inflation and Wartime Scarcity

Just as disputes over the distribution of wealth furnish the stumbling block for many otherwise excellent plans to obtain recovery from depression, so also they are the major problem in dealing with inflation. On matters of technical analysis, as a matter of fact, economists are in much closer agreement concerning the proper measures for controlling inflation than they are concerning the control of unemployment. But on the other hand the *political* problems are much more difficult. It is not too hard to get people convinced of the idea that an increase in purchasing power would be a good thing—"Nobody shoots Santa Claus." But the control of inflation on the other hand usually involves everything that is, in the short run, unpleasant. When we add to this the intense ideological frictions which are almost always involved in an anti-inflationary program, the problem becomes indeed tremendous.

To understand the dilemma it is necessary to remember briefly how it arises. An inflationary pressure exists either because people are trying to invest more money (build more factories, etc.) than the spontaneous savings of society will permit or else because people are trying to spend more money than the system has goods to supply. Usually both forces are in operation at once. Again, in time of war, we have inflationary pressure because the government is greatly reducing the standard of living in order to divert men and resources to fight the war. Let us first discuss the peacetime inflation.

One of the most widespread recent ideas among left-wing writers has been the notion that inflation is merely a matter of high prices and deflation of low prices. People with such an outlook are apt to assume that, if we keep official prices fixed by controls, we thereby "lick" inflation. Unquestionably a strong government particularly in time of war, with the special patriotic sanctions which war brings, can "hold the line" pretty well for a time by rationing and price control. In *all* cases, however, in which endless reliance has been placed on this method, it has broken down. The nemesis of price control is the black or "gray" market.

At first the success of a control program may be almost 100 per cent, and, misled by initial results, the authorities may think that endless amounts of unspendable money can be piled up. But as the discrepancy becomes greater and greater between what a man can legally buy and what his money nominally entitles him to buy, the effectiveness of legal controls is nibbled away in shady deals and growing black-market manipulation. One cannot predict precisely where or when the pressure will become too great. The situation has many intangibles. But one can say positively that, unless controls are buttressed by policies which deal effectively with the basic problem, they will collapse sooner or later.

But even if we decide to tackle the problem directly rather than through controls, there are still important value problems to be settled. The question is: Do we merely want to remove the immediate monetary sources of the inflation, or do we want to get at yet more basic problems? In nearly all cases the root difficulty is not merely a matter of money. The "excessive" creation of money, or increase in spending, practically always betrays some fundamental problem on the *production* side. Either certain business or government groups are trying to expand investment faster than the normal rate of voluntary saving will permit, or else the general public may be clamoring for a rate of increase in the supply of immediate consumption goods greater than existing production facilities can supply.

But in any event the modern bias against capitalist incomes will greatly hamper an effective program. In the case of inflationary pressure derived from excessive long-range investment—the case analyzed in Chap. 5—the capitalist pricing system would call for a higher rate of interest. This, in the first instance, would have the effect of "rationing" the scarce supply of credit and real resources and force a slowing down of the rate of construction. Over a longer period it might also act as an incentive for increased saving and hence make possible a somewhat faster rate of expansion. But when, as at the present time, there is a large government debt floated at a very low interest rate, the government authorities may be unwilling to allow the rate to rise. For, if the rate does rise, either the price of government bonds would decline or else the debt would have to be converted to higher yield securities—which would mean more taxes, and that would scarcely be popular.

On the other hand, if the banks are allowed to continue to lend to finance new investment projects, prices will be forced up and inflation will continue. If we refuse to raise the rate of interest and still want to prevent inflation, the only alternative will be direct government control of credit—which means centralized control of growth. Thus in the United States after the Second World War, the administration, on the one hand, has been unwilling to allow interest rates to go up, while Congress, on the other hand, has been unwilling to vote comprehensive controls of credit. In consequence the inflation was allowed to continue unchecked. Yet it must not be supposed that this inflation was altogether a social loss. Despite many injustices against teachers, widows of war veterans, and other fixed-income groups, the probabilities are that the rise of the national output has proceeded more rapidly than if we had held investment down to the relatively low rate of current voluntary saving that our soak-the-rich policies permitted.

The truth of the matter is that the existence of full employment and inflationary conditions puts us back into an "orthodox" economic world. In time of unemployment, saving, in the first instance anyhow, may actually hold back growth. But in time of inflation more saving will increase production, for, other things being equal, it will make possible a faster rate of increase of production especially where the construction of new plant and so on is concerned. The public, however, is apt to think only in terms of money. They will ask why could not redistribution, by taking money from the rich and giving it to the poor, help to raise consumption output? But in a time of full employment any important increase in consumption requires the building of new plants. Yet if we want to build new plants, without inflation, we shall need two things—more saving and more incentives to invest.

We have not yet completed our dilemma. As soon as we begin to talk of a need for more saving, the Keynesian analysis goes into reverse. Lord Keynes argued that in time of unemployment it was desirable to tax large incomes heavily in order to prevent "excess" saving. But by a parity of reasoning, if we want to *increase* saving, then we have a good reason for making our income-tax structure less progressive. The bulk of consumption is not the work of the upper income groups.

Higher interest rates, higher profits, greater relative taxation of the lower income groups! It would be difficult to conceive of a program more directly counter to many modern prejudices, and the amount of tortuous logic that has been used to avoid facing up to the problem has been remarkable. Yet the logic of the Keynesian schema is inescapable. Our left-wing writers, however, tend to be part-time Keynesians only and use his analysis only when it suits them.

The final problem is posed by the attitude of the labor unions. An intense jealousy of profit, coupled with an absolute unwillingness to face up to the basic fact of shortage, leads to endless demands for higher wages to "maintain the standard of living." And while such demands may temporarily benefit a particular group which for the moment has pushed its gains ahead of the rest, the continuing spiral is likely soon to overtake them and result in cries for yet more. Thus as in the case of antidepression policy the wage demands of the unions are likely to be the obstacle upon which effective policy will come to wreck.

If the United States is soon again drawn into a war, the consequences of these attitudes are likely to be most serious. An important war *must* reduce the standard of living of *all* income groups. There is no evading that fact. The only choice concerns the *method* by which the reduction is to take place. But our modern frame of mind will be apt to lead us to suppose that price control plus subsidies plus rationing can take care of the entire problem. Even if the money wage level should be kept unchanged —which is almost inconceivable in view of union attitudes—still black-market pressures will pile up. And the best efforts of left-wing economists will be concentrated upon blaming the scarcities on profits. In this connection it will help to quote from Lord Keynes regarding inflation after the First World War: [18]

> The Governments of Europe, being many of them at this moment reckless in their methods as well as weak, seek to direct

[18] J. M. Keynes, *Essays in Persuasion* (New York: Harcourt, Brace and Company, Inc., 1932).

on to a class known as "profiteers" the popular indignation against the more obvious consequences of their [the government's] vicious methods. These "profiteers" are, broadly speaking, the entrepreneur class of capitalists, that is to say, the active and constructive element in the whole capitalist society, who in a period of rapidly rising prices cannot but get rich quick whether they wish it or desire it or not. . . . By directing hatred against this class, therefore, the European Governments are carrying a step further the fatal process which the subtle mind of Lenin had consciously conceived. The profiteers are a consequence and not a cause of rising prices.

Summary

From all that has been said it will be seen that we cannot answer the question "Can we stabilize capitalism" by reference to economic factors alone. Definitely, we cannot give perfect stability and still retain that reasonable degree of economic freedom and decentralization upon which, we have seen, both growth and political democracy depend. On the other hand we do have easily accessible and well-known techniques whereby it is quite possible, economically, to say that there need never be a severe depression again. But the fundamental problem is ideological. Can the people be persuaded to permit adequate risk incentives? Can the unions be persuaded to restrain their wage demands during a depression and still more during an inflation? Can we convince our own people and the residents of the so-called backward nations of the desirability and the moral rightness of capitalist investment? On questions like these depends the real future of the capitalist system, and while it is easy enough to sketch the program which *ought* to be adopted, it is quite another thing to say whether it *will* be adopted. Yet one thing must be said. Many socialists and left-wing writers seem to feel that, by saying that the masses are not intelligent enough to manage a program of compensatory finance under democracy, they are thereby offering an argument for socialism. This cannot, however, be an argument for any liberal or democratic socialism. If the people lack the wisdom to manage part of the economic system democratically, on what basis can we possibly say that they are thereby proved fit to manage nearly all of it?

CHAPTER 8

The Prospects for Capitalism

AND NOW we come to the final question: What chance is there for the survival of a system retaining any essential resemblance to the one we have been sketching? The reply, it is submitted, depends largely upon the way we answer yet another query: Is the present crisis of democratic capitalism the result of a basic shift in social values, or is it merely the result of ignorance and misunderstanding?

In his book *Adventures of Ideas,* Alfred North Whitehead outlines a theory of the decline of civilizations in terms of boredom. He says that in every culture at its height one finds the culmination of a certain type of perfection. As long as adequate variations within that type are possible so as to retain freshness and verve, we continue to have high civilization. But when a particular form of perfection is repeated over and over again without variation, decline sets in. Either there is prolonged atrophy and slow decay or else a violent collapse.

Yet it may be maintained that one form of perfection is freedom itself, and one form of permanence, constant change. We have argued that, if men put their strongest emphasis upon such values as broad opportunity, rising living standards, tolerance, democracy, independence, change, and activity, then the capitalist system is the one best calculated to give them to us. But what if people are becoming bored with these values and wish instead to set up as their final aim such things as contemplation, serenity, security, and "participation"—even though it may mean the end of rising living standards, of independent opportunity, and probably of democratic government itself? In that case some alternative politico-economic system—"socialism," let us say, or comprehensive centralized planning—may seem to them the better choice.

But the trouble is that the question is seldom put that way. Throughout this book, it is true, we have tried to avoid the idea of a dogmatic iron-clad antithesis. Certainly there is plenty of room for variations within the type, within the framework of capitalist civilization. We are not merely confronted with a choice between centralized planning and unmitigated insecurity. One of the great wastes of any war, be it an international or an intellectual one, is that the energies which might normally be used for improvement are drained off into defense. Personally the author finds the most distasteful aspect of modern discussion to be the extent to which one has to spend one's time *stating* the problem rather than trying to answer it. It would be so much better to be able to explore the many ways available to us for reducing conflict instead of having to keep insisting that a minimum of conflict will always remain. I would so much prefer to occupy myself in discussing techniques of stabilization rather than in insisting that stabilization, in a growing world, can never be perfect. But the thing which keeps us from doing what we *can* do is the assumption of some people that we may easily achieve the impossible. Once, to be sure, we understand the problem and know our values we can go ahead toward improvement. In this connection, I should like to call attention to the many areas of social action indicated in the present volume: Work to conserve natural resources, to improve aesthetic and cultural standards, to make society sufficiently stable, to increase opportunity for all, and to prevent the concentration of too much power in single hands—all this furnishes an ample outlet for anyone's energy. But as long as we are obsessed with the idea that by some apparently quick, easy, *single* change, all our other aims will be automatically realized, then we are diverted from constructive action. Exploration of the limits of action is often a necessary prelude to successful action. It must not be confused with a policy of complacent inactivity.

Yet nevertheless there does come a point beyond which stabilization cannot be pushed without endangering growth, and centralization without endangering democracy—and by centralization I mean centralization of *policy* and not mere geographical distribution of units. But always we have a large body of writers whose one effort is to slur over and confuse our choice. The present crisis may not be due so much to a change in values as to the fact that the problem is no longer seen in perspective.

If there has really been a massive change in values on the part of the majority of the people, if men are really tired of change, growth, consumer sovereignty, and the responsibilities of democracy, then, of course, there is no real prospect for our civilization. Slowly the change in values will impose itself upon politico-economic life and the way be paved for aristocratic stagnation. In this case there will be no point in talking further about prospects. But on the other hand if the matter is not so much a change in values as a misunderstanding of the problem, then the survival or revival of democratic capitalism will depend upon two questions: First, can we persuade the people of their error *in time*? Second, even if persuasion fails but if the sheer force of circumstance makes the masses realize they have been cheated, will it then be too late for them to do anything about it? Let us begin by discussing the problem of persuasion.

It is scarcely too much to say that the full choice between socialism, or comprehensive, centralized planning on the one hand and capitalism on the other hand is virtually *never* presented in adequate balance in modern literature. This one-sidedness and inadequacy apply alike to cultural comparisons and technical economic analysis.[1] On the cultural side the Bohemian intellectual—

[1] Even Professor Schumpeter's *Capitalism, Socialism, and Democracy* (New York: Harper & Brothers, 2d ed., 1947), leaving aside its fatalism, fails to present the problem in full balance. For generally speaking,

fully qualified to dispose of the most knotty social problem by a hasty perusal of Thorstein Veblen or a few ideas from Karl Marx —constantly insinuates even in magazine fiction such ideas as the following: Business organization is a form of competition, competition is a form of rivalry, rivalry can sometimes lead to frustration and war; *therefore,* in climactic *non sequitur,* abolishing *that* type of rivalry will abolish *all* types of conflict.[2]

In the same way "aggression," "office politics," etc., are all ridiculed as if they were *solely* capitalist phenomena. But the true basis of comparison, we have seen, is not between business rivalry and a world without rivalry, but between different forms of rivalry. The left wing cannot validly argue that it will abolish conflict. All that it can logically try to maintain is that rivalry and politics for a government position is somehow *less* harassing and *less* of a source of potential conflict and ugly conduct than rivalry for business position. But its case is seldom trimmed down to such mundane terms—and if it were it would be tremendously less convincing—especially to those with practical experience of both careers.[3]

Turning from cultural ideals to technical economics one finds

---

Schumpeter contrasts dynamic capitalism with stationary socialism and hence greatly understates the problem of resource allocation in a growing socialist world. In addition, his discussion of the relationship of economic planning to democracy is, I am obliged to conclude, quite superficial. Compare Chap. 4 of this book with Chaps. XXII and XXIII of his. Yet it is ungracious of a pupil to criticize a teacher for not going so far into a problem as the pupil has done. What the pupil does he does *on the shoulders* of his teachers. As Schumpeter differed from Böhm-Bawerk I have differed from Schumpeter. This, however, does not affect my debt, my gratitude, and my affection.

[2] As to my meaning of the word "intellectual" see Schumpeter *Capitalism,* Chap. XIII, Sec. II, "The Sociology of the Intellectual." I am using the word here in Schumpeter's sense.

[3] I do not mean to say that government bureaucracy is worse than its business counterpart. I wish to insist only that it is no better.

the same one-sidedness. Essentially what is almost always done, for example, in texts on "comparative" economic systems, is to compare *stationary* socialism with *growing* capitalism. We have seen in this book that a growing *unrationed* socialism would encounter most of the same difficulties that a growing capitalism does. There would be the same difficulty about forecasting, the same "backlog" problem, the same tendencies toward excess capacity, and probably a still stronger pressure toward security sabotage and routine stagnation. In short, the basic forces making for cyclical maladjustment are not merely capitalist or monetary but derive instead in their fundamentals from the liberal values of consumer sovereignty and rapid growth. Yet the author is not familiar with a single modern text on planning that recognizes this fact.[4] The idea that some difficulties spring from conflicts in value standards which planning, as such, can never wholly reconcile is virtually unmentioned.

In this connection it may be worth while to quote the following from the noted Swedish economist, Bertil Ohlin: [5]

> In 1945 . . . most people thought that Sweden was well on the way to a depression . . . but the expected post-war inflationary boom—which Mr. Myrdal and some of his colleagues regarded as the predecessor of a depression—proved unexpectedly long lasting and intense . . . the real question in Sweden from the summer of 1946 [became] not to avoid recession but to reduce the inflationary pressure. . . . In January 1947 and in the following years the government presented an outline of an invest-

[4] Compare the author's *Economics of Disturbance* (New York: The Macmillan Company, 1947) and Abram Bergson, "Socialist Economics," in *A Survey of Contemporary Economics,* H. S. Ellis, ed. (Philadelphia: The Blakiston Company, 1948), p. 438. As already pointed out earlier in this book Dr. Bergson states my thesis somewhat inaccurately. I did not maintain that "large-scale" unemployment was inevitable under socialism. See Chap. VII in *Economics of Disturbance.*

[5] Bertil Ohlin, *The Problem of Employment Stabilization* (New York: Columbia University Press, 1949), p. 86.

> ment budget for the whole economy. There are stipulated sums for each kind of investment, and an analysis as to whether an investment should be maintained or reduced within the year or perhaps increased. Instead of restricting the volume of investment in 1946 and 1947, the authorities permitted it to increase up to the end of the latter year. . . . The problem was not seriously tackled until the latter part of 1947. It then proved difficult to restrict the labor force in the building industry quickly enough, and to bring about a transition of workers to export and consumer industries.

The reader should realize that the maladjustment described here was not simply a matter of miscalculation—if indeed it was a miscalculation at all.[6] There was also a head-on collision between the aim of rapid housing construction and the aim of inflation control. But how many lecturers to women's clubs on the "middle way" would refer to such a passage?

Yet another example of failure to consider full consequences is found in schemes like the "Brannan plan" for maintaining agricultural prices. As plans of subsidy and restriction they often make sense—on their own terms. Yet to avoid indefinite accumulation of surpluses and subsidies, quotas will be almost inevitable in many cases—barring war emergency. But how many realize that this will virtually freeze each farmer at a given level of *relative* prosperity? If the scheme really works, a better or more efficient farmer would receive little benefit from increases in skill, for quota revisions for superior productivity would be extremely difficult. Here, too, will be stability—but a severe limitation of opportunity.

Failure to assess alternatives, however, is nowhere more strongly marked than in labor-union literature—whether direct union propaganda or the more academic writing of sympathetic "labor" economists. By its claims the labor movement is a movement for

[6] Ohlin's passage should be compared with the chapter on "The Planned Businss Cycle" in Wright, *op. cit.;* also with Bergson, *op. cit.*

higher living standards, greater individual opportunity, more "democracy," and so on. But also it is a movement for "job security" and "cooperative management." Yet the two sets of aims are in frequent conflict. Effective democratic action often depends upon a conflict of leaders, difficult if not impossible to reconcile with tight organization. "Job security," as the worker usually understands it, that is, as an unending guarantee of security in that *particular* job, is in direct conflict with technical change and growth. The feeling of intimacy and "participation" conflicts with the efficiency of large-scale production. "Industrial democracy"—management "by" the workers—may be fully achieved without realizing the value of service to other labor groups. And so it goes.

Not long ago I attended a discussion of social problems at which certain union economists were present. In the course of the discussion I said that I believed the rise of unionism in America was linked with a shift away from the ideals of opportunity, competition, and rising living standards. The union representatives laughed at the notion. "Why," said they, "our only complaint is that business doesn't change enough, doesn't compete enough, doesn't put in enough new methods." "Yes," said I, "but you want job security do you not? And how is technical change to be combined with job security?" There was no answer. Yet the problem is vital. Even Dr. Lindbloom, though he has pointed out some of the conflicts of unions with capitalism, has not pointed out the far more serious conflicts of unions with growth! [7]

If people realized the nature of the choice and had deliberately chosen hierarchic stagnation, we should at least have some chance of establishing a reasonably stable society. But there is far from being any real understanding. Always, if the problem is considered at all, it is conceived in terms of a *single* final allocation of resources. No provision is made for *further* change and develop-

[7] Charles Lindbloom, *Unions and Capitalism* (New Haven: Yale University Press, 1949).

ment. This is the basic weakness of the whole neo-Veblenian school.

But there is a final difficulty, and that is the increasing breakdown of communication between groups in this country. For example, it is often to the interest of union leaders to isolate their rank and file from outside thought as much as possible. A constant stream of vilification and misrepresentation is poured forth in their organs, and all contrary suggestions are ignored. As Professor Schumpeter has remarked, a sneer is often the best way to parry an argument one cannot answer. Any doubts, however friendly or valid, are treated as an attack. If a labor economist wishes to continue to make money from arbitration fees, he must for the most part toe the line. A special premium is thereby put on the evolution of ingenious methods of obscuring the issue.

Equally important is the attitude of the intellectual. What the Jew was to the Germans, what the Negro has often been in the South, that the businessman now is to the American intellectual—a scapegoat group upon whom can be vented all the fears and all the frustrations of those criticizing them. For the intellectual is afraid. Read any article on the atomic bomb. And the intellectual, furthermore, is bewildered, and out of this fear and this bewilderment has come an intense will to find some easy remedy, some quick source of evil, which can readily be eliminated. So far, the businessman has proved the obvious butt.

The author has found that college sophomores come to him fully convinced of the following: If we are poor, it is because of the businessmen; if there is war, it is because of the businessmen; if the world is ugly, it is because of the businessmen; if democratic decisions are sometimes foolish, it is because of the businessmen; if we have unemployment, it is because of the businessmen; if we have waste, it is because of the businessmen; if we have inflation, it is because of the businessmen; if we have deflation, it is because of the businessmen.

In the light of such wholesale attacks and misunderstanding, the chances of bringing about a shift in attitude by persuasion alone do not appear good. If there were no other forces operating, our conclusion would have to be one of entire pessimism. Fortunately, however, there is a basic logic in the facts themselves which may impose understanding in spite of all the hostile forces now operating. Piracy always pays when pirates are few and nonpirates many. But when more and more of the economy is organized on a piratical basis, that is, when more and more groups use the slogans of planning or security or "participation" to entrench themselves by law against all further change, then the advantages of piracy become less and less and the growth of total product becomes slower and slower. In that case the results of security sabotage may become so obvious that they can no longer be ignored. Furthermore we now have the advantage of seeing a number of socialist and near-socialist economies in operation, and only the ignorant can any longer maintain that the mere nationalization of industry will magically dispose of the pressure-group problem.[8] Thus though we can expect little save bias and confusion from the intellectuals, there is still a hope in the common sense of ordinary citizens imperatively confronted by the facts.

We are thus brought up against another question. Suppose that the public does discover for itself that it has been cheated. Suppose that the masses really do want rising living standards and opportunity and find that the centralized routine state (whatever its name) cannot give it to them. What are the chances for a

[8] Tawney's magnificent rhetoric (*The Acquisitive Society*) is thus confronted with a large body of factual experience drawn from many countries. Yet as the author was preparing this chapter, he noted in the *Cavalier Daily* (a student paper of the University of Virginia) the statement that "if the mines were nationalized John L. Lewis would be out of a job," and upon questioning he found that the opinion derived from a professor of economics in a well-known university. All the strikes against nationalized industries in Europe and Australia appear to have gone unnoted.

political revolution or even a violent one? Here, too, one deals in imponderables and unpredictables. A good deal depends, of course, upon how concentrated and powerful the political authority has been allowed to become and how long the routine state has been in existence. A people which has been told for generations that businessmen are responsible for all their troubles and that the cure for everything is planning is not likely to note the true source of its woes very quickly. Always it will be said that the cure for *some* planning is to have more planning, that the bad effects of reducing inequality will be found in making incomes still more equal, and that the bad effects of concentrated power will be overcome by making it still more concentrated. And by the time the populace discovers what has happened it may be too late. Perhaps the most significant and diabolical modern discovery for the promotion of tyranny is the control which the modern state is now frequently able to obtain over the minds of the children so as to wipe out the race memory and, as it were, almost removes the brains of a society.

But at least we can say there is a chance, a chance that the people may wake up in time. After all, in the light of present world conditions, the one fundamental thing to realize is that capitalism once more makes sense economically. It is the most productive system, the one which gives the greatest opportunity, and the one which most curbs state power. We have, therefore, no right prematurely to bury our culture, for it may be that the sheer logic of the situation will overcome all the ideological pressures which we have detailed and start us once more on a great era of world expansion.

It may also be true that the growing international-mindedness of Americans and their growing contact with the rest of the world will induce a realization of the poverty and sufferings of other societies which may make us see our own system in an adequate light. Again, as we look beyond our own country, the Orientals would appear to be moving in exactly the opposite direction from the people of the West. While we appear to be adopting Eastern ideologies of noncompetition and security, they are avidly seeking the rising living standards and democratic opportunities of the Western world. Communism may thus in an almost Hegelian manner prove to be the missionary of capitalism in the Orient,[9] for it is inculcating values of Western civilization into Eastern minds and yet it cannot possibly satisfy those values. In other words, the Chinese are being taught to value kitchen sinks, but I do not believe that communism will ever be able to furnish adequate sinks on the scale that capitalism does. Thus there is the possibility that the Orientals, once finding that the planned economy cannot give them what they want, will turn once more toward the institutional framework which created Western wealth. Neither the United States nor England achieved its position as one of the wealthiest nations of the world through a planned economy, and the Orientals are not so stupid but that they will not someday recognize this fact.[10]

Two factors will be of crucial importance during this development. On the one hand there will be a number of well-meaning individuals who will urge that we throw away our principal strategic advantage and give large quantities of capital free to any country that wants it including the near-communist ones. If we do that, we risk the digging of our own graves, for it will be absolutely certain that no credit will be given to capitalism for any aid it supplies. The administrators of Communist regimes and, to some extent, of socialist regimes, will take all the credit for any resulting rise in living standard and attribute it to the administrative planning they have done, neglecting to mention that, without the productivity of American capitalism and the

[9] But in saying this I do not mean to be advocating assistance from us to the Oriental Communist—quite the reverse. See *infra.*

[10] India, for example, would seem to me to have more to learn, in the present stage of its development, from Adam Smith and Malthus—especially the latter—than from Hansen and Keynes.

savings of American citizens, none of these things would ever have been forthcoming.

No one should deny our moral obligation, after the Second World War, to do what we can to start Europe once more toward recovery. But may it not be true that that bill will soon be paid? Would not the United States from now on do well to become less uncritically generous than it has been so far? For the trouble is that much which we do give will be represented to the recipro-cants as "achievements" of socialism. It is time to insist upon some return before we give away our resources. If the worst comes to the worst and if social stalemate really confronts us with a secular inability to invest our total savings in the private market, then would it not be better to indulge in large-scale public works at home? Mercenaries cannot be relied upon indefinitely as allies. If it is *merely* a question of government investment in slum clear-ance in America or government (*de facto*) gifts for slum clear-ance in India, then the author believes that we would do well to look after our own people first. This is not in any way meant to imply an isolationist attitude. We should do all that we can to foster international lending and the creation of a reasonably free international economic market. But does it make sense gratuitously to build up collectivist economies for which we will receive neither thanks nor credit?

So much for the inadequacies of the left wing. Now let us con-sider what is much more important—the inadequacies of our own so-called conservatives and of our own alleged believers in capitalism. The author has called attention to many of these in his book *Democracy and Progress*.[11] It is his sincere conviction that the capitalists themselves are frequently the greatest enemies of their own system. There is, for example, a persistent tendency to recur to die-hard financial orthodoxy. But in addition the American businessman is far more impregnated with the ideology

[11] See especially my chapter entitled "Three Plans." The reader is re-ferred to this to fill in gaps in the present outline.

of secure routine than he realizes. We cannot tell the people of other countries that the protection of economic vested interests will inevitably cut off the progress of their society if we insist on protecting our own vested interests ourselves. The American tariff makes no sense whatever in the light of the perpetuation of capitalism or the future development of the world. In the same way a great deal will depend on the way in which our business concerns handle themselves in the matter of foreign investment. If we go into countries in an entirely ruthless manner and pay no attention to the welfare and development of our workers, then we must be prepared to reap the harvest of inevitable hatred. And for the same reason we should do well to subdue our megalomania and to make loans abroad rather than to insist upon owning abroad.

Again, the indiscriminate American attitude toward property may be a most serious handicap. We tend in this country simply to assume that capitalism is respect for property rights. We have seen that in any case this attitude can be misleading. But the property rights that we respect *here* are at least property rights obtained within the framework of the American economy which, whatever its shortcomings, has given greater opportunity and greater competition than almost any other ever known in history. Therefore, our property rights have been achieved in a social environment in which they are entitled to a greater degree of respect than private property which is the mere survival of feudal privilege. For example, if we ally ourselves indiscriminately with *any* owning interests, we shall find ourselves coming into Oriental countries pledged to all that is most reactionary and repressive, for instance, the fruits of a thousand years of feudal stagnation. We can scarcely claim to be the forerunners of democracy if all that we are going to do is to underwrite the results of aristocratic privilege.

Such stability as the French nation possesses is based upon the distribution of land to the peasants at the time of the French

Revolution. There was a political New Deal, so to speak, at that time. And in the same way there should be a reshuffling of the cards in many Asiatic countries so as to start people off once more on a relatively free basis. Property rights do not deserve too much respect unless they are accompanied by property opportunities. This is a truth which the American people in their foreign policy are in considerable danger of forgetting.

But if we keep in mind the values of opportunity, competition, democracy, productivity, then it is our capitalist society which is the truly revolutionary one—the only society which offers true hope to the masses for release from the long nightmares of tyranny. It is we, not the Marxists with their reactionary ideas of a good dictator, who have the truly constructive, the truly revolutionary ideal. Once that is recognized, then I think the case of capitalism becomes extremely hopeful.

Socialism, as I see it, has only one remaining advantage as against a liberal and constructive capitalism, and even that advantage is an illusion. Nevertheless, to give our treatment its full depth that advantage must be mentioned. In our account of the capitalist incentives and the capitalist ideals in their heyday, we largely omitted one vital factor. It must be remembered that during the Victorian period the great masses of the people were devoutly religious. Speaking from a purely neutral, scientific viewpoint this is a point of profound social significance, for it means that the demand of the human race for some final creed and final purpose in life was met by allegiance to an other-worldly hope. The teachings of orthodox Christianity—and of all other religions as far as that goes—have been that the kingdom of God cannot be found in this world. That furthermore is exactly what we have seen in our first chapter, although from an entirely scientific and material analysis.

But there are many people who cannot be satisfied by anything less than an *absolute* creed. They are the categorical finalists. They must have *absolute* assurance of ultimate truth, and if they cannot find it in religion, then the tendency is to seek it in economics or some other social gadget. The rule of the saints is to be ushered in by everything from a single tax to communism. All the bitterness and intolerance of religious controversy are transferred to the economic field. Whatever other characteristics the intellectuals may possess, they might all be described as belonging to the priesthood of the kingdom of God *on earth*.

But whatever merits particular ideas may have as aids toward the solution of particular questions and however imperative it is that we should do what we can to fulfill our social responsibilities, the fact remains that we cannot ever have a universal and perfect rule of love and peace in this world. A few groups of people who have undergone particularly harrowing spiritual experiences or have been vouchsafed contact with some great personality may *for a while* exemplify that rule of pure charity and love for which we all yearn. Thus the author has read accounts of the communal (not communistic) colonies in Palestine of formerly persecuted Jews which would indicate that, in this generation at any rate, something approaching the literal realization of the religious ideal may have been approached. But the attainment of such a social organization, it is submitted, is ultimately based upon the cultural qualities of people who have passed through harrowing experience. It would seem extremely doubtful that the second or third generation of these colonies would be able to hold the same spiritual humility as the founding generation. Over the long pull and on a large scale we do better to organize on a basis which makes some allowance for ignorance, for selfishness, and for differences of opinion. That was the final conclusion of Thomas Jefferson.

But the modern man, uneasy and troubled, cut off from the peace of a faith which his parents knew, is apt to feel that perhaps by establishing socialism he can have the satisfaction of feeling himself a part, as it were, of a band of priests and hence derive a feeling of purpose in life. A government servant is thus often thought to have the same moral satisfaction that the members of the priesthood are supposed to feel. But once we have passed the first fine frenzy of idealism which may attend the establishment of a socialist society, then it will be discovered that merely changing the name of the administrator from businessman to government official will not change many of the dilemmas which have been bothering society. Be good "for the good of the state" may be subjected to just as destructive a distillation by the scientific spirit and by selfishness as any of the other moral standards. The possibility of an other-worldly solution is one which human scientific knowledge can neither prove nor disprove. But the impossibility of perfection in this world is something which can be denied only because of a deeply *un*scientific prejudice. Attainment of ultimate certainty is always a matter between a man and the universe—not between "man" and the state.

Index